MISTY
The Music of
Johnny Mathis

Jakob Baekgaard

sonicbondpublishing.com

Sonicbond Publishing Limited
www.sonicbondpublishing.co.uk
Email: info@sonicbondpublishing.co.uk

First Published in the United Kingdom 2022
First Published in the United States 2022

British Library Cataloguing in Publication Data:
A Catalogue record for this book is available from the British Library

Copyright Jakob Baekgaard 2022
ISBN 978-1-78952-247-1

Typeset in ITC Garamond & ITC Avant Garde
Printed and bound in England
Graphic design and typesetting: Full Moon Media

MISTY
The Music of
Johnny Mathis

Jakob Baekgaard

sonicbondpublishing.com

Acknowledgements

I would like to thank some of the people whose knowledge about Mathis and his music have been crucial for the book. They include writers Tony Jasper, Vincent L. Stephens, Christian John Wikane, Michael P. Coleman, David Ritz, Jesse Green, Todd Everett, Charles Waring, Joe Marchese, and the late Joseph H. Manning.

I'm especially grateful for the insights from the producers, arrangers and musicians who have worked closely with Mathis: Robbie Buchanan, Kathleen Wakefield, Gil Reigers, Fred Mollin, Mark Portmann, Jay Landers, and Jorge Calandrelli.

Special thanks to Charles Waring and Joe Marchese who read the manuscript. Their suggestions for improvement made the book better. Thanks also to Joe Marchese for his work with the discography.

It has been a great privilege that Mr. Mathis himself agreed to be interviewed for this book. I would also like to thank his team that include Amy Farrell and Gil Reigers, who read the manuscript and provided useful comments and helped to source photographs for the book.

Thanks to Stephen Lambe and Sonicbond Publishing for the support and effort in getting this book into the world.

Mathis has always acknowledged the influence of his father and so I would like to end with a comment from my late father who once said that if there is music in the world, life can't be all bad.

Jakob Baekgaard, Ringe, Denmark, October, 2022

MISTY: The Music of Johnny Mathis

Contents

Foreword by Johnny Mathis

I've always enjoyed discussing the people behind my recordings as much as I enjoy singing the beautiful music they create. I was lucky that at about 18 years old, I was heard by George Avakian from Columbia Records singing at a local jazz club. And after recording my first two albums with George and then Mitch Miller, that's when the name "Johnny Mathis" just took off around the world.

In putting this book together and revisiting these songs, I am again grateful for the extraordinary help of the writers, arrangers, producers, musicians and friends around me. Those people were (and are) shining examples who could take just a little thing and make it sound wonderful.

Johnny Mathis
Singer
August 2022

JOHNNY MATHIS
COLUMBIA RECORDS

PERSONAL MANAGEMENT
HELEN NOGA

GENERAL ARTISTS CORPORATION
NEW YORK CHICAGO BEVERLY HILLS DALLAS MIAMI BEACH LONDON

Part One: Becoming Mathis

Introduction: Johnny Mathis: A Legend in the Making

It takes a lot to become a legend in music, but Johnny Mathis lives up to almost any criteria one can think of. He is a musical pioneer who was among the first to record thematically coherent albums, including Christmas records, and his classic collection of hits, *Johnny's Greatest Hits* (1958), that came out while he was still a very young man, started the trend of releasing anthologies of hits and is mentioned in the *Guinness Book of World Records* for its nine-and-a-half years run on the *Billboard* Top Albums Chart.

The recording industry has recognized Mathis's contribution to music as well. Three of his songs have been inducted into the Grammy Hall of Fame ('Chances Are,' Misty' and 'It's Not For Me To Say') and he has received five Grammy nominations for his music. In 2003, the ultimate acknowledgement came when he was awarded the Lifetime Achievement Award from the Academy of Recording Arts and Science.

When it comes to longevity, few artists are able to beat Johnny Mathis. He is the longest-running artist on Columbia Records, with over 17 million RIAA certified album and singles sold alone in the US. 86 years old, he is still touring and released his latest single in 2021.

A long life in the record business has resulted in many hits. Mathis has placed 50 songs on *Billboard*'s Adult Contemporary Chart and is the #6 all-time album artist in the history of *Billboard*'s Pop Album Charts. Most impressive is perhaps how he has changed with the times and recorded music in multiple genres. Hearing the records chronologically is like experiencing the changing history of pop music unfolded through the perspective of one artist. Underlining his status as one of the major players in music, Mathis has been canonized by Columbia Records and is one of the privileged few popular artists to get the massive box set treatment (boxes with 40+ discs). This exclusive club includes Tony Bennett, Johnny Cash, Miles Davis, Bob Dylan, and Elvis Presley.

Culturally, Johnny Mathis also stands out. As Karen Heller writes in her profile of Mathis in *The Washington Post*: 'Long before the terms 'multiracial' and 'gender-fluid' came into vogue, Mathis owned those spaces. He was a man in the vanguard but performing as a most traditional artist, with a catalogue of classics and a 29-piece band.'[1]

Vincent L. Stephens wrote a lengthy article in three parts that covers Mathis's complete recordings, except the singles.[2] It's an important reference for any discussion of Mathis's music. Stephens categorizes Mathis's music into different phases: 1. 1957-63: Signature sound. 2. 1963-67: Mathis @ Mercury. 3. 1967-77: The 'covers' era. 4. 1978-86: Mathis gets (adult) contemporary era. 5. 1986-present: Repertory singer. 6. 1980s Rarities. 7. 1958-2013: 'Tis the Season: Johnny Mathis does Christmas![3]

This book has separate chapters on the Global era and the Christmas albums as well, but otherwise, a different way of categorizing the music has been attempted. It's relevant to stress that Mathis's development happened as the result of collaboration. During his career, he has formed important musical relations with producers and arrangers. The importance of these relations is emphasized throughout the book, with chapters focusing on key collaborators in his career.

In contrast, little space is left for biographical information that's not directly or indirectly linked to the music. Tony Jasper has already written a thorough authorized biography of Johnny Mathis that ends in 1982 (The book was published in 1983). While he has a wide biographical focus, Jasper's book still contains valuable information about the music. Much important work on Mathis's music has also been done by a variety of writers and critics. Michael P. Coleman, David Ritz, Jesse Green, and Todd Everett have all covered his career with profiles, portraits, and retrospective articles.

Specific albums and songs have also been examined in detail by Joseph H. Manning, Christian John Wikane, Charles Waring, and Joe Marchese. Especially Waring and Marchese have covered many albums through their detailed notes to reissues of Mathis's music released on BGO and Real Gone Music, respectively.

In a way, this book can be seen as an extended set of liner notes, adding perspective and context to Mathis's whole recorded career. It's a companion to the music and hopefully, it will give listeners, old and new, the chance to reevaluate the records. The entry about Mathis on *AllMusic*, one of the most comprehensive online resources for reviews of music, clearly shows that there is a problem. A vast amount of his music has not been reviewed at all on the site.

To start a nuanced discussion of Johnny Mathis's music, the prerequisite is to listen to the records, ideally all of them. Whereas the familiar pattern with many artists is a phase of original inspiration and experiment followed by a recognizable form, Mathis has kept changing aesthetically and stylistically throughout his career. Despite his image as a romantic singer, he isn't a romantic artist. In fact, he is surprisingly unromantic. Mathis has no problem leaving an image of his old musical self behind, but on the other hand, he doesn't shun his past musical incarnations. This makes him hard to grasp as a music legend.

He doesn't fit the category of the traditional American-Italian crooner like Perry Como, Dean Martin, Frank Sinatra, or Tony Bennett. Nor can he be categorized as a jazz singer like Billy Eckstine, Johnny Hartman or Nat King Cole. He is too artful to be pigeonholed as easy listening, too open to popular music to be accepted as high art and he doesn't care about such distinctions.

Even his voice is in-between categories. Blurring perceived markers of female and male style, he moves effortlessly from the low to the high register, and he draws both on the rich legacy of Afro-American music and Western classical music.

Culturally, Mathis has been construed as a gay Afro-American crooner singing to a straight audience of white women, but the truth is more complex than that. It's just another attempt to make sense of a singer who isn't interested in fixed categories, whether cultural or musical. Mathis wants to sing all kinds of songs to all kinds of people. The only thing you don't find in his music is aggressiveness. His is a soft and dreamy universe far from heavy metal. In that sense, he could be considered a romantic if you leave out the *sturm und drang*.

Other legends have been reduced to a pregnant image: The Man in Black, The Chairman of the Board, The King. The private yet friendly and down-to-earth Mathis is not fit for traditional mythmaking drawing on biographical drama. People tend to remember the simple stories, but Mathis's musical story isn't simple. The image of Mathis as the romantic, easy listening icon has pervaded in public opinion, as far as the public knows him, but that image, while convenient for lazy listeners and critics, doesn't grasp what his music is about and why it matters. This book is an attempt to figure that out.

A City of Many Songs: Growing Up in San Francisco

John Royce Mathis was born in Gilmer, Texas, on September 30, 1935. Mildred and Clement Mathis had seven children and Johnny was their fourth child. The family moved to San Francisco when he was six and this was where he would grow up and gain his formative musical impressions. It was not only the city, but also the people around him that pointed Mathis in a musical direction, especially his father and voice teacher were important. 'My dad was a singer and that's the reason I sing. I heard him sing and I said, 'yeah pop, I will sing with ye.' I grew up in a household, I had six brothers and sisters, my oldest brother was a wonderful singer who sang jazz, and my sisters sang, and they sang the popular songs of the day, so I had all this music coming at me and then my dad, of course, who was a very pragmatic man, being the father of seven children, suggested that I take lessons, and my voice teacher was my absolute angel. She is the reason I sing to this time in my life.'[4]

The Mathis household wasn't poor, but they couldn't afford to pay for vocal lessons. However, a local voice coach, Connie Cox, was known for supporting musical talent from families that were not well-off and in Mathis, she recognized someone who had the potential to make a career out of music. Immediately she installed a professional approach to singing in him that helped develop his vocal range. 'I don't know how I got my vocal range, except that my voice teacher who was a wonderful woman who taught me free of charge for about ten or twelve years, from the time I was 13 years old. Her name was Connie Cox, and she said, 'you're gonna wanna sing all your life whether you can, or you can't, so let's learn to do it, and just the physical capability of opening the right vocal cords in your throat and things like that, physically, physically, physically, things that you're gonna do over and over again, so learn to do it properly, so you can sing the rest of your life.' And she instilled that in me and what an absolute revelation it was for me at such a young age to have that in mind all the time.'[5]

When it came to singing, Mathis had the discipline of an athlete, and in fact, sports was the only thing that threatened his future career in music. He liked playing basketball or practicing track and field and when he enrolled at San Francisco State College in 1954, he excelled in high jump and broke records. So great was his talent that in 1954-1955 the world high-jump record was within reach, and the Olympic selectors were interested. Eventually, he had to make a choice and he chose music. It provided a more solid prospect of a long-term career. Instead, sports, and especially golf, became a refuge from the world of showbusiness.

As it turned out, his past as a semi-professional athlete also had a positive influence on his music. Thus, Mathis attributes his remarkable breath control to his past as a dedicated sportsman:

'I think that came from my training on the high jump on the hurdler on the track team in college and what have you. My coach used to be adamant about, you know, your stamina, and I think that might have helped, who knows.'[6]

It wasn't the only case of the world of sports and music intersecting. As Mathis's biographer, Tony Jasper, points out. 'Oddly enough, it was a fellow athlete, a shot putter by the name of Johnny Bologna, who set him on the road toward a singing career. Bologna had a friend who ran a small club and realising Johnny was in need of a part-time job while he was training during the summer of 1955, he brought Johnny to the notice of the owner. Johnny was offered a weekend singing spot for ten dollars a night. His Saturday-Sunday jaunt at the tavern led him to a further summer job at Anne Dee's 440 Club across the road. His singing attracted wide attention, even, as some would say, 'a commotion.'[7]

Before Mathis took the stage as a performer, he immersed himself in all the music San Francisco had to offer. His own family introduced him to jazz. 'Jazz was brought into the house by my older brother and sister and I listened to contemporary stuff that my dad played on the piano, he couldn't read a note of music, he played piano beautifully, and he introduced me to extraordinary singers and musicians, and from the time I was about 13 years old, I frequented all the jazz clubs in San Francisco and everybody came there: Nat King Cole, Ella Fitzgerald, Sarah Vaughan, Lena Horne, all of these gifted people, and that's who I grew up listening to.'[8]

Nat King Cole's influence on Mathis is often highlighted. When the writer Steven Gaydos asked him what made Cole so great, Mathis elaborated, explaining Cole's style. 'No. 1: He was a great musician. No. 2: He had a limited voice and he only sang one way. He didn't get out of his register, and it was always musically sound. And it was always pleasing. He was so technically perfect, yet it always sounded simple. No. 3: he applied this style to all his songs, so he sang up-tempo songs so they sounded like ballads.'[9]

It's tempting to compare Mathis's style with Nat King Cole. A particularly idiosyncratic analysis has been done by the critic, Will Friedwald, who claims that Mathis's voice is piercing and mannered compared to Cole's. He concludes that Mathis's qualities as a singer are almost strictly sonic.[10] Friedwald's opinion is a keen reminder that beauty lies in the eye of the beholder, but he is right that there is a difference between Mathis and Cole, as there should be. Great singers are different personalities and stylists, not copycats. However, Cole and Mathis do have something in common. They are both masters in the art of the ballad and, in Mathis's words, 'technically perfect,' but they use their technique differently. If it could be said about Cole that he had a limited voice that he used to perfection, Mathis has an unlimited voice that he uses just as efficaciously. Like Cole, he can be soothing, wrapping the listener in a sheet of silky sound, but what Friedwald calls piercing is rather a tendency to use the full register of the voice, from the highest part to the lowest, sometimes stretching the voice as an opera singer. His ability to apply stylish ornaments might seem mannered to some who prefer a so-called natural style, but it really emphasizes that his voice is an instrument used by a trained musician and not an amateur. He doesn't swing that much, but his connection to jazz, a genre that was his first love and a crucial influence, lies in the way he elaborates on melodic lines and lets the music unfold its own story.

This is one of the reasons why Mathis has been able to work in so many different genres. He sings personally, but he never lets his personality get in the way of the music. Instead, the music becomes emotional through his personal investment in it. As Mathis has said: 'It's the most personal thing that I do is sing. 'Because I can't tell a lie. I want them to know exactly what I'm feeling.'[11]

In other words, Friedwald's claim that the qualities of Mathis's voice are almost strictly sonic, technique as an empty shell, misses the mark. Mathis just approaches emotion differently. Whereas many singers convey emotion and human warmth through their listeners' identification with their persona, Mathis creates a room that allows the listener to inhabit the music in another way. It becomes a shared space rather than a subjective story.

In a way, Mathis is a very private singer, but privacy doesn't mean that he is cold, impersonal, or emotionally distant, it just means, to paraphrase T.S. Eliot, that he uses an objective correlative, the song, to channel his emotions.

Musically, Mathis navigated easily between genres. If music is often linked to a place, Mathis moved from a jazz club to the opera. This was possible because he had an open mind and, early on, met people who were willing to share their musical world. One of these people was Mathis's voice teacher, who introduced him to classical music and took him to the opera. 'My voice teacher was an opera singer and so I had great compassion, working with her for those years when I was growing up listening to her, and all the operatic arias that she sang.'[12]

It's a love that still sticks with him to this day and two opera singers especially made an impression on him. 'I still have the love and passion for operatic music, which is the first music my voice teacher and I studied with, because they thought it would enhance my vocal range and that sort of thing. But in your heart, you always have this passion for certain music, I've always admired, and I'm very happy to have met some of the great voices in the world: Leontyne Price, Beverly Sills and on and on. I love operatic music, always have, and to hear Leontyne or Beverly Sills sing, it just knocks me out, I just love it.'[13]

Mathis also found inspiration in religious music. He went to church to hear it. 'I loved going to church, not so much listening to the preacher, because I had heard it over and over and over, but I loved listening to the voices in church and I went to a wonderful high school and some of my Jewish buddies would take me to shul with them and I'd go to temple with them and listen to the cantors singing.'[14]

The music of different languages also fascinated Mathis and it underlines what is perhaps the most essential thing to understand about his aesthetic: his all-encompassing infatuation with sound:

'You love sound. You love anything with sound. I grew up in San Francisco and joined a school with a lot of Latins, Germans, Italians and from the time I was a little kid, that's what my voice teacher and I did, we sang in French, we sang in German, and we sang in Italian. It was such a myriad, but I was a kid and kids do whatever is available and I was very fortunate in that respect, I had great appreciation from an early age for all kinds of music.'[15]

Summing up how living in San Francisco influenced his music, Mathis says, 'You're influenced, I think, by people that do something a little different from you as a singer and so you're always a little bit interested in whether I can do that or not. It was a never-ending opportunity for me, but I had all the advantages of growing up in San Francisco, where music was everywhere. There was the opera, there was rhythm & blues, there was jazz, everything, and I took advantage of all of it and even recorded a lot of things.'[16]

The first album that Mathis made was a jazz record. He didn't record it in San Francisco but in New York, the next big step in shaping a career as a professional singer. But before he left, he had to be discovered, and for that purpose, he needed help from someone: Helen Noga.

JOHNNY MATHIS
COLUMBIA RECORDS

PERSONAL MANAGEMENT
HELEN NOGA

GENERAL ARTISTS CORPORATION
NEW YORK CHICAGO BEVERLY HILLS CINCINNATI DALLAS MIAMI BEACH LONDON

Part Two: The Classic Columbia Years

Everything a Voice Can Do: Johnny Mathis (1956)

Helen Noga was the co-owner of the legendary jazz club, The Blackhawk. Mathis was brought to her attention when he played at the club. At the early stage of his career, it was a crucial meeting, according to Mathis biographer Tony Jasper:

'It was, of course, energetic, intelligent Helen Noga who kept Johnny together as person during these formative years. She was everything to him, from manager to substitute mother. Her time and energy was his and really, he wasn't on his own until 1964, following the sad affair which saw both locked in court action, and parting, the event almost coincided with the death of his mother. Helen had brought Johnny into a totally new environment – the cut and thrust of showbiz and the fickleness of public adulation.'[17]

Noga set Mathis's career into motion. She had the ability to make things happen, but she also gave him vital support on a psychological level. As he has later recalled:

'Helen made me feel that I could compete with other popular singers. I never felt secure about my singing. I felt that I sang well, but a lot of people do. And I felt I had no special attraction. In fact, I felt I had a lot of negative points. I wasn't forceful; I wasn't glamourous. I wasn't all those things that one is supposed to be to be successful ... But Helen made me feel something so that I could continue ... It didn't matter what you did one night – if you sang well – it's whether you could do it the next night, and the next night ... You have to make sure you outlast, outsing, outdo them forever, and she instilled that in me from a very young age.'[18]

Besides building Mathis's confidence, another important thing Noga had to do was to get him a recording contract. In fact, she had promised this to the Mathis family at the time when Johnny had to choose between a career in sports or music. The promise of a recording contract closed the deal and so she had to deliver, and she did. Noga reached out to George Avakian at Columbia Records, the label that would shape Mathis's career.

Avakian was steeped in jazz. While working at Columbia, he had been involved with projects profiling some of the greatest musicians in jazz, including Louis Armstrong, Fletcher Henderson, Billie Holiday, and Bessie Smith, so it was natural for him to place Mathis in a jazz setting, but Helen Noga wasn't glad about his choice. She was determined that the musical net would be cast wider than the jazz clientele, and so she pitched Mathis to Avakian and Columbia simply as an extraordinary singer and made sure that the first time he heard him was outside a jazz setting, such as her own place. Instead, she suggested that he hear Mathis at Ann Dee's 440 Club in San Francisco. Avakian recalls his meeting with the music of a 19-year-old Mathis in the notes he penned for the singer's debut on Columbia. 'The extraordinary thing about Johnny Mathis that night at Ann's 440 Club, just above the old Barbary Coast district, was that all the qualities you hear in this album was already there, although he had been singing professionally for less than three weeks. Helen Noga first heard him when Virgil Gonsalves, a baritone saxophonist whose sextet was working at the Black Hawk at the time, brought Johnny in for a Sunday afternoon jam session at the club. Helen was impressed by his potential, and told him, 'You know your jazz, but you can do more than work the jazz clubs; try the commercial places.' A couple of weeks later, Ann Dee heard him in a bar across the street from her place on Broadway and gave him his first job.'

'Before Johnny finished his second song, I knew I was going to sign him. He had so much that I was not surprised to learn that he was doubling weekends in an opera group production of Leonard Bernstein's 'Trouble in Tahiti.' Obviously, he had more training than most pop singers; his extraordinary breath control and sweeping range indicated that. He could do as many different things as four very different singers might and do them well. All he needed was experience and seasoning.'[19]

Part of that experience came when Mathis arrived in New York to record his debut album. 'I recorded a jazz album because I was signed to Columbia records by the head of jazz, and once I did the album, there was nothing for me to do, except to look for a job to sing locally in night clubs and I got lucky on a couple of occasions and I sang at a place called the Blue Angel where sophisticated people sang and then there was Bacon street with the jazz clubs I sang there and then I'd go to the opera, so I was all over the place vocally and God love them all because eventually, I got the opportunity to sing.'[20]

The venues were not the only places where Mathis got a chance to improve his craft as a singer. The debut album he recorded in March 1956, simply titled *Johnny Mathis*, was also a learning experience. He had always taken his voice seriously and leapt at the chance of acquiring new knowledge in the studio. He came in early for the sessions and watched how other artists worked to prepare himself. For the recording, George Avakian enlisted several notable jazz musicians, including arrangers Gil Evans and Teo Macero, bassist Ray Brown, drummer Connie Kay, trumpeter Art Farmer and saxophonist Phil Woods. The album was recorded in Columbia's famous studios, as Mathis recalls. 'We recorded the whole album in the Columbia Studios, which had been an old church that Columbia bought and converted into a recording studio. It was a wonderful place with lots of natural reverberation.'[21]

With the slogan 'A New Sound in Popular Song,' Mathis's debut was a lush and ambitious record designed to show every facet of his voice, and as such, it succeeded. The opener, 'Autumn in Rome,' is the first of two songs dedicated to the seasons, the other being 'It Might As Well Be Spring.' In a setting with chiming vibraphone and woodwinds blowing like a soft breeze, Mathis delicately paints a picture of Roman piazzas imbued with the nostalgia of lost love. 'Easy to Love,' on the other hand, is all smoky trumpet and swinging jazz-noir, with Mathis changing easily between a deep register and elegant light flourishes. He convincingly tackles 'Street of Dreams' that Tony Bennett made a hit, and the bleak barroom ballad of Frank Sinatra's 'Angel Eyes' is replaced with a feisty version filled with musical bravura.

One of the best tracks is a stunning version of Duke Ellington's 'Prelude to a Kiss' where the lyrics accurately describe what Mathis is doing. 'Though it's just a simple melody / With nothing fancy / Nothing much / You could turn it to a symphony / A Shubert tune with a Gershwin touch.' He also does a slyly swinging version of Ellington's 'Caravan' and his vocal chops come fully to the fore on a playful version of the Latin piece, 'Babalu,' a song previously covered by Billy Eckstine. It sounds like Mathis is roaring in a jungle, waking up all the animals as he invites everyone to a dance. It's a song exhibiting vitality and a surplus of musicality.

With his debut, Mathis showed that he could do everything with his voice. He could sing ballads, swing, and interpret standards made famous by other artists and still hold his own. He had no trouble finding his place in the company of the sophisticated arrangements and complex textures provided by Gil Evans, Manny Albam, Teo Macero, John Lewis and Bob Prince, but as the list of arrangers implies, the album was also a course prepared by many cooks and perhaps too sophisticated for a large audience whose palette suited pop rather than jazz. The fact is that Noga was right in her skepticism of Mathis being pitched as a jazz singer. The album didn't sell, but looking back, he still recognizes the importance of jazz in his life. 'The record companies are only interested in what sells and jazz has never been a big seller as far as music is concerned, no matter how great the musicians are. Some of my great times in my life was when I met Oscar Peterson, Dizzy Gillespie, Erroll Garner, all of these wonderful people who came through San Francisco and I heard when I was 12-13 years old, and I got to meet them and became pals with them and even sang with them and recorded with some of them later on. Human nature is human nature, if you want to be obstinate and not listen to that, 'cause it sounds different to what you're accustomed to, that's ok, but don't tell me what I can't listen to.'[22]

Mathis would continue to appreciate jazz and he also recorded jazz-influenced music from time to time, but his debut fundamentally changed any idea he might have had of becoming a jazz singer. It happened when he listened to the finished record. 'Once I heard myself replayed to me back, singing my so-called jazz interpretations, I felt that there were others who did it better: Ella Fitzgerald, Sarah Vaughan, I can name them. They had the natural qualities that were required to do jazz at a high level, I didn't have that. I enjoyed sticking my little toe in the water in that regard for a few times in my life, but then I settled into what I thought sounded comfortable when I heard it played back and that guided me as far as what I decided to continue to do vocally. Once I heard that my abilities were better suited to certain types of music, I felt more comfortable listening to myself do that.'[23]

It was clear that Mathis had to change his tune to get the big breakthrough he deserved and find a musical mode he was comfortable with. It required a new producer, a new arranger, a new sound and then something wonderful would happen.

A Wonderful Sound: The Percy Faith Recordings

Mathis's second album was also produced by George Avakian, but it was just a name on a sleeve. Truthfully, a new man had taken over, and he knew what he wanted: a sellable sound and a clear musical signature. That man was Mitch Miller, a legendary record producer and head of A&R at Columbia Records, famous for finding hit records and infamous for the dreck he sometimes pushed to his artists, including Tony Bennett, Frank Sinatra, and Rosemary Clooney. However, at this point, his manager Helen Noga's greatest concern was not whether the songs would be artful enough for Mathis, but whether he would make it at all, and so she went to Miller to see if he could help. Miller recalled the situation in his Television Academy Foundation Interview. 'She comes to the office, and she's crying and says, 'you gotta give him a chance.' I said, 'Helen, he obviously has talent, but let me find some songs for him. It will take us a few months to find songs that are suited for him.' We got these songs and we did this session and I got Ray Conniff, and Ray did these marvelous arrangements for him, and boom, he

MISTY: The Music of Johnny Mathis

had these hits, right off the bat: 'The Twelfth of Never,' 'Chances Are' and 'It's Not for Me To Say.'"[24]

The songs Miller calls attention to are all singles, but he doesn't mention another important single hit. Conducted by Ray Conniff, recorded September 21, 1956, and released November 5, 1956, 'Wonderful! Wonderful!' became one of Mathis's signature songs and reached number 14 on the *Billboard* charts. The hit provided the title for his second album, but bizarrely enough, the song wasn't included on the album and Conniff was nowhere to be seen. Instead, Mathis worked with another important bandleader and arranger, Percy Faith, who helped shape his sound on a string of albums.

Born in Canada, Percy Faith (1908-1976) started playing violin at seven and changed to piano at 10. At 14, he studied at the conservatory and began carving out a career as a concert pianist. It ended suddenly when he burned his hands severely in an accident. At that time, he was 18 years old and instead of the piano, he started focusing on composition and arranging, studying with Louis Weizman. He found work arranging for hotel orchestras, but his career really took off in the world of radio. He first started arranging for radio orchestras and eventually got his own radio program, *Music by Faith* (1938-40), whose popularity made a move to America possible. In the US, he worked at top radio stations NBC and CBS and became music director at Columbia Records in 1950. At Columbia, he both recorded in his own name and provided arrangements for other artists, as well as backing them with the signature sound of his orchestra. Faith became a pioneer of easy listening, softening the brass section, or skipping it entirely in favor of a warm bed of strings. His lush pop style suited Mathis perfectly.[25]

Wonderful, Wonderful (1957) was the first fruit of their collaboration. 'Will I Find My Love Today' immediately introduces a dreamy ballad style that fits well with other songs on the album, like the classics 'You Stepped Out of a Dream' and 'In the Wee Small Hours of the Morning.' It was still a period of transition, and there is a surprisingly brassy punch on the swinging 'Looking at You' that showed that Mathis hadn't forgotten his jazz roots, and he swings again on 'That Old Black Magic.' The brass volume is also high on 'Too Close for Comfort' and 'Day in Day Out,' underlining that the soft Percy Faith sound was not fully in place yet, but a significant change had happened. Before, Mathis was an adventurous artist singing with an orchestra so dynamic it could almost move into the foreground. Now the roles were in place; the orchestra, as lushly textured as it is, just provides the background, and as the liner notes point out, Mathis is 'holding his extraordinary technique in check except where it shows a musical end.'[26] In other words, compared to the debut, he sings in a simpler and subdued style like Nat King Cole.

If *Wonderful, Wonderful* was a promising beginning for Faith and Mathis, *Warm* (1957) was the fulfillment of the promise. *Wonderful, Wonderful* lulled the listener into a pleasant haze, only to break the ambience with a punchy brass section. In that sense, it was a failed mood album. *Warm* perfected the experience of artful easy listening without any disturbing swing interludes. The warm blanket isn't pulled away but stays on.

On the title track, thick romantic strings, harp, and classical piano provide a setting where Mathis can use the full strength of his voice. He is not holding back this time, making gentle falsetto flights, and exploring the dark, warm hues of the lower register. The overwhelming technique of the debut has been integrated into a romantic sound. Softly quivering vibrato is used on 'I've Grown Accustomed to Her Face,' an example of deep romantic balladry with dialogic strings. Mathis even challenges Frank Sinatra with his version of 'I'm Glad There Is You.' He reaches the same emotional layers as Old Blue Eyes and adds an otherworldly dimension of texture in tandem with Faith. The feeling of the album is summed up on 'The Lovely Things You Do' where Mathis sings: 'You make moonlight more than moonlight / you make heaven more than sky.' Simply said, *Warm* finds Faith and Mathis at the top of their game. Consequently, the listeners responded positively. The album entered *Billboard*'s top 25 of the bestselling pop LPs in the US and stayed there for 113 weeks. It also marked the first time a Mathis album charted in the UK.

It would have been the logical step to follow *Warm* with yet another romantic mood album, but Mathis had a very different concept in mind. He wanted to record a collection of religious music, as he explained in an interview with Michael P. Coleman. 'I decided to let my audience know that during my growing up years in San Francisco, I'd gone to the synagogue, to the Methodist church, to the Baptist church, and I wanted to sing some of that music.'[27]

The result was *Good Night, Dear Lord* (1958). True to his intention, Mathis embraces many different religious songs, including the Jewish 'Eli Eli,' the spiritual 'Swing Low, Sweet Chariot' and 'Ave Maria' in Schubert's and Bach's versions. Geographical boundaries and musical traditions are blurred as Mathis focuses on the praise of 'One God.' His voice both draws on gospel and classical religious music. He can paint the muddy depths of a 'Deep River' and the sunlight twinkling on the surface of the water.

Percy Faith once again provides congenial accompaniment. He moves from suspended strings and harp in the beginning of a slowly transcendental 'Swing Low, Sweet Chariot' to an interlude with the strings singing the melody. The climax is reached in a coda with Mathis's voice and the strings lifting each other in wordless wonder.

Together, Faith and Mathis create timeless hymns in a cyclical movement. The title track, the beautiful lullaby that begins the record, might as well be the end, and the versions of 'Ave Maria' that close the album are really two beginnings with Mathis as a cantor delivering the same text in different ways. The message of the album is clear: the longing for redemption is universal and humans sing the same songs of sin, hope and forgiveness everywhere. The tone on *Good Night, Dear Lord* isn't despairing or judgmental, it's comforting, and Mathis's soothing yet deeply felt interpretations bring the good news that these songs carry.

Good Night, Dear Lord was followed by another surprise. So far, the perfection of the Faith-Mathis sound had involved letting go of the swing element that disturbed the tranquil mood of *Wonderful, Wonderful*, but not only did Faith and Mathis return to swing on the appropriately titled *Swing Softly*, they dedicated a whole album to it.

The opening song, 'You Hit the Spot,' is a Trojan horse that begins as a classic Mathis ballad. Accompanied by piano, he purrs, 'you're as smooth as a kitten's ear,' but at the 1.14 mark, spinning turns into swinging and the orchestra enters with cool brass, acoustic guitars, and walking bass. Compare the brass section on 'You Hit the Spot' with 'Looking at You' from *Wonderful, Wonderful*, and it's clear that Faith has changed something. It's a far softer approach to swing with prominent use of acoustic guitar to create a crisp, light sound and the brass section is tamed.

The repertoire primarily consists of songs from movies and musicals, including an interpretation of Cole Porter's humorous tongue twister 'It's De-lovely.' It brings out every nuance of Porter's sophisticated play with the prefix de-, moving from classic combinations to pure Dadaistic joy culminating in the title's neologism. 'So please be sweet, my chickadee, / And when I kiss you, just say to me, / It's delightful, it's delicious, / It's delectable, it's delirious, / It's dilemma, it's delimit, it's deluxe, /It's de-lovely.'

Another Porter composition is the love song 'You'd Be So Nice to Come Home To' with seductive flutes and muted brass. Mathis also tips his hat to Nat King Cole on 'Sweet Lorraine' and changes the season from Cole's autumnal swing to a sprightly spring feeling, and he returns to the religious realm on 'Get Me to the Church on Time.' Here, it's less about spiritual comfort and more about the practical aspect of getting to the church in time as the piano and the orchestra simulate ringing bells. It's a song that underlines the light swinging mood of the album.

Continuing in the light mood, Faith and Mathis ended their collaboration with an album of Christmas songs: *Merry Christmas* (1958). It was the first of many Christmas collections to come. These albums will be discussed later to emphasize the significance of Christmas music as a separate body of work in Mathis's oeuvre. It was a genre that Faith helped Mathis explore, just as he helped pushing him in other musical directions while staying true to the commercial potential of pop. This experimental accessibility would be the hallmark of Mathis's career as his sound changed with the decades, always with a focus on a nice sound and nice songs.

Faith laid the foundation for this approach, and in his interview with Coleman, Mathis has said that he was one of the most important collaborators in his career. 'First of all was Percy, who wrote for me orchestral arrangements that were like the ones on his own records. He'd had a couple of hit records, and he just consented to work with me. It was kind of tough because he was a classically trained orchestrator, and some of the other people who were in the studio at the time were not. He said some funny things to those people when they'd ask him 'Why don't you do this?' or 'Why don't you do that?' I remember once he said, 'The reason I don't do that is because what I'm doing is perfect!' [Laughs] I said, 'Yeah! Right on!' Percy was one of my great, great heroes. I love him very much.'[28]

Summing up the importance of their association, Mathis says, 'Along the way, I've met some wonderful people who've been in my corner – probably because we enjoyed the same types of music – but Percy Faith was very, very important in my career.'[29]

Considering the importance of the collaboration between Faith and Mathis, it was hard to imagine how he could move on, but he didn't only bounce back after losing Faith, he made one of the most special albums of his career, and it would only take a voice and two guitars.

Making a Masterpiece: Open Fire, Two Guitars (1959)

Any worries that Mitch Miller would shamelessly exploit Mathis by providing substandard novelty songs were put aside from the beginning of their relationship. He found great songs and involved Mathis in the final choice for the albums and it paid dividends both commercially and artistically. Within the framework of Faith's elegant, easy listening orchestra, it was possible to make experiments with sounds and genres, adjusting each album like a tailormade suit.

It could be feared that when Faith departed, Miller would choose the pedestrian route and try to do more of what he knew already worked for the singer, but instead, he made one of the boldest choices in his career as a producer. The result is an album that stands out in Mathis's discography.

The cover of *Open Fire, Two Guitars* shows him in a living room in front of a fireplace. In the corner, there's a table with an acoustic guitar placed side by side with a coffee cup and an orange lamp without a lampshade. At the top, the album title is written by hand, followed by Johnny Mathis in big red letters and the song titles are also written by hand. It's an iconic cover that immediately points to the intimacy of the album. The setting is established on the title track with ascending and descending guitar lines that melt into a gently strummed chord that coincides with Mathis's voice: 'staring at an open fire / watching flames as they leap higher / brings forgotten thoughts to mind.'

The lyrics signal an album of introspection and the mood stays contemplative from the beginning to the closing chapter of 'My Funny Valentine.' Here, the twin guitars of Al Caiola and Tony Mottola provide an exquisite intro reminiscent of Bach. Such delicacy from the guitarists wasn't what Mathis expected. As he told Michael P. Coleman, 'That was a fun thing for me, because the two guys who played guitar on that, Al Caiola and Tony Mottola, wrote some music for a very popular program on CBS at the time, *Danger*, and it was a mysterious kind of scary television show. That was the only way I knew who they were when they showed up in the recording studio. It was quite a departure for me to sing with just two guitars and a bass. I LOVED doing that album.'[30]

In fact, Anthony Mottola (1918-2004) was used to accompany great singers. In the 1940s, he had backed Frank Sinatra in a trio inspired by Nat King Cole. Mottola later had the honor of playing on the only Sinatra recording with just one guitar and voice. In 1983, they recorded 'It's Sunday,' a late example of the autumnal string poetry that Mottola also provides on *Open Fire, Two Guitars*.[31] The other guitar, Al Caiola (1920-2016), adds further sophistication to the record. Caiola's association with Mottola goes back to when he was sixteen and they performed together on the children's radio show *Sally and Sam*. Their many years together shine through in the deep interplay. Like Mottola, Caiola played with some of the best artists, including Rosemary Clooney, Frank Sinatra, and Percy Faith.[32] They share an ability to play in many different genres, but jazz incarnated in the art of improvisation lies close to their heart and it can be heard in the music, as it's pointed out in the liner notes: 'The guitars second him splendidly, providing an embellishment here and there and enhancing the intimate feel of the entire program. Indeed, there is almost an atmosphere of improvisation, as if the songs were indeed being sung before an open fire, with two guitars somewhere back beyond the immediate glow.'[33]

If the guitars are back beyond the immediate glow, the bass, played by Frank Carroll and Milt Hinton, is even further back and almost unnoticeable, but it adds the deep bottom so the guitars can move freely around. They embellish the record with rich textures and melodies, but the center of it all is undoubtedly Mathis, and never has his voice shown such lushness and intimacy. The acapella intro of 'Bye Bye Black Bird' is achingly pure in the way the tones are stretched like the song of a lonely bird in the cathedral of nature. It's almost a shame when the shimmering guitars enter after seven seconds, but a sophisticated dynamic develops between guitars, voice, and the slow pulse of the bass. Chords ring into silence and the words, so sugar sweet with longing, fill the air. In the end, Mathis raises his voice in a featherlight falsetto flight with the echo of the melody in the background.

Highlight follows highlight. Different moods are painted, from a melancholy scene in an Italian café with a mandolin playing in 'I'll Be Seeing You,' to the softly strolling swing meditation of 'I Concentrate On You.' The guitars and voice seem to breathe with each other. Mathis's use of sustained notes, vibrato, jazzy phrasing, pauses, and tonal color is incredible. The guitars listen, respond, and create a sound so warm, delicate, and airy that the singer can only soar and be inspired.

The album is a timeless masterpiece that still resonates today. In 2020, the troubled year of the outbreak of the COVID-19 pandemic, The *Los Angeles Times* ran a piece with a top 35 list with records suitable for deep listening while in self-quarantine. One of the albums on the list is *Open Fire, Two Guitars*. Pop music critic Mikael Wood describes it like this: 'Neither over nor under-delivering on the promise of its title, this quiet 1959 classic is one of the romantic pop crooner's sparsest yet most sublime: just Mathis, his voice so supple it sounds almost wet, accompanied by guitarists Al Caiola and Tony Mottola in an expertly designed program of standards including 'When I Fall in Love' and 'Embraceable You.' Mathis could sing anything, of course; now in his mid-80s, he still can, as his recent rendition of Pharrell's 'Happy' (!) made clear. But with the arrangements as restrained as they are here, 'Open Fire' emphasizes depth of tone over breadth of ability. It's a dream to get lost in.'[34]

Open Fire, Two Guitars is a musical dream that only happened once. It's not surprising that the line-up wasn't repeated. Although it worked, it would be hard to recreate the magic of the record, but it's strange that neither Miller nor the producers that followed him learned a lesson that seems obvious: Mathis shines in a minimal setting. The reason is his voice is orchestral in its scope, so a large ensemble potentially takes the focus away from the pure wonder of his voice. Faith knew this and that's why he downplayed the effects of the orchestra, but nothing beats a minimal setting with a few instruments. Mathis went on to explore many different genres and lineups, large and small, but the sparse acoustic setting of his early masterpiece was already history. Instead, the next step was a return to the orchestral blueprint with a new arranger and conductor: Glenn Osser.

More than 'Misty': The Early Glenn Osser Recordings

Abe (Glenn) Osser (1914-2014), a son of Russian-Jewish immigrants, grew up in Munising, Michigan. Early on, he learned to play various instruments, taking up saxophone, piano, clarinet and not least, the violin, the instrument he would work with in full scale as an arranger and conductor. After high school, he studied music at Michigan University. He started with music education, adding practical knowledge of even more instruments to his repertoire, but ended up switching to music theory.

After he graduated in 1935, his impressive musical skills made him capable of working both as a multi-instrumentalist and arranger but arranging soon became Osser's call. His talent and diversity resulted in wide exposure as the arranger behind the Mets' theme song 'Meet the Mets,' and musical director and conductor for Miss America Pageant. He worked in strict musical settings as well, collaborating with prominent bandleaders such as Benny Goodman and Paul Whiteman. Like Percy Faith, Osser was involved with radio and he also landed a job as arranger and conductor for Columbia.[35] Here, he gained respect from the people around him, including recording engineer Frank Laico, who commented on Osser's work in an interview with Joseph H. Manning: 'He arranged his charts as if he wrote the songs himself. He had such a clear idea how to make an interesting arrangement for any song. He did so many different kinds of songs. He's a great artist.'[36]

In spite of Osser's talent, it was a tough job to follow Faith and the artistic and commercial success of the sparse *Open Fire, Two Guitars*, but Osser did the impossible and helped Mathis deliver another masterpiece: *Heavenly* (1959). In his notes for *The Voice of Romance: The Columbia Original Album Collection*, James Ritz underlines its significance. 'In the spring of

1959 – five months before his 24th birthday – Johnny came together with a brilliant orchestrator named Glenn Osser. By this time, Percy Faith – who had arranged all of the Mathis releases so far – was graduating from Columbia house arranger to bonafide recording artist himself and would soon release not only one of the greatest Columbia singles but one of the greatest singles of all time, 'Theme From A Summer Place.' The Columbia A&R department thought that the talented Osser might be a good fit for the particular Mathis talents. The result was *Heavenly*, the quintessential Johnny Mathis LP of his early period and which many consider his greatest album. It all came together here; the orchestrations, the production and particularly the voice. Not a false step in the whole procedure.'[37]

The success of the sound of Heavenly wasn't that it broke with what Mathis had previously done with Faith, but that it took some of the tested elements from their collaboration. For instance, the use of warm acoustic guitars in the bottom of *Swing Softly* is transferred into a ballad context and, once again, the violins play a significant role instead of the brass. The title, *Heavenly*, as well as that of its follow up, *Faithfully*, also points back to Mathis's religious roots on *Dear Lord*, but none of the albums are religious in the way the titles might imply. Instead, they focus on the spiritual aspect of love through serene interpretations of secular songs.

Moonlight, rainbows, and dreams are all over the material and the wistful mood is fleshed out by Osser's thoughtful arrangements. In a tribute, Jonathan Osser elaborates on his father's approach:

'When he arranged for singers, there was a subtle sophistication to his harmony – he didn't seek to transform the original song so much as to enhance it. But the sound was unique. One singer, who was moving from opera into the American Songbook repertory, commissioned some arrangements from my dad, and asked that he be liberal with 'Abe Chords.' Another singer said, 'You don't learn that kind of harmony in a conservatory.'[38]

Penned by Sidney Shaw and Burt Bacharach, the title track that opens the album is a fine example of how Osser works with strings on the album. After a sweeping intro with a suspended melody, the violins build up the tension with tremolo and Mathis croons the line 'What a feeling.' Then the line is echoed by an oboe, and there's a slight pause like a sigh, and Mathis sings the rest of the melody line, 'It's heavenly,' accompanied by celestial glockenspiel and dialogic strings. Then the clarification of the feeling comes when he sings, 'that's how it feels when you're with me.' The overwhelming emotions are mirrored in crescendo and Mathis soars and sings, 'Angels above could only be just that / as happy as we,' before he returns to the opening line with the strings once again using subdued tremolo. The opening is less than a minute. In that time, Osser and Mathis manage to stage a sophisticated drama that goes from subtle emotional tension to full-blown hymnic release. Osser uses strings like a writer would use full stops, commas, and interjections. The strings are not there to provide pompous ornament, they enhance the atmosphere of the song and the singer's interpretation. To achieve this, Osser brings incredible attention to the details of each song, but like Faith, he also has an ability to see an album as a complete narrative.

The title track is followed by an equally impressive interpretation of 'Hello, Young Lovers' by Rodgers and Hammerstein that once again uses tremolo to great effect before moving into a gently waltzing chorus with flutes and strings. Mathis catches a mood of wide-eyed wonder, serenading the young lovers as they move through life. He sings with the experience of one who has loved and hopes their trouble will be few as he wishes them all the best. He encourages them to be 'brave, faithful and true' and enjoy the moment, as he knows 'how it feels to have wings on your heels and to fly down a street in a trance.'

The key to understanding Mathis's sublime reading of the song is his ability to sing with total empathy and wonder and yet with the distance of one who is alone and looks at the lovers from afar. The narrator's empathy saves him from being bitter as he can imagine the young lovers' joy and relive his own love through them. In that way, memory and the moment right now intersect, and the song lifts itself from a melancholy past into a joyful present. This is underlined by the vital ending with the vocal stretching in exuberant defiance followed by a pregnant string coda.

Compare Mathis's 'Hello, Young Lovers' with the slowed-down autumnal ambiance of Frank Sinatra's interpretation six years later, and it becomes clear that Sinatra's version is great, but Mathis's is a masterpiece. Gordon Jenkins, a superb arranger, is too busy in his arrangement this time, preferring ornament over meaning, and while Sinatra also ends with an extended vocal line, it's an expression of defiance without real joy. Instead, the melancholy mood of someone who has lost his own youth and looks back pervades the song. The point is that Sinatra's interpretation is the easier choice and more conventional: the old man looking back at his lost years while giving the young lovers his bittersweet advice. His wings are clipped, but he refuses to accept that he can't fly. Mathis, on the other hand, flies on the strength of the young lovers. Sinatra's story is personal, imbued with the biographical meaning of the September of his years, but Mathis is personal in another way. He brings out the poetry in the song and makes it a hymn to love and lovers around the world.

Heavenly is filled with supreme love songs, but especially one song from the album has become a classic, and even today, as the music format of the masses has changed from hard copies to streaming, it is one of Mathis's most beloved songs with more than 13 million plays on Spotify. It was also inducted into the Grammy Hall of Fame in 2002. The name of the song is 'Misty.' Joseph H. Manning has written the definitive story of the song. He interviewed Mathis, who recalled how he ended up recording 'Misty'. 'I chose it, and there were several reasons. I heard Erroll Garner play it when I was in my early teens. I was frequenting a jazz club in San Francisco called the Black Hawk. Erroll played there about three or four times a year. One night, he played the song. There were no lyrics yet. I liked it a lot. I blurted out, 'Mr. Garner, I am going to record your song if I ever make a record.

Several years later, Johnny Burke had written lyrics to it, and I had fallen in love with an album that Sarah Vaughan had made with Quincy Jones. It was called Vaughan and Violins. I just loved their interpretation of 'Misty.' Erroll's business manager, Martha Glaser, heard somehow that I was going to record it, and she showed up at the recording studio. But we had a little problem because I was told to record a song from one of the current Broadway shows for which Columbia was planning to do the original cast recordings. That was going to push 'Misty' out.'

Well, that just couldn't happen, because there sat Martha Glaser waiting for me. By the time we got to the last song, which was 'Misty,' someone reminded me that I was also obligated to sing one of the Broadway show songs, and so we had a little argument over that. I said, 'Let's just do 'Misty,' and then sing the other song through and see which one comes out better.' When I sang 'Misty,' I remember the oboe solo, and that I just sort of came in at the wrong time with that high note. Well, it turned out to be a famous moment in the song. Looking back now, it was wonderful that it happened sort of accidentally on purpose.'[39]

While 'Misty' benefits from inspired moments like Mathis entering with his signature high note, the arrangement of the song was carefully planned. Glenn Osser told Joseph H. Manning: 'It was all written out. If you listen to it closely, Andy played block chords and the guitar played the lower notes in unison, just like in the George Shearing Quintet arrangements, except that I didn't use a vibraphone. Usually, when I do an introduction, I try to incorporate the main theme, paraphrased in some way. But this is one time that I didn't; it was a completely new composition. Behind it, I had the rhythm section and some violas and cellos sustaining harmony, just as a little cushion.'[40]

The pianist Andy Ackers has an important role on the recording since Osser decided to put the piano in the foreground, inspired by the fact that Erroll Garner was a master pianist himself. 'I knew that 'Misty' had been written by Erroll Garner. So I started off the arrangement with the piano on account of him. Then I decided that I wasn't going to have any violins come in at all until the second verse, when Johnny sings, 'And a thousand violins begin to play.' That business about him hitting that high note coming out of the instrumental break was his idea.[41]

The result of Osser's arrangement, Mathis's inspired singing and the fine playing of pianist Andy Ackers resulted in a classic recording that Mathis told Manning he still feels strongly about. 'It's the song I am most proud of because I did it myself. The other stuff was handled more or less by Mitch Miller or whoever was the producer of the moment. But I took it upon myself to do the tune the way I wanted to, and to have it actually become a signature moment in my musical career was the best thing that could have ever happened. I loved Erroll Garner so much. He was a wonderful musician, a genius really, because he couldn't read music. He never played the song the same way. He had all these amazing inventions he played before he started playing the melody. I was so proud that I had heard the tune when I was very young when there were no words to it, and that I kept my promise to record it, and I did it in a way that would last over a couple of lifetimes.'[42]

'Misty' was the first track on the second side of the record, so it could be feared that the album would lose momentum afterwards, but instead, the beauty continues and *Heavenly* ends with another highlight, 'That's All,' a standard penned by Alan Brandt and Bob Haymes. The song had already been cut by four singers who had shaped Mathis's own voice; Nat King Cole, June Christy, Billy Eckstine and Sarah Vaughan, so it was natural that he had a go at it himself.

Bobby Darin had made the song a big hit in 1959 with his up-tempo Latin swing version, but Mathis reaches back to the delicate art of Nat King Cole and the slow balladry of Billy Eckstine to create his definitive version. Introduced by Osser's achingly exquisite strings that don't mirror the melody as he often did in his introductions, a melancholy universe is established from the beginning. This isn't the shallow fun of Darin's version but a much deeper emotional ground that is mined.

Mathis enters together with softly tinkling piano and the paradox of a line, 'I can only give you love that lasts forever.' It unfolds the promise of romantic scenarios that are all the lyrical voice is able to give. The contrast 'are those, I am sure, who have told you / They would give you the world for a toy.' It's this paradoxical tension between a limited promise and unlimited love, unconditional surrender and infinite insecurity that carries the song. Mathis brings out the bittersweet longing of the lyrics and the culmination is the last verse that turns the motif around. From the 'modest' promise of eternal love, all the lyrical voice now asks is that love is returned. 'You'll be glad to know that my demands are small / Say it's me that you'll adore / For now and evermore / That's all.'

The first version of the final verse is sung with vibrato, followed by a waltzing interlude with acoustic guitars, strings, and oboe. The interlude seems to reflect the dream of a wedding waltz, but the dream is interrupted when the tempo slows down, and Mathis starts again and ends the song on a soaring light note. It's an ending that also brings the album full circle, from the heavenly ecstasy of being in love to the earthy longing of wishing someone special will return the love that is offered.

Mathis followed *Heavenly* with *Faithfully* (1959). Released the same year as the previous album, with titles echoing each other and a preliminary title track once again penned by Sidney Shaw and Burt Bacharach, it sounds like a musical twin, but *Faithfully* is a bit bolder and brasher than its predecessor. The focus is still on the solemn praise of romantic love as it is announced on 'Faithfully'. 'Faithfully, we will obey our love / Faithfully, all night and day, my love.'

Whereas *Heavenly* relied on tried and tested songs, its successor offered no less than five new songs and also dug up chestnuts like the pop hit 'You Better Go Now' and the title song for the 1953 movie *The Blue Gardenia*. This strategy worked because without the burden of previous interpretations and arrangements, Mathis and Osser got a chance to stretch out in a way they hadn't done before. Consequently, the sound is more melodramatic and experimental. On two songs from the Bernstein and Sondheim Broadway musical, *West Side Story*, 'Tonight' and 'Maria,' Osser uses a male voice choir on Mathis's suggestion, and especially on the latter, Mathis shows the full operatic range of his voice from the softest whisper to a dramatic vocal flight. It's a song that embodies a sensual approach to the song as Mathis gets lost in the pure sound of the name. 'Maria / the most beautiful sound I ever heard.' Maria is both a woman and music and the song is just as much a homage to music itself as it is a love song.

Mathis also uses the opportunity to stretch his voice on the serenade 'And This Is My Beloved,' a song taken from the musical *Kismet*. He covered 'Stranger in Paradise' from the same musical on *Heavenly*, but here he surrenders fully to the dramatic phrasings of the musical genre. Elsewhere, he returns to the standards with an ethereal interpretation of the Jimmy McHugh and Harold Adamson standard 'Where Are You?' However, the unexpected highlights of the album are two unknown songs.

The songwriters Abner Silver and Sid Wayne had already delivered a classic with 'Moonlight Becomes You' on *Heavenly*, but they surpass themselves on 'One Starry Night.' It has the operatic pop grandeur of the best musicals. Wrapped in Osser's wondrous arrangement with prominent use of harp and flutes, Mathis steps into an enchanted landscape and sings a cosmic love serenade that in less skillful hands would become clichéd, but instead, he lifts the pathos of the song and makes it a strength.

'Follow Me' was written by the multitalented showbiz legend Kay Thompson. It uses some of Osser's familiar tricks: the echo of the melody in the intro with strings and harp, and then a hovering flute melody repeated by the oboe, one of Osser's favorite instruments. Mathis enters and sings the simple word 'follow' with so much meaning it almost breaks the heart and the third time, he effectively adds the concluding 'me.' The drama of the song doesn't come from the melodramatic world of musicals but from a tension spun of the finest musical silk. Mathis once again uses vibrato and glissando, but in a much subtler way than the equally impressive 'Maria.'

Like *Heavenly*, *Faithfully* moves from romantic idealism to earthly longing and loneliness. The album ends with 'Blue Gardenia' where Mathis sings 'Love bloomed like a flower / Then the petals fell' accompanied by an orchestral emulation of falling leaves. But all is not lost because, as in 'Hello, Young Lovers,' the memory of love remains: Blue gardenia / Thrown to a passing breeze / But pressed in my book / Of memories.'

After the success of *Heavenly* and *Faithfully*, both top-selling albums peaking at number one and two on the *Billboard* chart, respectively, Mathis went deeper into the Broadway songbook with an album of ballads. The big question was how he would sing them. Would he prefer the melodramatic style of the musical or a more restrained ballad approach? *Faithfully* had shown he could do both things on the same album, but the result was also a less homogenous album than *Heavenly*.

The answer is immediately given on the first track of *Ballads of Broadway* (1960). 'Moanin' Low' is mellow and laidback. Accompanied by piano, Mathis hums the intro before he introduces the lyric. 'Moanin' low, my sweet girl, I love her so / Though she's mean as can be / She's the kind of girl needs the kind of a man like me.' The last part is delivered with silky bluesy phrasing, and even when the strings enter, there's no doubt that the main instrument is the piano.

No less than five songs are co-written by Richard Rodgers, among them 'Dancing On The Ceiling' and 'Spring Is Here' where the strings once again take the center stage, but generally there's much more of a band feeling this time with softly tugging acoustic guitar and bass clearly in the mix on tracks like 'Don't Blame Me' and the concluding 'The Party's Over.' Conceived as one part of a double album, with the other being *The Rhythms of Broadway*, *Ballads of Broadway* is a consistent set of lovely interpretations of standards without making too much of a fuss. At this point, Osser wasn't taking Mathis in new directions, and yet the last album of their early years was a departure for them in both good and bad ways.

Johnny's Mood has the dubious honor of presenting the first real clunker on a Mathis album, and it even comes as the opener. On the surface, everything about 'I'm Gonna Laugh You Out of My Life' goes by the book. A fine intro with strings introduces the song and then Mathis comes, but instead of building tension, he almost immediately starts with the high notes and his voice seems uneven and restrained without its usual natural elegance and pacing. The nadir is the sudden tongue-click pronunciation of 'hard' at the end of one of his signature vocal flights. To top it off, Osser inserts a trumpet coda that comes like a deus ex machina. It's an awkward ending to a surprisingly faltering song.

Fortunately, things already get much better with the second track, 'Stay Warm.' This time the brass element is used thoughtfully and introduced from the beginning. Mathis croons convincingly in tandem with the trumpet and the vocal flights are once again beautiful. Even the use of a trumpet coda works this time and wraps up an early highlight of the album. Hereafter, it's smooth sailing with a string of excellent songs, including strong readings of the standards 'The Folks Who live On The Hill' and 'April in Paris,' both including trumpet.

The prominent use of trumpet ends up being one of the strengths of the arrangements and the album that started so frustratingly turns out to be another winner. For the next albums, Osser stepped back while other arrangers provided something that had been missing in Mathis's music for a while: swing.

Specialists of Swing: Ralph Burns and Nelson Riddle

Mathis's move towards a more swing-oriented sound had already been prepared while he worked with Glenn Osser. When he did his double album of songs from Broadway, the rhythmical side, *The Rhythms of Broadway* (1960), was left in the capable hands of Ralph Burns.

Ralph Burns (1922-2001) studied piano as a child and later attended New England Conservatory. Through the recommendation of the stellar big band singer, Frances Wayne, whose family he had lived with, Burns joined the Charlie Barnet Orchestra as a pianist and writer. He quickly made the big band scene aware of his talents and so Woody Herman snatched him, and he became a crucial component of Herman's legendary first herd, eventually moving from the piano chair to composing and orchestrating. Inspired by Duke Ellington and Billy Strayhorn, Burns' writing flourished. In the fifties, while still writing for Herman, he made the first recordings under his own name, including the masterpiece *Spring Sequence* (1955).

Outside jazz circles, Burns also scored film soundtracks and he was an orchestrator for some of the most successful shows on Broadway, among them *Chicago* and *No, No, Nanette*. He was also involved with Richard Rodgers and orchestrated his musical *No Strings*.[43]

When Burns began his collaboration with Mathis, he was hot. At this time, Burns was also recording with another notable Columbia artist, the singer Tony Bennett, and he had certainly proved that he knew how to handle swinging rhythms, which was required of the second side of the Broadway project: *The Rhythms of Broadway*.

The unknown part of the equation was Mathis himself. He had shown he could swing sporadically on his debut, but the few hard brass arrangements by Percy Faith didn't work so well. Instead, Faith and Mathis found the perfect formula when they began to *Swing Softly*, as their album from 1958 was called. Would the lush and richly textured instrument of Mathis's voice adapt to snapping, cracking, and cooking big band swing? Put another way, could he swing hard as well as softly?

The answer comes on the opener 'Everything's Coming Up Roses.' It starts with a dramatic brass fanfare, but then things slow down, the violins enter and Mathis croons, 'I had a dream / A dream about you, baby / It's gonna come true, baby / They think that we're through.' It's closer to Scott Walker's grandiose ballads than jazz, but something happens. Mathis sings 'but baby,' letting the last word ring with vibrato and a tingling piano enters accompanied by a fast, lightly swinging drum rhythm and the walking bass starts. The weather forecast predicts swing. There's silence for a moment and Mathis sings 'things look swell,' and the moment he gets to 'swell', the brass breaks through, and from now on, there's no way back and Mathis swings himself through a series of big brass punches, swirling violins, and impossible breaks, and he ends with an extended powerful vocal. It's like a fighter getting into the ring and this start should knock everyone out who is foolish enough to claim that Mathis can't swing hard.

The momentum is kept with the tracks that follow. The brass volume is consistently high, but Mathis matches the swinging power of the orchestra with his adroit voice. It's a joy to hear his take on 'Guys and Dolls,' 'I Could Have Danced All Night' and 'A Cockeyed Optimist' and his force as a ballad singer also comes through on a hybrid song like 'I Wish I Were In Love Again' that combines swing, ballad and cabaret.

A highlight is the reading of four Cole Porter songs. Mathis is simply one of the best interpreters of Porter and the reason is quite simple: few people are better at misbehaving with music. Cole Porter was in love with words and their rhythms. Peruse his lyrics and they are filled with supreme strings of alliterations, assonances, repetitions, metaphors, and homophones. Speaking of homophones, listen to the way Mathis elegantly brings out the double meaning of 'Letts' and 'let's do it' in a passage from 'Let's Do It': 'Lithuanians and Letts do it / Let's do it, let's fall in love.' It requires perfect pronunciation, a sly sense of rhythm and musical timing to redeem a conceit like this. Ella Fitzgerald, another shrewd Cole interpreter, has it and Mathis has certainly got it. His reading of 'Let's Do It' might be the definitive version and it puts Will Friedwald's preposterous claim that it's not worth hearing Mathis sing standards to shame.[44] The only problem with Mathis's interpretations of Cole Porter is there are not enough of them. He could have made a whole album of Porter tunes, but he never did.

Four songs in this ideal musical setting with Burns are also something, and any way you cut it, *The Rhythms of Broadway* is a success. Helped by Burns' superb arrangements and band, it revealed a hard-swinging Mathis who had lost none of his sophistication in the process. The question was if he could keep up the pace when he got the chance to collaborate with another specialist of swing: Nelson Riddle.

Arranger and conductor Nelson Smock Riddle (1921-1985) will forever be remembered for the rich musical legacy he created with Frank Sinatra in the fifties when they perfected the art of the concept album and created such classics as *In the Wee Small Hours* (1955), *Songs for Swingin' Lovers* (1956) and *Only the Lonely* (1958). Before he started working with Sinatra, Riddle had cut his teeth as arranger for Bob Crosby and worked as staff arranger for NBC Radio in 1947. He also studied with Mario Castelnuovo-Tedesco and Victor Young.[45]

His association with Capitol Records, and eventually Sinatra, began with his work for Nat King Cole. Riddle was the arranger behind Cole's hits 'Mona Lisa' (1950) and 'Too Young' (1951), and the success of the songs paved the way for a long musical relationship and further success with Sinatra and other iconic singers like Rosemary Clooney, Ella Fitzgerald, and Peggy Lee.[46]

It was Mathis's new producer Irving Townsend that made the collaboration between Mathis and Riddle happen. He had taken over the reins after the epic effort of Mitch Miller, who had proven that it was possible to combine chart-topping pop and art. It was Miller who had turned Mathis away from jazz because his jazz debut didn't sell well, so in a way, it was ironic that Mathis's new producer took him back in a musical direction that Miller had mostly shunned.

However, Townsend is perhaps most famous for producing Miles Davis' *Kind of Blue* (1959), the best-selling jazz album of all time. Seen in that perspective, it's not surprising that Townsend saw both the commercial and artistic potential in taking Mathis's music in a jazzy direction. The result was two very different albums. One would be one of his most eclectic efforts so far and the other a stringent swing album.

Mathis and Riddle began their collaboration with the surprisingly adventurous *I'll Buy You a Star* (1961). It spans different versions of swing from the heavy booming brass of 'Ring the Bell,' of course with sounds of bells, to the metamorphosis of the title track that starts as a smoky piano ballad only to become a dynamic Latin big band piece with congas and marimba. An even lighter version of the swinging conga sound is explored on 'Sudden Love,' sweetened by flutes and strings, while 'When My Sugar Walks Down the Street' strolls along with woody walking bass and muted trumpet in relaxed style.

The use of choir, first introduced by Glenn Osser on *Faithfully* (1959), is also explored. Easy listening prevails on 'Wherever You Are It's Spring' and 'Oh, How I Try,' but the choir is elevated into art on the slow oriental beauty of 'Magic Garden,' sporting softly chiming triangles, operatic voices and sweet call and response patterns in the midst of arabesque strings and flutes.

Riddle is not only working wonders on a lush soundscape like 'Magic Garden,' but also sprinkles stardust on a standard with his arrangement of Charlie Chaplin's 'Smile,' described by the *AllMusic*-writer Joe Viglione as 'elegance suspended in space.[47]' It's not only the elegance but also the emotion that is suspended. The key to understanding the song has always been the tension between sadness and happiness, as expressed in the opening verse, 'Smile though your heart is aching / Smile even though it's breaking / When there are clouds in the sky, you'll get by / If you smile through your fear and sorrow.' Pathos and sentimentality can easily overshadow the unsettling tension of smiling 'through your fear and sorrow', but Riddle keeps the melancholy undercurrent in the song and the strings never exhilarate in pure joy but hang suspended in midair like 'a tear may be ever so near.'

As usual, Mathis explores a wide spectrum with his voice but digs even deeper into the lower register with burnished bass notes, delicate dark shadings, and a powerful tenor less light and nasal. There's no better way of illustrating this difference than comparing the endings of the ballads 'Love Look Away' and 'My Heart and I.' The former is an example of the dark tenor, while the latter is lighter and brighter.

Taken as a whole, *I'll Buy You a Star* is a triumph of textures and a rich musical painting, but commercially it didn't fare so well. It reached number 38 on *Billboard* magazine's album chart and stayed there for 23 weeks. Seen in that perspective, it was not surprising that the approach for Mathis's second album with Riddle was different.

Recorded in April 1961, only two months later than *I'll Buy You a Star*, *Live It Up!* is a no frills-big band swing album. The difference is clear if you compare the opening title tracks of the two albums. Whereas 'I'll Buy You a Star' was an artful metamorphosis from piano ballad to sophisticated Latin swing, 'Live It Up' is uncomplicated big band jazz at full throttle from the beginning. The tempo is slowed down on the ballad 'Just Friends,' and afterwards, Mathis successfully returns to Cole Porter on the lovely 'Ace in the Hole.' There's a bit of doo-wop spice on 'A Cold Rainy Day' while the big band swing continues with 'Why Not' and 'I Won't Dance.'

The easy-going mood of the album is underlined by the humorous 'Johnny One Note.' Although it is written by Rodgers and Hart, the song, taken from the Broadway musical, *Babes in Arms*, is closer to a novelty song than a standard. Ironically, it tells about a Johnny that can only sing one note, hardly Mathis, and when it's told in the lyrics that he can't hear the instruments like the brass, the drum, the flute and the trombone, the specific instruments answer each time.

The ballads are a rare sight, but 'Crazy in the Heart,' introduced by a saucy saxophone solo, is a slow jazzy delight. However, tempo is the name of the game, and this is emphasized with the cooking closer, 'Love,' a zestfully funky Latin big band piece propelled by restless congas. It's the highlight of an album that doesn't have the artistic quality of the predecessor, but in return, it was a commercial success. It reached number 14 on the *Billboard* album chart and stayed on the list for 39 weeks.

Unfortunately, the success didn't make Irving Townsend stay and Riddle also left. The collaboration only lasted for two albums, but it made an impression on Mathis, who recalled the experience of working with Riddle in an interview with Buddy Seigal. 'The songs I recorded with Nelson Riddle I was very proud of, simply because at the time we recorded them, he was on top of the world. I never thought that Nelson would ever bother recording with me. When I hear some of those songs, I get very nostalgic.'[48]

It wasn't an easy job for Mathis' next producer, Ernie Altschuler, to find a proper replacement for Riddle, a living legend at the time, but instead of finding someone with an illustrious resume, Altschuler's alternative had his best work ahead of him and would just begin his golden era at the same time he recorded with Mathis. His name was Don Costa.

Weaver of Sound: The Don Costa Trilogy

Ernie Altschuler knew something about finding the combination of a hit and a superior sound. He had produced Percy Faith's smash hit 'Theme from a Summer Place' and could now look forward to working with a singer whom Faith had previously backed. Altschuler chose an arranger and conductor, Don Costa, who had already made a name for himself and was moving up fast. In a *JazzWax.com* post about Don Costa, Marc Myers wrote, 'The studio guitarist-orchestrator came to prominence in the mid-1950s when he was hired by ABC-Paramount as the start-up label's A&R chief. Costa was the pen behind Steve Lawrence and Eydie Gorme at ABC-Paramount and other artists such as Lloyd Price and Paul Anka. Frank Sinatra hired Costa in 1962, and he wound up arranging quite a few of the Chairman's champion swingers for nearly 15 years. But between gigs at ABC and Reprise, Costa worked for Columbia.'[49]

At Columbia, Costa made three albums with Mathis: *Rapture* (1962), *Johnny* (1963) and *Romantically* (1963). Together they could be considered a trilogy that epitomizes all the work Mathis had previously done at Columbia. Costa goes back to the recorded heritage and delivers his own take on the Mathis sound that widens and deepens the picture. He has a particular reference that is evident both aurally and visually. If the cover painting of the first Mathis-Costa collaboration, *Rapture*, feels like a déjà vu, it's because it's painted by Ralph Wolfe Cowan, who also did the cover for *Heavenly*. Just like Glenn Osser built on the legacy of Percy Faith, Costa continues to refine the lush orchestral sound introduced by Osser, but it's also possible to hear links to Faith and Riddle. At the same time, his arrangements also have a unique quality and are justifiably praised by Myers: 'Without mincing words, Costa's string work for Mathis is sensational. Rather than merely create lush gardens for Mathis to run through, Costa's writing for strings (and choir on some tracks) rises up to Mathis' delivery level, cushioning the singer's power and taking the edge off his high-end vibrato.'[50]

Mathis was also impressed by Costa's musicality. He was quoted by Joe Marchese, who wrote the notes for the compilation *60th + 1 Anniversary Classic Singles & Favorite Songs*, saying, 'He was one of the most extraordinarily gifted individuals that I have ever known,' Mathis notes of Costa. 'He was the kind of musician who could do what he did at any moment during the day or night. In other words, he carried his gift of music with him all the time. Of course, he was very generous in sharing it with me. He would come to the studio without having the arrangement done, and he would do it on site, and do it fast, and that successfully!'[51]

Costa was a fast arranger, but that didn't prevent him from being original. The crucial difference between Osser's and Costa's approach to arranging lies in Myers' observation that the string work takes the edge off Mathis's high-end vibrato. Osser often highlighted the drama of Mathis's voice through his arrangements, and he used the tension between the orchestra, the voice, and a single instrument to great effect. He was particularly happy about the oboe, the harp, and as a late addition, the trumpet.

While continuing the orchestral elegance of Osser, Costa primarily works horizontally instead of vertically. If the string sounds don't make up gardens that Mathis can run through, as Myers aptly puts it, they could still be enjoyed as a landscape of sound with many splendid details, but it's not merely a beautiful background. Mathis's voice and the music are woven together and one of the finest achievements of Costa is perhaps that he illuminates the voice as an instrument in the orchestra, not outside it. Just listen to how the different instrumental parts and Mathis coalesce in the beginning of 'You've Come Home' or the smoothly sublime orchestral cushioning of his voice on 'The Love Nest.'

A textbook example of the art of ambience can be found in 'Lament (Love, I Found You Gone)' that uses a contrast between the dreamy atmosphere of the intro, underlined by harps, and the deep register of Mathis's voice as he sings, 'the night was cold / and the wind was high / the moon grew old / in a restless sky / then came the dawn / with a pagan song / through weeping eyes / I found you gone.' It's a complex tone poem encapsulated in the first minute of the song that reflects the melancholy movement from night till day and an underlying sense of loss.

Just to show that Costa also masters the dramatic elegance of Glenn Osser, the album closes with a symphonic reading of the standard 'Stella By Starlight.' It's an epic ending to an album that introduces Mathis's new collaborator in the best possible way, and on the next album, Costa proved that he dared go to places where Osser hadn't gone before when he used a big band to supplement the sound of the orchestra.

Costa's second album with Mathis, simply titled *Johnny* (1963) is the inconvenient part of the trilogy because it doesn't fit with the aesthetic of the other two albums, both collections of beautiful ballads conceived in the spirit of Glenn Osser.

Instead, *Johnny* is an eclectic affair that includes most of the things that Mathis had done before, and so the title fits an informal musical portrait of the singer. On the first two tracks, 'Easy Does It' and 'The Most Beautiful Girl In The World,' Costa uses a big band but avoids the hard swinging approach of Ralph Burns and sweetens the sound with choir to achieve an easy listening version of big band swing. The music really comes to life when the choir is used to create a gospel feeling that harks back to *Dear Lord* on the vibrant version of Duke Ellington's 'Jump for Joy.'

Mathis also returns to Cole Porter on the pantheistic 'I Love You' where daffodils, hills, birds, and the breeze sing the eternal song of love to the accompaniment of strings and light Latin percussion. The motif of the wind, this time as a scent 'like a perfumed woman,' returns in the reading of Frank Loesser's standard 'Joey, Joey, Joey.' It's hard to think of someone who could coax more musicality out of the simple sound of 'Joey' than Mathis, and he brings out all the lovelorn longing that is possible in his crooning of the name.

Ballads abound and the playfully baroque intro of 'When the World Was Young' mimics the coming of spring, but quickly turns into an elegy that recalls the nostalgia of 'Hello, Young Lovers,' this time with an irrevocable sense of loss that can't be redeemed by the optimism of youth. The mellow memory of love also pervades 'Miss Butterfly,' with echoes of Japanese music. Elsewhere, an entire dream world is created in 'Weaver of Dreams' where Mathis croons, 'I'm in your spell and there's no cure / I'm lost for sure / 'Cause you're a weaver of dreams / And I'm in love with you.'

Once again, Costa uses a dramatic ending on 'No Man Can Stand Alone' that leaves all caution to the wind and rolls out the big romantic arsenal with bombastic strings and a coda of pompous percussion fireworks that would leave Osser blushing.

In the final part of the trilogy, *Romantically*, Costa returns to the template of the ballad album. Once again, there's a reference to Osser with the title echoing *Heavenly* and *Faithfully*, and Mathis returns to the theatrical sound that he covered so well on his version of Bernstein's 'Maria,' but while keeping the sound in technicolor, Costa adds subtle musical layers and achieves the paradox of outgoing intimacy in his arrangements of 'Getting to Know You' and 'The Sound of Music,' both penned by Rodgers and Hammerstein.

It has previously been noted that Mathis is a congenial interpreter of Cole Porter, but it could be just as tempting to compile an album of his interpretations of Rodgers and Hammerstein. Since he had sung a superb version of 'It Might As Well Be Spring' on his Columbia debut, he had successfully explored their songbook and 'Getting to Know You' and 'The Sound of Music' are among his most convincing takes on songs by the famous pair. With the help of Costa, Mathis achieves a rare theatrical intimacy that is both ethereal and grandiose. Especially 'The Sound of Music' is a stunning example of majestic textures with marching acoustic guitars, softly singing brass, whispering flutes, and sweeping violins. Glockenspiel and harps support the dreamy ambience with the choir like a rising tide underneath the operatic surge of Mathis singing lyrics that might as well be a self-portrait. 'My heart wants to sing every song it hears / My heart wants to beat like the wings of the birds that rise from the lake to the trees / My heart wants to sigh like the chime that flies from a church on a breeze / To laugh like a brook as it trips and falls over stones on its way / To sing through the night like a lark who is learning to prey.'

If 'The Sound of Music' is a perfect musical fairy tale, then the illusion is partly broken on 'It's Only A Paper Moon.' It trembles between make-believe and magic, a chugging orchestral piano ballad that both feels heavy and light as air. Elsewhere, the stark reality of time is shown in 'To Young to Go Steady' and 'September Song.' On the former, the problem is being too young, and the latter laments the coming of old age. Before Sinatra would cut his signature version and make it the title song of his 1965 album, Mathis shows the way with a voice as varied in autumnal colors as a mosaic of leaves changing from burnt red, light yellow and brown to faded green. Mathis wasn't in his twilight years, but he had certainly come a long way since his beginning and had moved from a promising singer to a superstar.

The Costa trilogy did well. *Rapture* reached number 12 on the *Billboard* chart, while *Johnny* peaked at number 20. *Romantically* was the least successful of the albums, peaking at number 23, but no matter what, Mathis had proved that he was a worthwhile investment, and his next step was to move away from Columbia to gain complete artistic freedom and start his own label, Global Records, under the auspices of Mercury Records. He even managed to bring both Osser and Costa with him. It looked like the ideal situation, but looking back, Mathis would later think of his Global years with mixed feelings. Freedom meant no one would be there to influence him, but the most attractive thing about his new position also turned out to be his biggest problem.

Johnny Mathis

Part Three: The Global Years

A Ship Without A Sail: The Global Years

In 1963, Mathis moved to Mercury Records, where he would oversee his own imprint, Global Records, with ownership of all his masters and total control of the music. His association with Mercury lasted three years and produced a staggering amount of material, including ten albums, an unreleased collection of Broadway songs, and a slew of singles. It was an unparalleled burst of productivity but also a patchy period without the unifying vision of a long-term collaboration with a producer or orchestrator. Instead, Mathis produced himself, worked with a producer on a single release and collaborated with different arrangers and conductors.

In the liner notes to a boxset of his collected Global recordings, he talks candidly about these years. 'When we decided to go to Mercury, I was young and inexperienced. At Columbia Records, most of my best work in the studio was achieved by concentration and good focus. I'd had the good fortune of working with people like Percy Faith and Glenn Osser, who made decisions for me. They had wonderful taste, and I would always go along with whatever they chose for me. Now, all of a sudden, I was in charge of my own decisions in the studio, and I didn't have someone to guide me on what I was doing, right or wrong. I was pretty successful at the time, so everybody thought that maybe I knew what I was doing...

But I wasn't a producer, and I didn't realize until then how important producers were and how much they assisted me in my work. I tried to do what I could, but I had no idea what would be good for the market. So I just concocted things, but I was expected to be a professional and have my charts thought out, and I wasn't good at it.'[52]

In the words of one of the songs he released during his time at Global, Mathis was 'Like a ship without a sail.' Left with his own instinct of what would work musically, the irony of Mathis's freedom is that it resulted in some of the most conservative choices of his chameleonic career. He did take steps forward, especially with the Latin American album, *Olé* (1964), and the introduction of modern pop songs in his repertoire, but overall, he stuck to the material he knew: classic pop in the shape of standards, Broadway tunes and movie songs.

It's telling that his first album for Global was a Christmas album, a concept Mathis had already tried out successfully at Columbia. This album, *Sounds of Christmas* (1963), will be discussed later. His next album, *Tender Is the Night* (1964), also followed a familiar template; the ballad album, and relied on an orchestrator he had already worked with before. The point is not to say that Mathis made subpar music while he was at Mercury. In fact, despite the quantity of the records he put out, the quality of the music is remarkably high. One reason is the supreme shape of his voice; another is that, after all, Mathis wasn't completely alone on his musical ship. Old friends and new collaborators would show up and help him.

Old Acquaintances: Don Costa and Glenn Osser

Don Costa had already been reunited with Mathis on the album, *Sounds of Christmas*, but only as a producer. On the second Global album, *Tender Is the Night* (1964), he assumed his previous role as arranger and conductor while Mathis produced the record. The result was a classic ballad collection, up there with their previous collaborations, which is saying a lot, but something was also different this time. Costa's approach is much more vertical, favoring dramatic waves and movements while relying less on sophisticated sound tapestries. Indeed, certain instruments also play a crucial role. The use of glockenspiel and piano is especially prominent. The former adds ethereal ambience while the latter provides the relaxed jazzy mood of a cocktail piano and lyrical flourishes.

The span between the intimate and the dramatic is reflected in the songs. 'Call Me Irresponsible' and 'I Can't Give You Anything But Love' are delivered in the smooth baritone style of his early idol, Nat King Cole, whereas the theatrical catharsis of 'Where Is Love?' and 'Somewhere' show the full operatic range of his voice.

The album is perfectly paced, and the use of drama is never overdone. There's also a thematic coherence to the songs, as when the image of the sailboat appears in the title track that mentions 'a sailboat in Capri' and the motif returns in 'A Ship Without a Sail,' and just as the album begins with an ode to the night, it ends with the lightly waltzing wizardry of 'Tomorrow Song.'

The closing piece is one of two new songs penned by Bart Howard, the other being the ballad 'Forget Me Not.' Mathis has always been good at introducing new songs by writers he liked, and Howard was one of them. 'Bart was a lovely, quiet, sophisticated gentleman, and a dear, dear friend, who liked to play the piano and write songs. He would have been the last to tell you that, but he desperately wanted to have a successful song, which he finally did when he wrote 'Fly Me To The Moon.' Before that, though, he had written a vast amount of songs, and I recorded lots and lots of them. He was very important to me, keeping my focus on not just listening to music that was available, but also to try and find something that was a little more interesting.'[53]

It says something about the quality of Howard's songs that they don't feel out of place in a collection of timeless songs, among them 'Laura' that Mathis has mentioned as one of the key songs in his repertoire because of the poignant Costa arrangement.[54]

Overall, *Tender Is The Night* was a success, both artistically and commercially, climbing to number 13 on the *Billboard* chart. In spite of this, except for a series of singles, the album marked the end of Mathis's musical relationship with Costa, but another old friend eventually took over: Glenn Osser.

Osser also collaborated with Mathis on his Christmas album, *Sounds of Christmas* (1963), but it took two more years before he returned to deliver what is arguably one of the greatest albums of the Global era: *Love Is Everything* (1965). In fact, the album harks back to Mathis's glory years on Columbia. Not only does Osser return, but the album is produced by Al Ham, another Columbia acquaintance who had worked alongside Mitch Miller as associate producer on the albums *Goodnight, Dear Lord*, *Swing Softly* and *Merry Christmas*. However, Ham's crowning achievement came when he solely produced the masterpiece, *Heavenly*. *Love is Everything* almost reaches the same heights, but the most interesting thing about the album is how the approach to arranging is changed.

The twist of the Global years is that they reverse the positions of Costa and Osser, so Costa made his most Osser-inspired album with *Tender is the Night*, whereas Osser himself explored the texturally layered approach that Don Costa perfected on his trilogy. This doesn't mean that Osser doesn't use his subtle dramatic curves. They are there from the very start on the silky 'Never Let Me Go' and the magical merry-go-round 'A Thousand Blue Bubbles,' but instead of working with signature instruments and motifs, he explores a colorful canvas of sound and creates a dream to get lost in. Whether it's using the wistful touch of acoustic guitar and piano on the title track, with echoes of Glen Campbell, or light Latin percussion and sweeping orchestral curves on 'Come Ride the Wind With Me,' Osser's musical palette is broader than before.

The repertoire covers songs from several decades, spanning the 30s to the 60s, but in Mathis's versions, they get a timeless quality as he gives profound readings of ballads like 'Young and Foolish' and 'This Is All I Ask.' Even the potentially kitschy cowboy song, 'One More Mountain,' which recalls Lee Hazlewood, gets a deep treatment, so it becomes a grand emotional statement and a worthy way to close the album.

Like Costa, Osser recorded a batch of singles with Mathis, but he was also involved in three other Global albums. His appearance on *The Sweetheart Tree* (1965) was very limited, he just provided the arrangement for the movie song 'Mirage,' but he was the arranger and conductor on five of the twelve tracks on *The Shadow of Your Smile* (1966), a surprisingly successful patchwork that showcased all the types of songs Mathis could do from easy listening swing to Broadway tunes, Brazilian ballads, folk, and modern pop.

The slowly waltzing arrangement of the Beatles classic 'Yesterday' is both airy and mournful, adding a humming coda from Mathis, and Osser catches a celestial feeling of *saudade* on Jobim's 'Quiet Night of Quiet Stars (Corcovado)' with Mathis singing perfect in Portuguese, just as he breaks into flawless French on another Beatles song, 'Michelle.'

Osser always had a knack for bringing out the best in Mathis's Broadway tunes and this is also the case with the triptych that closes the album: 'On a Clear Day You Can See Forever,' 'Melinda' and 'Come Back to Me.' 'Melinda' goes back to the operatic grandeur of 'Maria' while the other two reveal a surprising influence from Burt Bacharach, an artist and songwriter whose songbook Mathis would explore much more in his career.

In fact, a Bacharach composition appears on the next and final Global album with Glenn Osser: *So Nice* (1966). In an arrangement without choir, Mathis's voice gets the chance to reveal its full orchestral scope on 'What the World Needs Now,' without losing any of the subdued sophistication characteristics of Bacharach. Another highlight is a trio of songs from the musical *Man of La Mancha*: 'The Impossible Dream,' 'Dulcinea' and 'Man of La Mancha (I, Don Quixote).' The conductor on two of these songs wasn't Osser, but Jack Feierman, who played an important role as a key collaborator in the Global years in tandem with Allyn Ferguson.

New Partners in Sound: Jack Feierman and Allyn Ferguson

In a period of frequently changing collaborators, Jack Feierman and Allyn Ferguson provided some stability and were involved in many Global releases, either together or separately. Jack Feierman (1924-2016) grew up in Omaha and studied piano as a child before switching to trumpet as a teenager. He eventually chose to pursue a career as a conductor and studied orchestral conducting techniques at the New York Eastman School of Music. As a trumpeter, he played with Count Basie, Stan Kenton and Woody Herman, and he worked as a conductor for Mathis, Natalie Cole and Frank Sinatra.[55]

Allyn Ferguson (1924-2010) played the trumpet like Feierman, but he changed to piano when he was seven years old. He ended up working as a prolific arranger and composer, who scored several soundtracks for TV programs, and he also had a Chamber Jazz Sextet that collaborated with the poet Kenneth Patchen.

Feierman's and Ferguson's knowledge of jazz served them well when they collaborated on the most intriguing Mathis release during the Global years, the Latino-flavored *Olé* (1964). The idea for the album came from Mathis himself: 'The concept of this album was all mine. I had been hanging out with Miles Davis for a while, and he introduced me to a film called *Black Orpheus*. I fell in love with the music and over the years, I have recorded almost every aspect of its soundtrack. That was the genesis for the album itself.'[56]

Two songs from *Black Orpheus* ended up on the album. On 'Manha De Carnival (Morning of the Carnival),' the intimate picking of an acoustic guitar accompanies a soft humming that later transforms into Portuguese song as sensual flutes enter. A breathtaking coda of swiveling guitar and vocal concludes the piece. More vibrant than this ethereal ballad is the 'Samba de Orfeu' with Mathis singing nothing but la-la-la as a choir of children joins him in a samba party propelled by lively percussion.

The soundtrack to *Black Orpheus* introduced bossa nova to the world before the singer Astrud Gilberto and saxophonist Stan Getz, and the music penned by Antonio Carlos Jobim and Luis Bonfa made them international stars.[57] Jobim is acknowledged in a medley containing two of his lesser-known songs, 'Generique' and 'Felicidade,' co-written with Vinicius De Moraes. Like the two songs from *Black Orpheus*, the medley both contains the restless sound of samba percussion and the breezy stylings associated with Jobim, but the interesting thing is that the two approaches overlap, making the music akin to watching a sunset on a quiet beach while a carnival is heard in the distance.

Another Brazilian composer, Heitor Villa-Lobos, is also explored. Mathis himself has been critical about his own reading of 'Bachianas Brasileiras (Parts 1-3)'. 'This was a composition that, as a singer, I often used for my vocal exercises. If I were to do it today, I'd probably rest my voice between the various parts, but when I recorded it that wasn't the case. As a result, it may sound a bit labored, but I'd give myself a C for effort on this selection.'[58]

In spite of his own reservations, it's hard to think of someone who would be better suited for bringing out the feeling of a Brazilian Bach with a touch of Latin opera. Mathis thrives in the lush minimalism of the chamber strings and it certainly isn't a failed experiment but a road that could have been pursued even more.

Mathis also revisits a tune from his debut, 'Babalu,' and there is a notable difference this time. Gone is the youthful testosterone. It's like drinking a powerful wine that has aged, mellowed, and developed finer nuances. It's indeed a Brazilian take on 'Babalu' that swings and dances elegantly, using strings, acoustic bass, and percussion.

A contrast to the Brazilian flavors of the album is the Spanish-tinged opener 'Granada,' written by the Mexican composer Agustin Lara, and 'La Montaña' by the Spanish composer Augusto Algueró Dasca.

Overall, *Olé* proved to be a successful artistic experiment, but unfortunately, it didn't fare well commercially. Quite unusually for Mathis, it didn't even enter the *Billboard* chart.

This was not the case with the previous Ferguson-Feierman collaboration, *The Wonderful World of Make Believe* (1964), which reached number 75 and stayed on the charts for ten weeks. It was an album with a clear concept, as Greg Adams points out in his review for *AllMusic*: 'The theme is fantasy, from imaginary locations ('Camelot,' 'Shangri-La') to fanciful yearnings ('I'm Always Chasing Rainbows,' 'When You Wish Upon a Star') to vague, idealized realms ('Beyond the Sea,' 'Beyond the Blue Horizon').' Adams concludes that *'The Wonderful World of Make Believe* is strictly an album effort – no standout single tracks here – but it's an enticingly dreamy effort and Mathis sings superbly.'[59]

There is a Bart Howard jewel on the album. The otherworldly waltz, 'Sky Full of Rainbows,' belongs among Howard's best songs, and 'Shangri-La' proves that a minimal setting with just piano and voice works wonders for Mathis, but unfortunately, the intimate experiment isn't fulfilled, and an orchestra enters in the middle of the song and provides a grand finale that is also a little too safe.

The safe bets continued with *This is Love* (1964), the album that preceded *Olé*. If *The Wonderful World of Make Believe* was just a good and solid album, *This is Love* feels more like a classic Johnny Mathis collection. Whether it's the cover painting, once again painted by Ralph Cowan, or the choice of songs, including three songs from Nat King Cole's repertoire and two pearls from Bart Howard, the album just has that special something and this is underlined in a brief note from Mathis: 'Just a postscript – because love songs, of all songs, speak for themselves. For me, this recording has been a labor of love – because of my fondness for the songs and for these simple new settings. And most of all, because of my pleasure in singing them for listeners who understand so well – listeners like Allyn Ferguson and Jack Feierman – and you.'[60]

While the songs are all love songs, they span different genres, from the slowed-down big band piece 'Put on a Happy Face' and the bluesy 'Limehouse Blues' to the bossa nova of 'The End of a Love Affair' and the sensual jazzy ballad 'Under a Blanket of Blue,' complete with smoking saxophone. Speaking of smoke, 'The Touch of Your Lips' is all velvet and smoke and the reference to Nat King Cole is felt in the sonorous bass notes of the phrasing.

Once again, Mathis includes Bart Howard in his program and 'What Do You Feel in Your Heart' and the closer, 'Fantastic,' are both top-shelf Howard songs sung with delicate feeling. They are wrapped in lovely arrangements that include a wealth of instrumental details like the brief appearance of a baritone saxophone at the 2.55 mark in 'Fantastic.'

At Global, Mathis also did another project very close to his heart, but unlike *This Is Love*, his *Broadway* album planned for release in 1964 was shelved until it materialized in 2012 on a double release with *Love is Everything*. In his review for *AllMusic*, Al Campbell offers a possible explanation for the delay. 'At the time, Mercury felt the album was too upbeat and not the type of romantic material Mathis had been so successful with during his previous tenure with Columbia.'[61] Mathis himself has later expressed his satisfaction of finally seeing it in print and compliments Allyn Ferguson 'whose arrangements on this album are truly wonderful.'[62]

Hearing the album is akin to discovering a lost treasure. Here is the album where Allyn Ferguson finally reaches the level of Faith, Costa, Osser and Riddle, and not least Ralph Burns, whose *Rhythms of Broadway* (1960) is a kindred spirit. However, Burns was swinging hard while Ferguson is much more intricate in his arrangements, as Mathis has also pointed out: 'Lots of interesting rhythm patterns from Allyn. He was a taskmaster. He was very, very smart and he always put that into his music. He was very esoteric as far as his jazz was concerned. I just sort of tagged along. I enjoyed the challenge and vocally, I think it worked. I was quite enamored at the time with Lena Horne and I think a lot of it reflects that.'[63]

Broadway opens with the cooking R&B swing of 'Ain't It De Truth' followed by 'Get Out of Town,' the first of two Cole Porter compositions, the other being 'Ridin' High.' Mathis once again proves that he is a supreme interpreter of Cole and makes the music swing, but surprisingly the most Cole-like lyrics don't come from Cole, but from Burton Lane and E.Y.

Harburg on the song 'When I'm Not Near the Girl I Love.' Harburg has penned lyrics for such standards as 'Brother Can You Spare a Dime' and 'April in Paris,' but here, he indulges in a string of alliterations and wordplay perfectly executed by Mathis.

For once, the strings are mostly left in the background or left out entirely, and when they appear, they often serve a surprising purpose, as when they show up in the up-tempo Latin big band swing of 'Comes Once in a Lifetime.' Even a song like 'You Better Love Me' that starts as a classic ballad with strings gets a rhythmical twist and suddenly swings halfway through. Nothing is predictable on *Broadway* and the only sure thing is the joy the music brings as Mathis sings and swings his way through the repertoire.

Ferguson's last album with Mathis is a patchwork produced by Norman Newell that included the work of many different orchestrators, including Glenn Osser. However, *The Sweetheart Tree* (1965), like the albums that followed; *The Shadow of Your Smile* (1966) and *So Nice* (1966), proved that many cooks can make an excellent dinner. It opens with a trio of songs arranged and conducted by Tony Osborne. The jazzy 'A Wonderful Day Like This,' with walking bass and brass, sets things in motion, but the album quickly settles into ballad mode. 'Arrivederci Roma,' complete with mandolin and sighing strings, is the kind of Italian ditty that Dean Martin would love to sing, while 'Clopin Clopant' changes the scene to France and sidewalk cafes accompanied by accordion.

Ferguson enters the picture with 'This is Love,' co-written by Newell. Surprisingly, the song was not included as the title track of the album from 1964, but here the beautiful ballad finds its place as Mathis serenades the different shapes of love. 'I'll Close My Eyes' is another ballad with a lovely arrangement by Ferguson, but this time Tony Osborne takes care of the conducting. The interpretation of 'Danny Boy,' written by the English songwriter Frederic Weatherly and based on the traditional Irish melody 'Londonderry Air,' finds Ferguson conducting an arrangement by Geoff Love. It has the right balance between pathos and sentimentality so inherent in the lyrics. Mathis gently lifts the song and ends on a stunning falsetto flight.

More magic happens on 'The Skye Boat Song,' a majestic arrangement of a Scottish folk song. In fact, the song is about a king. It tells about the journey of Prince Charles Edward Stuart from Benbecula to the Isle of Skye as he fled from government troops following his defeat at the Battle of Culloden in 1746. The original lyrics include a reference to the defeat.

'Burned are their homes, exile and death / Scatter the loyal men; / Yet ere the sword cool in the sheath / Charlie will come again.'

Mathis leaves out this fourth verse and also the second verse with references to the war, and instead, he focuses on the journey at sea, starting with the chorus, but here he also leaves out a line, replacing the second line, 'Onward! the sailors cry' with the fourth line that is repeated twice, so the chorus goes like this: 'Speed, bonnie boat, like a bird on the wing / Over the sea to Skye / Carry the lad that's born to be king / Over the sea to Skye.' He then moves on to the first verse, where the lines 'Loud the winds howl, loud the waves roar, / Thunderclaps rend the air' are emulated by the strings and then comes the last part of the verse with a rare direct reference to the war 'Baffled, our foes stand by the shore, / Follow they will not dare.'

The music gains its strength from a combination of the wild drama at sea and a celestial sound emphasized by harps. The song is often interpreted as a slow waltz and this is also the case here, but it's something more than a traditional historical war ballad. Instead, it becomes an almost otherworldly tale of existential longing supremely realized through Mathis's heartbreakingly beautiful voice. It's later mentioned in the third and final verse that 'Rocked in the deep, Flora will keep / Watch by your weary head.' Flora is the historical Flora MacDonald who helped Charles escape, but it doesn't matter so much here because Flora becomes the muse of hope in an existential sea of despair. Mathis sings the song, so it rises above its historical circumstances and it can be understood intuitively on a human level.

The final Ferguson contribution almost reaches the same staggering heights of 'The Skye Boat Song.' It's a bold and sophisticated interpretation of the standard 'Autumn Leaves' that is explored as a classic grand concerto with choir and elements of rolling Spanish guitars, harking back to Ferguson's and Feierman's *Olé*.

The album also includes noteworthy contributions from Lincoln Mayorga, who conducted and arranged the title song written by Henry Mancini, whose work Mathis would later explore in depth. Mayorga also conducts 'Mirage' with an arrangement by Glenn Osser. The wistful movie song closed the US version of the album, but three other tracks have later been added as a bonus: 'If Love Were All,' conducted and arranged by Tony Osborne, and two songs, 'Try A Little Tenderness' and 'If I Had You,' arranged and conducted by Alyn Aynsworth, whose orchestral work on Ray Noble's sweeping ballad 'The Very Thought of You' also made it to the original album.

Mathis's eleventh album for Global and his swansong for the label was *Johnny Mathis Sings* (1967). Among fans, it is known as 'the red and white album.'[64] Mysteriously, no orchestrators are credited this time. The back of the cover just shows Mathis in a garden with a big bouquet of white flowers. Mathis has also picked a nice bouquet of songs on this album, as Joe Viglione points out in his *AllMusic* review. 'These dozen tunes are grade A, and sequenced very nicely.'[65] Viglione especially highlights Mathis's version of Bobby Hebb's song 'Sunny': 'When Sunny Gets Blue' appeared on the immortal Johnny Mathis Greatest Hits package, and here he does his own follow-up, a marvelous study of Bobby Hebb's 'Sunny', a slow tempo rendition songwriter Hebb has stated he is most proud of.'[66]

Among the other tracks on the album are two very nice Burt Bacharach songs, the classic 'Always Something There To Remind Me' and the less familiar 'Saturday Sunshine,' as bright and light as the title suggests. Too light for its own good is Mathis's version of the Beatles hit 'Eleanor Rigby,' marred by an overdose of kitschy organ, but Henry Mancini's 'Lovers in New York' is a great topic song about the city that never sleeps sung sophisticatedly by Mathis.

Another interesting songwriter is Bert Kaempfert, whose hit, 'Strangers in the Night,' made by famous Frank Sinatra, Mathis tackles in a hushed version that wisely avoids competing with the lush romanticism of the chairman. Mathis later returned to Kaempfert, who became the first songwriter that was covered by Mathis in the extensive songbook format.

Taken as a whole, *Johnny Mathis Sings* is a solid album, but also proof that Mathis's albums benefitted from the steady involvement of a distinctive orchestrator and/or producer. In that sense, *Johnny Mathis Sings* marked the end of a road taken. After this album, Mathis went back to Columbia and once again worked with determined producers and arrangers who lifted his work and took him in new directions.

Before it's time to pick up the story of Mathis's epic run with Columbia, it's worth taking two detours that cover two musical formats where his work for Global and Columbia overlap: the single and the Christmas album.

Part Four: Singles and Christmas Songs

The World in a Grain of Sand: The Singles

There are several aspects to consider when trying to describe the artistry of Johnny Mathis: He is a connoisseur of songs, who has always appreciated the craft of great songwriters, no matter the genre, he is a master of moods, who investigates the atmosphere and emotions a song conveys, and finally, he is a purveyor of pure musicality. Listening to Mathis, one can enjoy the care that goes into the phrasing and the richness of textures from the dark to the light register.

These aspects of Mathis's art are unfolded through the trajectory of his albums that are impressively varied. However, it's also an extensive journey and instead of going on an odyssey with the long players, one can also take a short trip with the singles. They give insight into his world through a medium that is like a grain of sand compared to the castles of the albums. But in their own way, the singles can be just as intriguing, and it's important to remember that Mathis got his breakthrough as a singles artist. His debut album had just flopped when Mitch Miller came to the rescue and reintroduced him as a hit artist with the songs 'Wonderful! Wonderful!' and 'It's Not for Me To Say' that marked the first time Mathis hit the charts, reaching number 14 and 5, respectively.

The singles that will be considered here are the songs that were not part of the album packages. As Didier C. Deutsch explains in his notes to *Johnny Mathis: The Singles*:

'Columbia released two kinds of singles: songs recorded individually and released as stand-alones, if you will, and songs extracted from specific albums to call attention to these albums.'[67]

At Global, the practice of releasing stand-alone singles continued, and taken together, these stray songs make up an important body of work. At the time they were recorded, the singles seemed ephemeral, and Mathis has explained that the process of recording them was different than recording an album. 'When we recorded the albums, we usually spent 3-4 days to do about a dozen songs. But when we recorded the singles we had three hours to do four songs. Why four? I have no idea. But that was the norm.'[68]

It may be that the singles didn't justify the same time and attention as the albums, but they were nevertheless done professionally with top orchestrators. Many of them also worked with Mathis on his albums, including Percy Faith, Glenn Osser, Ralph Burns, Don Costa, Allyn Ferguson, Robert Mersey, Ernie Freeman, Al Capps, D'Arneille Pershing, Gene Page and Ray Ellis. Yet, one of the most important collaborators, Ray Conniff, only turned up on the singles, although his work was included on an album collection simply titled *Johnny's Greatest Hits* (1958).

Released in March 17, 1958, contrary to his album debut, *Johnny's Greatest Hits* showed the full force of Mathis as a hit artist. It spent three weeks as number one on the *Billboard* charts and the album had its last appearance on the charts over ten years later. In the process, it earned both Gold and Platinum certification. The orchestrators who helped Mathis get such staggering success were two Rays: Conniff and Ellis.

Even though he was only associated with Mathis for a short time, Ray Conniff played a significant part in his career. It says something about his influence that seven of the twelve tracks on *Johnny's Greatest Hits* had his musical signature.

Ray Conniff was born on November 6, 1916, in Attleboro, Massachusetts. His mother played piano and his father played trombone and was the leader of a local band. Instrumentally, Conniff followed in his father's footsteps and started playing the trombone, but he also had a knack for arranging and his arrangement of 'Sweet Georgia Brown' for the dance band he played in was the first of many to come.[69]

Eventually, Conniff moved to New York as a young man to pursue a musical career and he ended up playing with Bunny Berrigan, Bob Crosby, and Artie Shaw. His big break came when Mitch Miller discovered him in the early fifties and made him house arranger for Columbia. Among others, he worked with the singers Don Cherry, Johnnie Ray, Guy Mitchell, Frankie Laine, Marty Robbins, and not least Johnny Mathis, with whom he recorded a series of singles, including such pearls as 'Wonderful! Wonderful!' b/w 'When Sunny Gets Blue,' and 'It's Not For Me To Say' b/w 'Warm and Tender.'[70] However, the single that has gone down in pop history is the awe-inspiring combination of 'Chances Are' b/w 'Twelfth Of Never.' Mathis has later recalled how the B-side was a gamechanger: 'At first we were told that we needed a second song for the other side of the record, and that it was not an important song, just something that had to be on the flip side. So all along, it was my feeling that those were songs that were not supported by the company because they were not interested in them. The success of 'Twelfth Of Never,' which was on the flip of 'Chances Are' took everyone by surprise. After that, everyone was a little more careful about what was put on the other side of a single record.'[71]

The song starts intimately with a harp as the only accompaniment and Mathis singing the lines: 'You ask how much I need you, must I explain?

/ I need you, oh my darling, like roses need rain.' It takes a true artist to transform the borderline banality of these lines into a profound expression of longing, but Mathis does it. Then an acoustic guitar enters, and he establishes the connection to the title: 'You ask how long I'll love you; I'll tell you true: / Until the twelfth of never, I'll still be loving you.' Eventually, the strings enter and lift the song until it returns to the quiet combination of harp and voice. A coda of strings and choir wrap up the combination of chivalric folk balladry and lush pop.

The A-side is an even bigger hit and once again, it starts intimately, this time using light acoustic guitar and cocktail piano. Mathis is crooning with silky vibrato and elegant long lines that are balanced by perfect staccato punctures. Just listen to how he sculpts a line like, 'Guess you feel you'll always be the one and only one for me.'

The strings are also there and get an interlude with brass, but the real orchestral wonder of this song is how Mathis manages to sound both elevated, ethereal, and relaxed, lifting the song out of the atmosphere of a bar and into a starry universe.

Like Percy Faith, Conniff would move on to pursue a career in his own name, but his short stay with Mathis was important and set the stage for him as a hitmaking romantic crooner.

Ray Ellis took over after Conniff in the singles department and continued to provide hits, five of which ended up on the classic greatest hits compilation: 'All the Time,' 'When I Am With You,' 'Come to Me,' 'No Love (But Your Love)' and 'I Look at You.' Born in Philadelphia, July 28, 1923, Ellis' way into arranging was encouraged through his stint in the military where he handled arranging duties with the U.S. Army Band. As Percy Faith, Ellis also worked in radio before he moved to New York in 1954. Once again, Mitch Miller recognized a talent and gave him a job as staff arranger for Columbia. Among his significant early achievements were his arrangements for Mathis and his work on the Billie Holiday masterpiece *Lady in Satin* (1958).[72]

Ellis continued the romantic style that Conniff had made the foundation for, but at the same time, he introduced new elements like the twang of an electric guitar on 'Come To Me' and slightly increased orchestral volume that brought out the melodramatic side of Mathis on 'All the Time.' He also experimented with swinging brass on 'Teacher, Teacher' and arranged a superb mood piece, 'Let It Rain,' with vibraphone raindrops and sensual saxophone. He even used flamenco guitar on 'Stairway to the Sea' and time and time again, proved that it was possible to stretch the sound of the romantic ballad.

Some of his most delicate orchestrations were made in 1961. Among this batch of songs, the highlight is a single that deserves the same iconic status as the combination of 'Chances Are' b/w 'Twelfth of Never.' 'Laurie, My Love' b/w 'Should I Wait (Should I Run to Her) contains one of the finest interpretations of a genre Mathis had become a specialist in: the portrait. In fact, the lyrics to 'Laurie, My Love' make it quite clear: 'This is a portrait of Laurie, my love,' and what a portrait it is. It has the light feeling of Laurie that 'walks down the street' and the music mimics the change of the seasons that also becomes a metaphor for a psychological transformation from cold isolation to the cosmic revelation of love: 'Gone are the winter snows / Your lips have melted the frost / Now like a leaf that blows / When I am in your embrace / I am lost, lost in time, / Lost in space, lost in wonder.' Mathis made other portrait singles like 'Jenny,' 'Marianna' and 'Gina', but none of them surpass 'Laurie, My Love.'

The B-side 'Should I Wait (Or Should I Run to Her)' combines sighing strings with subtle chamber jazz feeling and Mathis's supreme expression of longing, considering whether he should 'run with heart in hand to her.'

Ellis and Mathis followed up with another strong single, 'Wasn't the Summer Short' b/w 'There You Are,' once again nailing a wistful feeling of nostalgia, loss, and longing. Like 'Laurie, My Love,' 'Wasn't the Summer Short' also uses the seasons to reflect a psychological change, but this time it's disenchantment rather than ecstasy: 'Autumn comes all too soon. / Midsummer madness dies. / Nothing is quite the same when leaves / Turn gold 'neath September skies. / Why did we let this magic time go by?'

Ellis didn't let the musical magic go by, but he wasn't the only one who did an excellent job with the singles. Familiar collaborators from Mathis's albums like Glenn Osser, Ralph Burns and Don Costa also lent a helping hand, and when he moved to Global, the collaboration with high-profile arrangers and conductors continued. One of his projects involved Quincy Jones as a conductor on eight singles. Most of these recordings were never released, but 'All I Wanted' b/w 'Listen Lonely Girl' (1964) made it to wax and both sport fine arrangements by Claus Ogerman. While 'All I Wanted' is a somewhat generic ballad, 'Listen Lonely Girl' has the feeling of a sparkling pop song written in the style of Burt Bacharach. Another song, 'Two Tickets and a Candy Heart,' arranged by Torrie Zito, is simply too sugar-sweet and accentuates a problem with the songs Quincy Jones did with Mathis; the material wasn't quite up to scratch, and it says something that one of the most interesting songs is the shelved 'Reserved for Lovers' by an uncredited writer, a dreamy, jazzy ballad delivered with casual elegance.

When Mathis returned to Columbia, he adapted to the changing sounds of the times and collaborated with arrangers and producers that helped shape his albums, people like orchestrators Robert Mersey, Ernie Freeman, D'Arneille Pershing and Gene Page, and producers Jerry Fuller and Jack Gold. There would also be time for a fleeting and yet substantial pairing like the single 'Wherefore and Why' b/w 'Last Time I Saw Her' (1970) containing two songs by singer/songwriter Gordon Lightfoot conducted by Perry Botkin Jr. Especially on the latter, Mathis tugs at the heartstrings and reaches the same level of emotional poignancy as Glen Campbell's version, once again proving that he could easily handle the transition from Broadway to heartfelt singer/songwriter folk-pop.

Before his stay at Global, and after, Mathis also found time to record singles in a genre that was close to his heart: Christmas music. A gem is his collaboration with Gladys Knight & The Pips 'When A Child is Born' b/w 'The Lord's Prayer' (1981). But singles were not enough. He explored this genre in depth on his many Christmas albums that constitute a special chapter in the Johnny Mathis story.

Songs for the Season: The Christmas Albums

Every music genre deserves to be treated with respect, but that isn't always the case. Christmas music seems to incarnate both the best and worst aspects of the music industry. At its worst, it's a tactless celebration of commercialism, and at its best, it has the quality of uniting people in a timeless message of love and forgiveness. It's true that Christmas is the season of presents, but the greatest gift is the love given by God through Jesus.

Christmas is the time of love, but it's also the season of sadness. It's a time when the absence of loved ones is felt. Whether it's someone who has passed, someone who is far away, or just someone who isn't there, Christmas can be a reminder of how hard it is to be alone, and yet it is also about realizing the blessing of those who are here.

In short, Christmas tunes are songs of innocence and experience. They are songs for children and grownups, pop songs and psalms. A celebration of generosity, but also the expression of the very human desire of wanting things.

It's the great achievement of Johnny Mathis that he takes Christmas music seriously as an art form and shows how many different moods and sounds the songs can span. His love and respect for Christmas is simply a part of him, and that is also the reason why he decided to sing Christmas songs in the first place, as he has said to Michael P. Coleman, commenting on his first Christmas album: 'I come from a big family and Christmas was a big deal for us, so I decided to make a Christmas album. And lo and behold, it became a very high point in my career. I think that album and those Christmas albums that followed it are the greatest accomplishments I've ever had because I loved nothing more than having my parents listen to my music and be pleased with it. If you can imagine having a parent have people come to them and say, 'Oh, it's not Christmas without your son singing a Christmas song!' – they were over the moon about it!'[73]

Merry Christmas (1958) was made with Percy Faith and his orchestra and was the first Christmas album Mathis did. Not only was it a good start, it's a masterpiece in the genre. It was also a commercial smash, perhaps his greatest success ever, certified 5X Platinum and it's still selling solidly.

The album combines traditional Christmas carols and holiday hits. The common denominator is the quality of the songs, as Mathis points out in his personal note to the album: 'some of the most beautiful music I know is contained in these songs.'[74]

Another asset is the superb arrangements of Percy Faith, the best he ever did with Mathis. This is Faith the sound sculptor making lush landscapes that lift the songs into tiny symphonies. Just listen to the opening 'Winter Wonderland,' a carousel of sweeping strings and chiming bells with Mathis 'walking in the winter wonderland.' It's Christmas magic set into music. 'The Christmas Song (Chestnuts Roasting On An Open Fire)' slow things down and Mathis croons sweetly, accompanied by an operatic choir. There's a clever use of a musical quote when 'Jingle Bells' turns up the second time Mathis sings that 'Santa's on his way / he's loaded lots of toys and goodies on his sleigh,' and the quote is repeated in the coda.

The sound of jingling bells turns up again on the whimsical 'Sleigh Ride,' filled with giddy instrumental effects and Mathis playing along with charming vocal detours. On the other hand, he digs deep into balladry on the touching 'Blue Christmas' and 'I'll Be Home For Christmas' that both show the serious side of the season as he aches with longing, singing about coming home for Christmas, if only in a dream.

The dream theme continues in a precious reading of 'White Christmas.' Introduced by an elegiac solo violin voice and heavenly choir, Mathis once again sings with such delicacy and feeling that lines such as 'I'm dreaming of a white Christmas / With every Christmas card I write' become a poignant expression of yearning. It all ends with a Mathis signature, a prolonged vocal line, and Faith's circular string motif spiced by thoughtful use of vibraphone.

The arc of the album moves from secular earthly frolic and sadness to the spiritual beauty on the B-side of the album, containing the amazing 'O Holy Night,' ending almost in a whisper, 'What Child is This (Greensleeves),' bathed in harp and choir, and the booming vocal proclamation of 'The First Noel.'

The two worlds, the secular and the spiritual, are then united on 'Silver Bells' that takes the scene to the city with the sweet sound of silver bells, laughing children and shoppers rushing home. Mathis then concludes: 'Christmas makes you feel emotional / It may bring parties or thoughts devotional / Whatever happens or what may be / Here is what Christmas time means to me.'

On the album, Christmas is innocence, joy, sorrow, sadness, giddiness and earthly desire, but in the end, the album is wrapped up with two religious songs: 'It Came Upon The Midnight Clear' where the Babel of complex human emotions is redeemed and 'Silent Night, Holy Night' that announces the coming of Christ.

Merry Christmas was a hard act to follow, but somehow Mathis came up with an album that didn't disappoint at all. Part of the reason for this was that he didn't try to duplicate the sound of his Christmas debut. Instead, three of his most important collaborators were gathered to customize a leaner and lighter sound than the plush technicolor of the predecessor. Don Costa produced, the lovely arrangements were penned by Glenn Osser, and Jack Feierman conducted the orchestra and chorus. The multilayered textures were kept but expressed with fewer musical voices. In other words, if *Merry Christmas* was a pop symphony, then *The Sounds of Christmas* is closer to chamber pop.

The approach to the choice of songs was also different this time. While the album includes some Christmas classics like 'Have Yourself a Merry Little Christmas,' 'The Little Drummer Boy' and 'Rudolph the Red-Nosed Reindeer,' there is also space for some less familiar songs like 'Christmas Is a Feeling in Your Heart,' 'A Marshmallow World' and 'The Secret of Christmas.' The album even includes two new songs, 'Have Reindeer, Will Travel,' and the title track 'The Sounds of Christmas,' both written by Jerry Livingston and Paul Francis Webster. Although very different, both are quality songs.

'The Sounds of Christmas' brilliantly uses the conceit of hearing in a string of virtuoso variations in the lyrics, 'Snap and crackle of the yuletide log / Popcorn popping in the grate / Neighbors knocking at the old front door / Drop in to help celebrate / The sounds of children / Laughing sounds of girls and boys / Playing with their Christmas toys / Silver bells that jingle on the tree.'

These musical scenes of sound could be justified as a mood painting in itself, but like a Shakespearean sonnet, there's a volta that adds a surprising twist and turns the song into an elevated expression of romantic love. 'But of all the sounds of Christmas / No sweeter sound could be / Than the Merry Christmas kisses that my love gave me.'

Musically, the song is just as clever, ending with a quotation of 'Deck the Halls.' The play with words and music continues on 'Have Reindeer, Will Travel' that humorously describes the ride in Santa's sleigh while acknowledging the heritage of Johnny Mark's iconic 'Rudolph the Red-Nosed Reindeer,' once again referencing the names of the reindeers.

The religious songs don't take up as much space this time, but 'Hallelujah Chorus' from George Frideric Handel's Christmas Oratorio, *Messiah*, concludes the album, and the song is highlighted by Mathis along with 'The Carol of the Bells' in his notes for *The Complete Global Albums Collection*. 'For this album, I decided to record the 'Hallelujah Chorus' and the 'Carol of the Bells'–I just sang my part, the part that all the tenors sing in these particular compositions. I had no problem about doing it, my only concern was how I would get my voice to be predominant if I sang only one part of the melody. You know, when you're young, nothing frightens you. The fact that I had sung these songs in school for years, with all kinds of choirs, I thought, why not, let's do it. And as the years went on, people got used to hearing those songs at Christmas time.'[75]

Indeed, people like hearing Mathis singing Christmas songs, then and now. The album spent two weeks on *Billboard*'s Christmas Albums sales chart, a chart that was established in 1963. The following years, it would show up on *Billboard*'s seasonal LP chart and today, it deserves the status of a Christmas classic, not quite up there with *Merry Christmas*, but close.

Mathis's next Christmas album, *Give Me Your Love for Christmas* (1969), emphasized the secular side of Christmas, starting with a swinging big band version of 'Jingle Bells Rock' before moving into ballad territory with an old favorite, 'Have Yourself a Merry Little Christmas,' covered on the previous album. 'The Little Drummer Boy' is revisited as well and there are takes on the standards 'My Favorite Things' and 'What Are You Doing New Year's Eve.'

The highlights come at the end of the second side of the LP. Burt Bacharach's 'Christmas Day' contains a moral message delivered through Hal David's lyrics: 'learn to give / try to live / each day like Christmas Day.' It could easily be too much, but Mathis sings these words sincerely like a

Left: Hitting the high note. JM singing in the studio.

Right: 'I settled into what I thought sounded comfortable when I heard it played back.' JM with headphones in the studio.

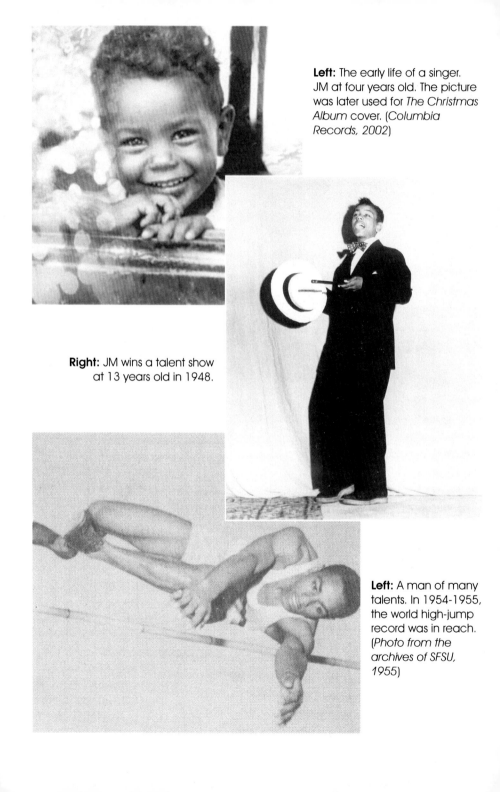

Left: The early life of a singer. JM at four years old. The picture was later used for *The Christmas Album* cover. (*Columbia Records, 2002*)

Right: JM wins a talent show at 13 years old in 1948.

Left: A man of many talents. In 1954-1955, the world high-jump record was in reach. (*Photo from the archives of SFSU, 1955*)

Above: JM at 22 years old in the studio. (*Sony Archives*)

Left: Classic beauty. JM formal portrait next to a column, taken in the late 1950s. (*Columbia Records*)

Right: JM jumps while playing tennis in the late 1950s. (*Columbia Records*)

Left: A meeting of stars. JM with Elvis on the set of one of The King's movies during the late 1950s.

Right: Not completely alone. JM with arranger Allyn Ferguson, his close collaborator during the Global years.

Above: First impressions. JM in the studio recording his debut with George Avakian and Bob Prince.

Below: Life of a pop star. JM with his parents reading fan mail in the late 1950s.

Above: Hitmaker. JM with producer Mitch Miller who turned him into a pop star after the disappointment of his debut.

Below: Into the music. JM singing in the studio in the late 1960s.

Above: The element of swing. JM in the studio in the 1960s.

Right: Kindred spirits. JM with arranger and songwriter Henry Mancini in December 1968. In 1986, they recorded the album *The Hollywood Musicals*.

Right: JM didn't relax much as this promo shot from 1969 suggests. That same year, he released three albums.

Below: Shaping the sound. JM with early idol and friend, Nat King Cole.

AGENCY: CHARTWELL ARTISTS, LTD.
9720 WILSHIRE BLVD.
BEVERLY HILLS, CALIF.
TEL. (213) 273-6700

Johnny Mathis

Left: Man's best friend. JM with his dog Henry on a signed promo shot from 1970.

Below: Live is where the music lives. JM sings onstage in the UK in the 1970s. (*Photo: Tony Russell*)

Right: There is more to life than music. JM cooking at home in the 1970s.

Below: In Royal company. JM with Farrah Fawcet Majors and Prince (later to become King) Charles in 1978.

Left: Soul man. JM in the 1970s when he started recording soul and disco.

Below: The epitome of elegance. JM on stage in the 1980s.

Right: Extraordinary voices. JM with his friend and fellow singer Barbra Streisand, recording in the studio in the 1990s.

Below: JM, Fred Mollin and Jay Landers in the studio for *Let It Be Me* recording.

Above: Guitars play a key role on *Let It Be Me.* JM is surrounded by strings in Nashville. (*Photo: Becky Fluke*)

Below: JM and Fred Mollin's Nashville crew during the recording of *Sending You a Little Christmas* with guest star Billy Joel.

Above: Women with wonderfully wide vocal ranges. JM with Dionne Warwick and Deniece Williams during a lunch in 2013.

Below: A singer of love songs. JM sings at a party in 2015.

Above: A special time of the year. JM in Kahala Resort Honolulu in December 2018.

song of hope from a sinner and the real prayer comes in the closing track, 'The Lord's Prayer,' a symphonic ending to an album that doesn't reach the heights of the previous albums. Still, it's a fine set of Christmas songs with solid arrangements by Ernie Freeman.

The most interesting thing about the fourth Christmas album, *Christmas Eve with Johnny Mathis* (1986), is the return of Ray Ellis, who played an important role as an orchestrator on many of Mathis's greatest singles. He contributes arrangements for 'Toyland,' 'Jingle Bells,' 'The Christmas Waltz,' 'We Need a Little Christmas' and a medley of 'Christmas Is for Everyone' and 'Where Can I Find Christmas?' The result is a mixed bag from the fairytale elegance of 'Toyland' to middle of the road pop swing on 'Jingle Bells.'

Another notable guest is Henry Mancini, who conducts a medley of his own songs, 'Every Christmas Eve' and 'Giving (Santa's Theme)' from the movie *Santa Claus: The Movie*. Once again, Mathis finds the emotional grandeur in these songs without succumbing to sticky sentimentality, and Mancini's arrangements capture a magic mood, using bells, choir, and ascending violins.

Overall, *Christmas Eve with Johnny Mathis* (1986) is his smoothest Christmas album, and the absence of the religious songs isn't a strength. However, even without the religious aspect, Mathis still paints an entertaining and emotionally involved portrait of Christmas.

So far, while keeping the high musical standard of his Christmas albums, Mathis had not been able to match the beauty of his Christmas debut, *Merry Christmas*. *Sounds of Christmas* came close but *Give Me Your Love for Christmas* and *Christmas Eve with Johnny Mathis* were only good, not great, and the question was if Mathis would ever reach the heights of his debut.

The answer came when he released *The Christmas Album* in 2010. It is immediately established that the album is something special with the bold beginning, 'Joy to the World,' which announces the birth of Christ with classical fanfare, vibrant violins, and pompous choir. A less skilled musician would easily drown in this ocean of sound, but Mathis rides the wave as his voice rises forcefully above it all, bursting with joy, committing himself to the message of love.

The album was produced by Robbie Buchanan and he fondly remembers the session. 'It was definitely a lot of fun making the record. With the natural combination of Johnny's voice on Christmas songs, it was a joy. One of the highlights was doing the Tom Snow song, 'Heavenly Peace.'It is actually quite a difficult piece to pull off both vocally as well as instrumentally. However, Johnny worked very hard on it (on his own time), and came in and nailed it. He was very well prepared for everything and left nothing to chance…a total professional.'[76]

On 'Heavenly Peace,' Mathis sings ', once the choirs quiet down and sing their last Amen / What happens then?' The answer to this question is found in the title. The feeling of heavenly peace changes between a quiet whisper and an ecstatic embrace with choir. Another layer is added when secular and religious love overlap in a setting changing between the sublime setting of a mountain and the everyday scene of a street, 'And it's all about peace can be found on a mountain top or an avenue / In the silent night, in the light of day, in the way I feel when I'm with you.'

The religious theme continues with 'Away in a Manger' whose hushed beauty is supported by quiet harps and mellifluous choir, and then Mathis sings a heartbreaking pop symphony of secular love on a 'Christmas Love Song,' keeping the balance between the spiritual and the secular as the two worlds overlap in a timeless theme of love.

It's all very solemn, but Mathis has always embraced the contrasts of Christmas from joy to sadness and seriousness to silliness, and so it's fitting that 'Frosty the Snowman' is thrown into the mix. Mathis has sketched some of the most poetic portraits of women, but he sings just as tenderly about Frosty 'with a corncob pipe and a button nose / And two eyes made out of coal.'

The informal feeling of joy continues on 'Have a Holly Jolly Christmas,' but once again, Mathis takes a U-turn with the serene 'Oh Little Town of Bethlehem,' including a solo violin intro, a glockenspiel interlude and, not least, the subdued vibrato of his own voice, supported tastefully by fleeting glimpses of orchestra and choir.

The dynamic between quietness and movement continues with the irresistible pop swing of 'I've Got My Love' that uses a catchy hook delivered by the choir. The apotheosis of the album comes on the medley of 'Snowfall/Christmas Time Is Here.' In a swirling landscape of sound where flying snowflakes are reflected by dissonant strings, Mathis conveys a feeling of being exposed to the sublime universe of nature, but then a transition happens to a cozy piano ballad and 'Yuletide by the fireside / And joyful memories there.' The cozy feeling doesn't last, though. In the end, the swirling violins return.

On the closing tune, 'Merry Christmas,' Mathis puts it all in perspective and unites the secular and spiritual motifs, the family and the church, as he sings: 'May the ones you love be near you / with the laugh of friends to cheer you / when the church bells ring / like the angels sing / and you hear the joyful hymn they chime/hang a wish for me / on your Christmas tree / for a very merry Christmas time.' It's a beautiful ending to an album where Mathis successfully conveys his poetic view on Christmas.

Christmas is also about singing together and so it makes sense that Mathis's sixth Christmas album, *Sending You a Little Christmas* (2013), included a heavy dose of duets. There's a refreshing approach to the art form, so the album embraces classic vocal duets with Billy Joel ('The Christmas Song'), Gloria Estefan ('Mary's Boy Child'), Natalie Cole ('Have Yourself a Merry Little Christmas') and Susan Boyle ('Do You Hear What I Hear'), but also a meeting between Mathis and the pianist Jim Brickman on 'Sending You a Little Christmas,' a double duet with Vince Gill and Amy Grant on a medley of 'I'll Be Home for Christmas / White Christmas' and a collaboration with the vocal group, The Jordanaires ('Home for the Holidays').

Even though the album sports some familiar songs from Mathis's Christmas repertoire, they are reworked, so the duet with Susan Boyle on 'Do You Hear What I Hear' comes across as a completely new composition, getting an air of the Scottish highland combined with a feeling of 'We are the World.' As strange as it sounds, it works.

Mathis also sings alone, and one of the jewels is his take on Donny Hathaway's Christmas soul classic, 'This Christmas.' Soul is just one of many genres on the album, there's also a rootsy reading of 'Home for the Holidays' with crying pedal steel and the deep river vocals of The Jordanaires.

Once again, the album shows Mathis's eclectic take on Christmas and his reading of Irving Berlin's standard 'Count Your Blessings (Instead of Sheep)' closes the album on a spiritual note.

Musing on the significance of the Christmas albums, Mathis says, 'It'll probably be my legacy and I'm so happy that it makes a lot of other people happy.'[77]

Part Five: Return To Columbia

Flying Home Again: Up, Up, and Away (1967)

The Christmas albums span Mathis's entire career and the same could be said about his label, Columbia Records. After his brief affair with Global Records from 1963 to 1966, Mathis returned to Columbia in 1967 and has been there ever since. However, as Charles Waring points out, something had happened with the label while Mathis was away: 'Columbia was a different label to the one he left in 1963. Its new president was Clive Davis, an ambitious, Harvard-educated attorney who had previously handled Columbia's legal affairs. His promotion from legal counsel to head honcho was an unprecedented move that would quickly set a trend in the music business and begin a systematic corporatization of the record industry, where lawyers and accountants (the so-called 'bean counters') began to make important creative decisions.'[78]

Clive Davis took a very active role in bringing Mathis back to Columbia. In his biography, *Clive: Inside The Record* Business, he tells how he admired Mathis's style and campaigned actively to get him back. Davis did his homework and studied the albums Mathis had made at Global and found out that most of them were not major copyrights. In other words, there were no hits to drive the sales forward. Davis wanted to change this pattern by applying what he referred to as the 'formula.' The formula meant that every record had to have huge contemporary hits that had already proven their value in the market. Instead of the old Mathis singing old hits, he wanted the old Mathis to sing new hits. It wasn't a matter of changing the artist, but rather a case of changing the repertoire. Davis was aware of every little detail. For instance, he knew that such a detail as the fact that the records had begun to be packed in plastic wrapping had an impact. Without a chance of hearing the music before buying, many consumers relied on the track list and wanted recognizable hit songs. Davis was ready to cater to the listeners' preferences. He was also aware of the effect of the cover and title. With a mathematical approach, he figured out that they accounted for a 20% impact on the sales each, leaving 60% to the music itself. It was all about selling the product and keeping an eye on the mainstream audience by selling records that were middle of the road (MOR). It meant not being too artful or hip, but on the other hand, not too old and dated. Davis had an analytical approach to aesthetic matters.[79]

Earlier in the history of Columbia, Mitch Miller was the one who sometimes pushed easy hits at the expense of art and originality, but knew how to sell music. Now it was Davis's turn to be the both admired and criticized merchant of music. To some of the people Davis worked with, the producers and A&R men, he might have come across as too cold and calculating, but others, like Robert Mersey and Jack Gold, could see the idea and managed to keep the balance between art and business. Sometimes there would be conflicts, and it's clear that throughout his career, Mathis has had mixed feelings about some of the contemporary hits that have been presented to him. He has voiced his opinion about the songs, but he has also remained pragmatic and open to recording all kinds of material. His return to Columbia saw him exploring new musical territory from the beginning, but an old friend would be there to ease the transition from classic to contemporary pop.

Released on October 23, 1967, his Columbia comeback record, *Up, Up, and Away*, not only reunited him with his old label, but also marked the return of Glenn Osser, who once again delivered excellent arrangements. This time with a lighter touch than the plush orchestrations of *Heavenly* and *Faithfully*.

Penned by modern pop maestro Jimmy Webb, the title track underlined the new approach that Clive Davis had set into motion. Webb is known for songs like 'Galveston,' 'Wichita Lineman,' 'MacArthur Park' and 'By the Time I Get to Phoenix.' 'Up, Up, and Away' is another popular Webb tune and is performed as an airy bossa nova.

The lyrics, taking the perspective of a balloon, are perfectly suited to Mathis's dreamy universe as he sings: 'The world's a nicer place in my beautiful balloon / It wears a nicer face in my beautiful balloon / We can sing a song and sail along the silver sky / For we can fly, we can fly.' There is not a trace of sadness as the balloon becomes a metaphor for the uncomplicated joys of music and love. The poetic playfulness is even underlined by a cheeky reference to Antonio Carlos Jobim's iconic bossa nova, 'The Girl from Ipanema', at the end of the song.

Adding to the contemporary feeling of the album, no less than three songs are taken from a film released the same year as the record. *Doctor Dolittle* is perhaps best known in the 1998 version starring Eddie Murphy as the eccentric doctor who talks to animals. Before that, it was a motion picture musical with limited success, but later it became a cult favorite. Part of the reason for that could be the English composer Leslie Bricusse's songs that have the literary sweetness of the best Broadway compositions. 'Where Are the Words' and 'When I Look in Your Eyes' are both vintage Mathis ballads, while 'At the Crossroads' is an existential song about finding the right path, choosing between left and right, day or night, or dark or light, concluding that 'only my heart can know.' Indeed, the heart also sings as Mathis ends the song with his signature falsetto that soars in the sky, up, up and away.

While the triptych of songs from *Doctor Dolittle* represented the classic pop sound of Johnny Mathis, it was the sound of yesterday. Instead, the modern pop of the title track was closer to his new aesthetic shaped by the producer, Robert Mersey. Mersey also conducted and arranged a song on *Up, Up, and Away*, and the fact that 'Misty Roses' spent two weeks at number 40 on *Billboard*'s top 40 list of easy listening songs showed that he was on to something. Introduced by dreamy vibraphones, the song finds Mathis crooning with gentle vibrato in an elegant setting using cocktail piano, shuffling acoustic guitar and a breeze of romantic strings.

If 'Misty' was the iconic song of his classic pop sound, then 'Misty Roses,' written by the folk singer/songwriter Tim Hardin, proved that Mathis was ready to change with the times and explore a modern pop expression, which nevertheless kept his sophisticated approach to songs intact. Robert Mersey helped him on this journey that prepared his eclectic adventures in song for decades to come.

The Pleasures of Pop: The Robert Mersey Productions

Robert David Mirsky (1917-1994), better known as Robert Mersey, came to Columbia in the early 1960s and worked as a producer and arranger. Before that, he did arrangements for the famous songwriting team Leiber and Stoller. He also had a taste of pop stardom himself. In 1959, he recorded the instrumental hit 'Tracy's Theme' under the name Spencer Ross. As the man behind the scene, Mersey was most influential, and at Columbia, he worked with an impressive roster of singers, including Aretha Franklin, Andy Williams, Barbra Streisand, Mel Tormé, Patti Page, and not least, Johnny Mathis.

Mersey's first collaboration with Mathis was *Up, Up, and Away*, but it was a transitional record that still showed the notable influence of Mathis's old collaborator, Glenn Osser. With the next album, *Love Is Blue* (1968), Mersey continued producing but also did the arranging and conducting and shaped a sound closer to the vision he had presented on 'Misty Roses.' It was a vision that brought Mathis closer to modern songcraft while retaining his roots in classic pop.

As a singer, Mathis had grown up with the classic pop concept that separated the songwriter and the singer. As a rule, the great songwriters like Cole Porter, George and Ira Gershwin, Richard Rodgers and Lorenz

Hart, Jerome Kern and Irving Berlin didn't sing their own songs. Hoagy Carmichael and Johnny Mercer were exceptions to the rule. Most of the songwriters were associated with Broadway, Tin Pan Alley and Hollywood show tunes, and they looked at songwriting as a craft, a craft they were very good at, so good that their legacy constitutes what has been called the Great American Songbook.

Classic or traditional pop had its heyday in the 1940s until the mid-1950s and Mathis made his debut in 1956 at a time when rock 'n' roll was taking over, but as his popularity showed, rock 'n' roll didn't prevent the concept of classic pop from being relevant. Part of the reason for this was that rock 'n' roll didn't break fundamentally with the separation between the songwriter and the singer. It wasn't Elvis who wrote 'Hound Dog' and 'Jailhouse Rock,' but Jerry Leiber and Mike Stoller. Still, rock 'n' roll challenged classic pop with an emphasis on rhythm and simpler song structures, and most of all, it was responsible for the divide in pop music taste: Rock 'n' roll became the music of choice for teenagers, and classic pop was branded as adult pop. New target groups were developing and eventually, the separation between songwriters and singers also started to dissolve.

The real change happened when rock-inspired groups like The Beatles started to write their own material and singer/songwriters such as Joni Mitchell and Bob Dylan boomed in the 1960s and 1970s. The idea of writing your own material based on tradition was already inherent in folk, country, and blues music, and eventually, the idea of the original artist who expressed personal feelings became the norm. By the end of the 1960s, Mathis included more contemporary singer/songwriter material as a supplement to the classic pop he specialized in.

Mathis had already started singing contemporary pop songs while he was at Global. When he returned to Columbia, Mersey accelerated the inclusion of modern material pushed by Clive Davis and the record company: 'The record company, of course, was always concerned about sales. I was more concerned about the quality of the songs and at that time, I had probably gotten a little annoyed with the music that was presented to me, popular music at the time. We had obligations as far as the record companies were concerned to try to sell records and they would give us their idea of what would sell. He (Mersey) was in charge of getting the music for me to sing.'[80]

Mersey's masterstroke, possibly influenced by Clive Davis, was that he often found modern pop songwriters who had a connection to the aesthetic of classic pop. Burt Bacharach is one of the most prominent examples. With no less than four songs on *Love is Blue* (1968), the follow-up to *Up, Up and Away*, Bacharach is featured heavily on the album and provides the opening song, 'I Say a Little Prayer,' sporting a Mersey arrangement which has a surprisingly playful classical break and coda.

His connection to Brill Building pop underlined that Bacharach was a professional songwriter, but he was also a distinctive artist in his own right. One of the things that made him modern was his pregnant use of rhythm. Just listen to the four songs on the album and it's there. Besides great melodies and harmonies, the hallmark of classic pop, 'I Say a Little Prayer,' 'The Look of Love,' 'Don't Go Breakin' My Heart' and 'Walk On By' all have a signature rhythm that is just as important as the melodic hook, and so the modern listeners' craving for rhythm is satisfied while the melodies and Hal David's brilliant lyrics give Mathis plenty to work with.

Once again, Mathis explores the songwriting of Jimmy Webb with a very good version of 'By the Time I Get to Phoenix,' although it doesn't reach the heights of the iconic interpretations done by Glen Campbell and Isaac Hayes. However, his profound reading of Lennon and McCartney's 'Here, There and Everywhere' lifts the Beatles song from a low-key piece with skeletal electric rhythm guitar and doo-wop harmonies to a pocket symphony that fleshes out the classic pop potential of the song.

If 'Here, There and Everywhere' transformed a modern pop song into a standard, then the arrangement of Mancini and Mercer's classic pop song, 'Moon River,' has the feeling of a Western ballad, using acoustic guitar and harmonica. It showed that Mathis could go both ways. He could sing contemporary pop with a classic feeling and give a classic pop song a contemporary twist.

Mathis's next album, *Those Were the Days* (1968) continued to explore modern pop. The eclectic program of songs includes a fine interpretation of Paul Simon's 'The 59th Street Bridge Song (Feelin' Groovy)' and a kitschy take on The Doors' 'Light My Fire' whose simple structure in terms of melody and harmony doesn't do anything good for Mathis. The lyrics, far from his subtle sensualism, are also a mismatch with an open declaration of carnal lust. It must have been a case of the record company trying to pitch a hit to him without understanding his aesthetic. Fortunately, he wouldn't pursue the music of The Doors further, but he delved much more into the music of Bert Kaempfert whose 'Every Time I Dream of You' is one of the best songs of the album.

Mersey's fourth and final production for Mathis was dedicated entirely to Kaempfert. *Johnny Mathis Sings the Music of Bert Kaempfert* (1968) has the honor of being Mathis's first songbook album, and it's very strange that no one had thought of recording a book of songs before, especially considering Mathis's admiration of Ella Fitzgerald's songbooks and his love of great songwriters like Cole Porter, Rodgers and Hammerstein, and Bart Howard, all of whom deserve a book of songs interpreted by Mathis, but never got it. Instead, their songs are scattered across various albums.

In the fifties, Frank Sinatra had proven that concept albums could be a commercial success, but he relied on mood albums. Focus on a songwriter was a more abstract idea to sell to an audience. In fact, Clive Davis wasn't keen on concept albums at all. He believed they were 'always a turn-off in the MOR market.'[81]

It was also more or less a coincidence that Kaempfert got a songbook album, but the fact that Kaempfert wrote contemporary hits might have softened Davis. Mathis's stature as an international star allowed him to frequently travel to Europe and it was here that he met the German-born Kaempfert, whose songs had already caught his attention. As he recalls in an interview with Roger Catlin: 'I had just started going to England on and off, and then on one of my occasions, I just went on across the channel to Germany. I'd always been a fan of the music of Bert Kaempfert, and got a chance to work with him. Ha! I hope I'm not giving out too much information, but I had never had schnapps before. So I went over there and we got pretty heavy into schnapps before dinner and what have you. So now when I listen to that, I kind of remember that!'[82]

Fortunately, the album also includes plenty of musical schnapps, among them such timeless songs as 'Strangers in the Night,' 'Spanish Eyes' and 'L-O-V-E.' They have been interpreted by some of the greatest singers like Frank Sinatra and Nat King Cole, but Mathis gets to the heart of Kaempfert's music as he swings gently and croons the maestro's easy-listening ballads with smooth sincerity.

The album was recorded in Hamburg and although Robert Mersey is credited as the producer of the album, he wasn't present at the session.[83] Instead, the music was arranged and conducted by Kaempfert's collaborator, Herbert Rehbein, who also gets co-writing credits on several tracks, including the lush ballads 'If There's a Way' and 'Lady' that both sound like classic pop done the Mathis way. At this point, Mathis was both in the past and the future, not really caring about the distinctions between classic and modern pop.

Drummer Rolf Ahrens played regularly for Kaempfert and was among the musicians used for the session. He was quoted by Joe Marchese, who wrote the notes for the reissue of the album, as stating how impressed he was by Mathis's approach to the music. 'During the recording session, instead of going for normal playbacks, Johnny Mathis chose to sing live, along with the orchestra.' He continued, 'The result was one of the most sensitive interpretations ever [of Kaempfert's music].'[84]

The sensitivity that Ahrens notices was also due to the circumstances of the recording studio, Studio Hamburg. Mathis told Marchese about the special effect of the place: 'Its acoustics were so loud that I thought I was singing too loudly. I ended up singing as softly as I could. I was tip-toeing with all these songs because it was so vibrant in the studio.' He discovered that the hushed style melded well with the repertoire. 'There were no big, crashing sounds. It was all smooth and round; there was no attack. I was trying to fit into that. Occasionally, I found myself singing too softly.'[85]

The result was a feeling of orchestral intimacy and as Marchese concludes: 'His beautifully ethereal, sensual vocals meshed sublimely with Rehbein's elegant, swirling orchestrations.'[86] Starting out with the only song not penned by Kaempfert, 'Wonderland By Night' immediately introduces the dreamy ballad universe of the album. Accompanied by acoustic guitar, choir and light strings, Mathis sets the scene as he sings of stars and a floating yellow moon. His voice is just as celestial, moving in spiraling curves that outshine the strings in richness and depth. It's a quintessential example of his ability to project an entire universe in a song.

When the program of Kaempfert's songs starts, the lyrics are grounded in visual impressions. Both 'Spanish Eyes' and 'Strangers in the Night' are about observations and the exchanging of glances. In 'The Lady Smiles, ' Mathis sings, 'Every time the lady smiles / her brighter world is what I see.' The lyrics connect the songs to the physical world, but Mathis's interpretations rise above what is immediately felt and seen. Frank Sinatra's iconic version of 'Strangers in the Night' is a staged drama that paints a concrete picture of two strangers and tells their story in song. Mathis shifts the focus from the strangers to the night, emphasizing the misty mood of the music itself in a way that is much more sophisticated. Just compare Sinatra's rough scatting at the end of the song with Mathis's closing vocal flight, so delicate and unrestrained, that it feels like the air itself is singing. Sinatra is on the street, humming, while Mathis is up in the air. Both versions have their qualities. Sinatra is the master of dramatic storytelling, whereas Mathis brings out the pure beauty of sound itself. In that sense, he is closer to classical music than pop. Interestingly, when Mathis talked about the qualities of Kaempfert's song 'The Times Will Change' to Joe Marchese, he also drew parallels to classical music: 'There were so many lovely songs,' Johnny acknowledges, 'but that's the one that still fascinates me. It's very, very engulfing and almost operatic in feeling.'[87]

The word operatic might suggest an image of a belting singer but listening to the gentle vocal of 'The Times Will Change', nothing could be further from the truth. Instead, the operatic element comes across in the arc of the music. Extended vocal lines, dramatic turns and a clear feeling of spatiality brought out by the different layers of instruments all add to the classic quality of the song.

Adding variety to the album as a whole, the soft swinging songs of 'Danke Schoen,' 'Remember When (We Made These Memories),' 'If There's A Way,' 'L-O-V-E' and 'It Makes No Difference' compliment the pure ballads with a tasteful sense of dynamics. Mathis has come a long way since the brassy punch on *Wonderful, Wonderful* that disturbed the tranquil mood of the album. Even when the brass volume is high on the big band swing of 'L-O-V-E,' a Nat King Cole signature, the hard edge of the brass is toned down.

The only scratch is the misleading cover image of Mathis posing in movement with arms spreading out. It does little justice to the dreamy mood that dominates the record. Other than that, Bert Kaempfert had every reason to be satisfied with the result and he also expressed his thanks to Mathis and arranger Herbert Rehbein in the liner notes, adding a humorous hint to his own songs. 'Johnny has always been one of my favorite artists. What he does is unique and his interpretations of the songs are in a class by themselves, pure Mathis. Watching him work with Herbert, and listening to his renditions of these songs that I had heard sung by many others in many languages, was a high point in my career that I shall never forget. 'Danke Schoen,' Johnny. I 'L-O-V-E' you.'[88]

In an eclectic period, the Kaempfert album was an inspired moment of unity, exploring the voice of a single composer. First released as a standalone album in Europe, it was later combined with a compilation of Bacharach tracks on the double album *Johnny Mathis Sings the Music of Bacharach & Kaempfert* (1970), providing proof of how good the result could be when Mathis sang songbooks. It would still take a very long time before he returned to the songbook concept. Instead, he followed the template that Mersey had developed, mixing all kinds of contemporary songs, simply enjoying the pleasures of pop.

Mersey left after the Kaempfert album, and it would be the job of a new producer to polish his method. As it turned out, the collaboration became one of the longest-lasting associations of Mathis's career, even surpassing the long run of albums he did with Mitch Miller. The name of the producer was Jack Gold.

Middle of the Road: The Early Jack Gold Productions

Jacob (Jack) Gold (1921-1992) knew all aspects of the record business. He worked as a producer, songwriter, and singer, and before he came to Columbia, he had been involved with small labels, taking care of the business side as well as producing. At Columbia, his collaboration with Mathis would stretch across three decades, from the end of the 1960s to the beginning of the 1980s.

Mathis still remembers him fondly, both as a producer and as a friend. 'He was a lovely man. He was physically impaired, he couldn't walk, so he had to use crutches, a terrible, terrible thing, but he was a lovely human being, a wonderful man. I learned a lot about compassion from working with him. He had plenty of time to do what he did because of the fact that he couldn't get around, so he spent a lot of time listening to music and giving me suggestions about what he thought would be relevant to me. He was a genuinely wonderful human being in my early singing career and I just loved him. He was a lovely, lovely man, who gave me nothing but good ideas. Because by the time I met Jack Gold, I had been successful with my music, but he really opened my interest level as far as what directions musically I could go if I wanted to, and I always have wonderful memories of him. He was a wonderful, wonderful man.'[89]

There's no doubt about Gold's dedication to Mathis. He suffered from Parkinson's, which made work difficult, but he still had Johnny as his top priority. Tony Jasper quotes an interview with Paul Green from 1978. When working had become even more difficult, he still wanted to hold on to Mathis: 'Given the talent and application Johnny's got, rather than do ordinary things I only want to do great things, and make great records with him for another year, or two or three.'[90]

There's no way of underestimating the influence Gold had on Mathis's music. He rebooted his career at a time when sales were starting to go down and reestablished his relevance as a hitmaking artist. It didn't come all at once. 1978 was the crucial year when things really started happening commercially and artistically with the single, 'Too Much, Too Little, Too Late,' and the album it was taken from, *You Light Up My Life*, and its follow-up, *That's What Friends Are For*.

In the beginning, Gold would mainly provide stability. *Love Theme for Romeo & Juliet (A Time for Us)* from *1969* was his first production, followed by four other records: *Give Me Your Love for Christmas* (1969), *Raindrops Keep Fallin' on My Head* (1970), *Close to You* (1970) and *Love Story* (1971). None of them stands out and their most important quality is that they continue to document Mathis's survey of the Burt Bacharach songbook. As Joe Marchese explains in his liner notes to the reissue of the double album, *Johnny Mathis Sings the Music of Bacharach and Kaempfert*, Mathis had a long history with Bacharach. 'Johnny's history with Burt Bacharach dated back to September 1956. Just months earlier, Bacharach– then a staff writer toiling at Paramount Pictures' publishing company, Famous Music – had first teamed with lyricist Hal David at the suggestion of Famous honcho Eddie Wolpin. Though their earliest songs were primarily novelties like 'Peggy's in the Pantry,' 'Underneath the Overpass,' and 'The Morning Mail,' they had the opportunity to work in a more mature vein when Famous assigned them to write for Johnny Mathis. The new singing sensation was to appear in an MGM film, Lizzie, starring Eleanor Parker as a woman with three personalities. Mathis would perform their new song in the movie. The fledgling team came up with the ballad 'Warm and Tender.' Columbia slotted their tune as the B-side of 'It's Not for Me to Say,' also performed by Johnny in Lizzie. Not only did 'It's Not for Me to Say' reach the top five on the Hot 100, but it was included on Johnny's Greatest Hits, the groundbreaking hits collection.'[91]

In Marchese's notes to the reissue of *Johnny Mathis Sings the Music of Bacharach and Kaempfert*, Bacharach himself is also quoted, commenting on Mathis's qualities as an interpreter of his songs and he also tells how that first recording changed his own situation financially. 'Whenever I heard that Johnny Mathis was recording a song of mine, I knew I was on safe ground – that the performance would be special and unique. When 'Warm and Tender' was recorded, it helped me out financially in an unusual way. You see, 'Warm and Tender' was the B-side of 'It's Not for Me to Say', which turned out to be an enormous hit for Johnny, and having the B-side meant I got paid as much on record sales as the writers of the A-side. I thank you for that, Johnny, and a big thank you for all of the songs of mine that you have done.'[92]

Mathis also appreciated Bacharach. As he explained to Joe Marchese, he liked the challenging elements of the composer's style. 'All of Burt's stuff was quirky, as far as his melodies and his rhythm patterns were concerned. The time signature would stop and go! I thought it was wonderful.'[93]

Fortunately, the structural complexity of the songs isn't a hindrance to tunefulness or emotional depth and Hal David's poetic lyrics add another layer to the songs. Mathis's interpretations include such Bacharach-classics as 'I'll Never Fall In Love Again,' 'Raindrops Keep Falling On My Head,' 'They Long To Be Close To You' and an essential addition to Mathis's list of portrait songs: 'Alfie.' The information in the text about Alfie is almost non-existing. Still, Mathis brings flesh and bone to the name. This isn't the pure infatuation with sound found in 'Maria' or 'Joey,' but an example of Mathis's ability to portray all the existential anguish offered in the questions posed by the lyrical voice. It's a very human portrait, but one that really portrays the one who is asking rather than the one who is asked.

Other than enhancing Mathis's repertoire of Bacharach compositions, the albums are solid efforts that use the template that Mersey introduced, covering songs by Jimmy Webb, Paul Simon, The Beatles, and many others.

It's hard to say what Gold missed with his early productions, but when he stepped back a bit, and allowed room for another producer, Richard Perry, and Mathis himself, something positive happened. The concept of *You've Got a Friend* (1971) wasn't different, as the subtitle said, Mathis still sang 'Today's Great Hits,' but the sound was more intimate. An example is the sparse beauty of his own production of Carole King's hit, 'You've Got a Friend,' carried by piano, harmonica, bongos and D'Arniell Pershing's string arrangement, or his soulful reading of the Bee Gees hit 'How Can You Mend a Broken Heart.'

Jack Gold was still involved. He produced two ballads taken from movies, 'If' and 'For All We Know,' both arranged and conducted by Al Capps, but it's Pershing's arrangements and the productions by Mathis and Perry that lift the songs on the album. Seen in that light, it's strange how the excellent take on the Holland-Dozier-Holland song 'Reach Out' and another convincing Beatles interpretation, 'Golden Slumbers,' were left out, but even without these songs, the album rises above the five previous Gold productions.

Mathis himself was skeptical about the result of the collaboration with Perry. In Joe Marchese's liner notes for the reissue of the album, he summarizes the experience. 'Somehow it didn't click,' Johnny remembers. 'Richard and I became pals, but that was it. We didn't work together very much in the studio. We were searching for a direction, and we never quite found it.'[94]

Perhaps it's the flawed, composite nature of the album, marred by the search for a sound, which makes it a more interesting album compared to the previous albums produced by Jack Gold that relied too much on a safe formula.

For the next album, Gold was back, but this time as an executive producer with Sid Feller producing. The concept this time seemed so obvious it's a puzzle that Mathis hadn't tried it before, but *In Person* (1971) was in fact, his first live album and successfully merges the past and present. Writing about the album on the blog *Riffs, Beats & Codas* in his survey of Mathis's music, Vincent L. Stephens says, 'Mathis's approach to Vegas-style entertainment is very different from Elvis, Engelbert Humperdinck, or Wayne Newton – and that is a good thing. Taking some of his '50's classics and his new role as a conduit for '70's soft pop, he represents the past and present quite strikingly on this live set. Mathis's self-effacing style runs counter to the Vegas schlock aesthetic and allows the songs to shine. If the 'Close to You/ We've Only Just Begun' medley plays to the hit status of these songs in the early '70s (hence the immediate applause), his medley of Errol Garner's 'Misty'/'Dreamy' and several signatures is for the ages. He also showcases a refreshing sense of humor on Ivor Novello's 'And Her Mother Came Too,' some soulful grit on 'Come Runnin,'' and showcases his robust vocal mettle on Brel's 'If We Only Have Love.' If you want a quick summary of what he is capable of as a vocalist, entertainer, and artist, this is an excellent start.'[95]

In Person marked the end of Gold's first phase as a producer for Mathis. He returned in 1975, beginning his most fruitful period with the singer that included an album that would boost his career. However, in 1971, Gold wasn't the man that could add new dimensions to Mathis's sound. He left that job to other producers who brought Mathis closer to soul music.

Soul and Inspiration: The Jerry Fuller Productions

'Soul and Inspiration' is a song penned by Barry Mann and Cynthia Weil that was a hit for the Righteous Brothers, but it also shows up on the third Mathis album produced by Jerry Fuller, *Me and Mrs. Jones* (1973). The title succinctly sums up what Fuller brought to the Mathis sound: soul and inspiration.

Singer, songwriter and producer Jerry Fuller, was born in Fort Worth, Texas, on November 19, 1938. Both of his parents liked to sing and early on, his mother, Lola, taught him and her other three children how to sing. When he was 11, he formed the Fuller Bros with his brother Bill and after high school, he recorded his first song for Lin Records, 'I Found a New Love,' and moved to Los Angeles. Here, he pursued his own music and worked as a demo singer for Hollywood publishers and writers. Eventually, he got a songwriting contract with the label Four Star Music where he wrote more than 400 songs. In 1967, he became a staff producer at Columbia and discovered Gary Puckett and Mac Davis. He also worked with Mark Lindsay, O.C. Smith, Andy Williams, and Johnny Mathis.

Fuller produced a string of Mathis singles, starting in 1971 with Jimmy Webb's 'Evie,' and when he left Columbia the same year to start his own Moonchild Productions, they continued working together. From 1972 to 1973, they did four albums together: *The First Time Ever (I Saw Your Face)*, *Song Sung Blue*, *Me and Mrs. Jones* and *Killing Me Softly with Her Song*.[96]

These albums are so unified in sound and aesthetic that they could be considered a tetralogy. Like the best producers before him, Fuller understood how to create a link to Mathis's past while creating a new sound. Robert Mersey and the early Jack Gold productions had revitalized Mathis as a modern pop balladeer, but they had also lost some of his orchestral grandeur and emotional urgency. Fuller brought it back and added a touch of soul and a pinch of jazz and made Mathis soar, or as he sings on 'Corner of the Sky' from *Me and Mrs. Jones* (1973): 'Rivers belong where they can ramble / eagles belong where they can fly / I got to be where my spirit can run free / gotta find my corner of the sky.'

Fuller collaborated closely with Mathis and even sang backup vocals on some of the songs. They had respect for each other and enjoyed working together. In Joe Marchese's liner notes to the reissue of *The First Time Ever (I Saw Your Face) / Song Sung Blue*, Fuller comments on the process of preparing the albums. 'I used to make little tapes for him,' the producer reveals. 'He'd come in from being on the road and I'd have a whole batch of songs for him. He'd have maybe a couple of songs that other people had presented to him as well, and we'd go over the material and pick the songs. He wasn't familiar with some of the songs that I laid on him, so we'd get with the arranger and say, 'Yeah, I'd like to do that.' Then I would get a keyboard guy in to play it, and I'd sing along with it and show him the song. I'd give him the recording of me singing the song, followed by just the piano for him to take on the road and rehearse with it. He'd never have it in front of him when he was singing. He had it memorized! He did his homework and was very ready to go.'[97]

'Corner of the Sky' is a perfect example of a song that combines the past and the present. Penned by Stephen Schwartz, it's a Broadway musical tune, a genre that Mathis knows inside out, but it's played as a modern pop song. It starts with a pretty gospel-infused piano intro before ascending into the chorus with choir and strings, while a propulsive electric bass and ticking drums drive the rhythm forward. The prominent place of the electric bass in the mix is a new thing in Mathis's music and adds an understated groove to the orchestral scope. It can be found even in a shimmering acoustic ballad like 'Alone Again (Naturally)' from *Song Sung Blue* (1972), a song that became a staple in his repertoire and meant a lot to him as he revealed to Tony Jasper: 'It's so sad, so touching. I get great satisfaction out of singing the song on so many occasions. In 1974, of course, it had its own poignancy for me when my father died and so both of my parents were dead.'[98]

'Too Young' was another important song from the album and proof that Fuller understood where Mathis came from. He told Joe Marchese how the song, one of his own favorites, ended up on the album. 'My favorite track was 'Too Young.' Johnny and I had the same idol, and it was Nat Cole. I asked Johnny if he'd ever done 'Too Young.' He said, 'No. Nat did it, you know.' I said, 'Well, it's time you did!' I just loved it. I got with D'Arneill Pershing and said, 'I mean no offense whatsoever, please, but I want you listen to the album Love is the Thing by Nat Cole, and I want you to basically go to school on Gordon Jenkins-type arrangements.' He said, 'You got it! I love him too, you know!' So that's where those strings came from. That song is meant to be done that way.'[99]

The choice of the song 'Happy' on *Me and Mrs. Jones* is also interesting. Although never included in the actual soundtrack, it's associated with the Motown-produced movie about Billie Holiday, *Lady Sings the Blues* (1972), with Diana Ross playing Holiday, and shows the connection between soul (Ross) and jazz (Holiday), at least in theory. With layers of glockenspiel and strummed and fingerpicked acoustic guitar combined with swirling strings and dramatic choir, the song itself is closer to majestic pop. The writers are Smokey Robinson and Michel Legrand, and Legrand also appears elsewhere. The medley of 'I Was Born in Love with You / Summer Me, Winter Me' from the movie *Summer of '42* is included on *Me and Mrs. Jones* but is produced by Jack Gold.

Fuller is the producer of a song from the same movie, 'Theme from Summer of '42 (The Summer Knows)' that shows up on *The First Time Ever (I Saw Your Face)* along with another Legrand song from the TV movie *Brian's Song*: 'Brian's Song (The Hands of Time).' All three songs are co-written with Alan and Marilyn Bergman. Mathis would later dedicate one of his rare songbook albums to the music of Legrand and A. & M. Bergman: *How Do You Keep the Music Playing? The Songs of Michel Legrand and Alan and Marilyn Bergman* (1993).

A better synthesis between pop, soul, and jazz than 'Happy' can be found on 'Me and Mrs. Jones.' It became a huge hit for Billy Paul, who recorded it in 1972, and just a year later, encouraged by the record company, Mathis takes up the baton with a version that's perhaps even jazzier and adds a big band touch to the brass arrangement while the signature sound of the strings is kept intact. Although he was doing a good job with it, Mathis told Tony Jasper he wasn't fond of the song. 'Anytime you have to take a song or take words and over, say, a period of three bars make up your own melody, it really isn't much of a song. But then I sing the songs they want me to sing.'[100]

Closely related to 'Me and Mrs. Jones' is the reading of James Taylor's ballad 'Don't Let Me Be Lonely Tonight,' carried by bittersweet strings and brass, acoustic guitar, and piano. The jazzy touch can be found in the softly swinging accompaniment from the drums played with brushes and the sensual saxophone solo, but the greatest horn is Mathis as he fills the song with emotions of regret, longing and mourning that come across in perfectly paced pauses, curved lines, understated vibrato, and gentle humming.

The influence of orchestral folk music can be found on the acoustic title tracks from *The First Time Ever (I Saw Your Face)* and *Song Sung Blue*, written by Ewan MacColl and Neil Diamond respectively, but the most important musical influence on the four albums produced by Fuller is soul. Songs by George Clinton ('Life and Breath'), Bill Withers ('Lean on Me'), Gamble & Huff ('Me and Mrs. Jones') and Stevie Wonder ('You Are the Sunshine of My Life') are introduced into the repertoire along with Fuller's own 'Show and Tell,' written specifically for Mathis. Mathis's reading of the song is the epitome of musical elegance, but Al Wilson would raise the emotional stakes and top the charts with his cathartic version recorded in 1973, a year after Mathis.

As proven by a comparison with Wilson, Mathis's strength as a soul singer isn't the ability to transmit raw emotion but a more understated brand of soul singing. Nobody understood that better than Thom Bell. He had already provided songs for Mathis while Fuller was working with him and the sophisticated songs, 'Break Up to Make Up' and 'Betcha By Golly Wow,' both originally written for the soul group, The Stylistics, were a perfect fit. Bell and Mathis told Joe Marchese about the song, with Bell detailing the origin of the complex structure: 'One of my background singers majored in music. In one of her theory classes, a professor told her something to the effect of 'there's never been a song that, when you modulate, it goes back to the key that you came from.' I said, 'What?' He said that once you make the modulation, if you go to F-sharp or G or G-sharp–wherever you go–the song never comes back to the original F. I said, 'Get outta here!' He said that's impossible to do. Man! I went home and played... Now listen to 'Betcha By Golly Wow' and see how many keys that thing changes in just the beginning!' Mathis immediately took to Bell's sophisticated pop-soul stylings. 'I always, always loved his songs. I couldn't wait to sing one, and 'Betcha by Golly Wow' appealed to me as much as some of the later ones I'd eventually learned. It was a revelation for me to meet and later work with him. I was always just amazed that he even knew who I was. I just wanted to get to know him and see if I could sing some of his songs, and it just worked out beautifully.'[101]

'Break Up to Make Up' and 'Betcha By Golly Wow' clearly showed the potential of a collaboration between Bell and Mathis. That potential would be realized with the two albums they did together. It was the beginning of a deeper journey into soul.

Deeper into Soul: The Bell, Bristol and Florez Productions

If Jerry Fuller was the first producer that introduced Mathis to soul material, Thom Bell took him further in this direction and fleshed out his potential as a soul singer. With Bell in the producer's chair, Mathis got success in the R&B market that had previously been untapped, as Bell explains in an interview with Christian John Wikane: 'He'd been labeled a pop act and that's who he was. It was a total rebirth for him in areas that the label skipped over because they hadn't needed those R&B stations, though they would have helped with more sales. We got airplay on stations where he'd never gotten airplay before. He got sales where he'd never gotten sales before.'[102]

Not only did Bell deliver commercial success in new musical areas, he also helped create two artistic highlights in the Mathis canon, *I'm Coming Home* (1973) and *Mathis Is* (1977), with the former standing out as a genuine masterpiece. One of the reasons why the albums work so well is that Bell brought his own aesthetic approach to the projects. He had already pioneered the Sound of Philadelphia with Kenny Gamble and Leon Huff but added new layers to the symphonic soul sound that fitted Mathis perfectly.

Born in 1943, Bell had already listened to Mathis as a teenager and thought of him as the heir to Nat King Cole. He was serious about singing himself, teaming up with Kenny Gamble in his vocal group, The Romeos, but it was his talent as an arranger, producer and songwriter that would make him famous. He had studied classical music as a child and his lush string arrangements became an essential part of the Sound of Philadelphia.

Before he worked with Kenny Gamble's and Leon Huff's iconic Philadelphia International Records, Bell had already cut his teeth as an arranger, songwriter and producer for Cameo-Parkway and he got his breakthrough working with the vocal group, The Delfonics, on the Philly Groove label. The song 'La-La Means I Love You' went to No. 4 Pop in 1968 and was a sign of great things to come. His production and songwriting for The Delfonics, foreshadowed the Philly Sound with lush layers of horns and strings, as exemplified by the 1969 hit 'Didn't I (Blow Your Mind This Time). Bell continued having success with vocal groups when he came to Philadelphia International Records (PIR), but in the early phase of his association with PIR, he was mostly a musician and arranger as well as a partner in Gamble and Huff's publishing company, Mighty Three Music. His important productions outside PIR included the first three albums on Avco by the vocal group, The Stylistics, whose early hit, 'Betcha By Golly Wow,' (1971), written by Bell with lyricist Linda Creed, was covered by Mathis.

There were already close ties between Columbia and Philadelphia International, which was distributed by Columbia's parent label CBS, and Bell had proven his worth as a producer, so the idea of a collaboration certainly seemed within reach, and Bell was eager to work with Mathis. In the end, it came to be, and their partnership got a flying start with the album *I'm Coming Home* (1973).

Bell has made a point out of emphasizing that his music cannot be reduced to a template of the Sound of Philadelphia. Like Mathis, he can't be pinned down musically. Both were interested in branching out and that's what they did on the album.

I'm Coming Home consists of original music. Mathis sat down with Bell and songwriting partner, Linda Creed, and his musings became the inspiration for the songs. As he explained to Christian John Wikane: 'They wanted something, so I told them. That's the way they got the idea of the album. They're talking to me and getting my thoughts about different things. I thought that was the most marvelous thing. Nobody had ever done that before.'[103]

Mathis has always been a master of making his music personal instead of private. This time his own life provided the material for the songs, and yet, the result is timeless and universal, as when he sings about the problems of being too kind on 'Foolish': 'Folks say I'm naturally kind / I'd like to think that they're right / They say I'm kind but in their minds / They're really laughing at me.'

Indeed, there is a natural sweetness about the album. It's light, deep, intimate, and lush. While the influence of the symphonic sound of Philly soul is certainly there, the album is more than that. This is underlined by the title track and opener. Its catchy use of a triangle motif is supplemented by breezy chords on Rhodes, softly suspended strings and a brass arrangement inspired by Burt Bacharach. It's no wonder that it became a number one hit on the *Billboard* Easy Listening chart. An even bolder move is the epic 'Life Is A Song Worth Singing.' The song starts out as a funky instrumental odyssey in the mode of a blaxploitation soundtrack, with Bell's inventive use of sitar, a trademark he perfected in many of his productions, including 'Didn't I (Blow Your Mind This Time).' Mathis enters around the three-minute mark, emphasizing that 'life is a song worth singing / sing it.'

The next song, the ballad, 'A Baby's Born,' examines the link between innocence and experience and the circle of life: 'winter never seemed so cold / you grow old / and time has slipped away / yesterday was just a dream / faded schemes / now turn silver-grey / as old friends pass away / and yet / a baby's born.' Using elegiac strings, piano, Rhodes, and shimmering bells, the song rises forcefully in a funky crescendo with horns.

As a contrast to the philosophical songs, the Latinized funky pop of 'Sweet Child' is just as light and catchy as the breezy flutes and rolling marimba that adorn it. On the other hand, 'Stop, Look, Listen (To Your Heart)' is a convincing exercise in deep soul balladry. Much emphasis has been placed on the technical aspects of Mathis's voice, but here is a chance to hear how naturally he changes emotional register from the exuberant joy of 'Sweet Child' to the wounded introspection of 'Stop, Look, Listen (To Your Heart).' Anyone who claims that Mathis isn't an emotional singer just needs to hear him singing the opening lines: 'You are alone / all the time / does it ever puzzle you? / Have you asked why?' There's such delicate use of pause and vibrato, as every word is softly carried into the other. Pauses can be effective to convey emotion but can easily descend into staccato patterns that break the musical flow. Mathis can both hold an emotional line, slow it down and stop it without interrupting the flow like he is balancing in midair without falling.

Bell also had an important role in making Mathis explore new vocal territory. As Joe Marchese points out in his notes to *Life Is a Song Worth Singing: The Complete Thom Bell Sessions*: 'Bell focused on the expressive, seductive and romantic qualities in Mathis' lower register, leading the singer to explore a new area of his familiar voice.'[104]

The musical journey on *I'm Coming Home* is wrapped up with 'I Just Wanted to Be Me,' a symphonic soul pop song with funky breaks and Bell's sense of detail revealed by a marimba in the background. The song suitably tells about the existential journey of coming into your own. It was something Mathis and Bell did musically without denying their past. The result was an album that was very special, not only to Mathis but also to his father. 'It was my father's favorite album that I made. My dad and I were inseparable all our lives. He was my best pal. He would sit and listen to I'm Coming Home ad nauseam. Every time I play it, I think about dad. I start sobbing because my dad had that album on every time I ever saw him.'[105]

I'm Coming Home would not mark the only time that Bell and Mathis worked together. They reunited three years later for the album *Mathis Is* that was recorded in 1976 and released the following year.

Although not as highly profiled as the predecessor, the album nevertheless shows Bell and Mathis at the top of their game. With the exception of a wonderful reworking of The Spinners' 'Sweet Love of Mine,' the album once again sports all new material, but this time written in tandem with Bell's nephew, LeRoy M. Bell, on the majority of the tracks. LeRoy Bell's partner in the soul group, Bell & James, Casey James, also collaborates with Thom Bell on the track 'World of Laughter.' It has an irresistibly swinging pulse that combines funk and jazz with sweet doo-wop choir.

Sherman Marshall, who penned the 1973-hit 'I'm Doin' Fine Now' for the group, New York City, also shows up as a collaborator with Bell on the anthemic Philly soul ballad 'Hung Up in the Middle of Love.' The rhythmical drive in the chorus, propelled by brass and strings, is already prepared by the use of spinning percussion. The introduction itself is a perfect study in how Bell works with rhythmical cues that are integrated with the strings while the sophisticated time signatures continue in the song. Mathis is never thrown off the beat but floats elegantly above it, and yet, he retains an earthy funkiness that Bell brought into his vocabulary by emphasizing the rhythmical elements that his great early arrangers like Percy Faith and Glenn Osser didn't bring into play.

Bell, on the other hand, was also enriched by working with a singer as musically complete as Mathis. It gave him the opportunity to branch out beyond the template of Philly soul, and he took it. As Mathis says: 'He was interested in me because he had been involved in R&B all his life and he loved the idea of branching out a little, you know when you only do one kind of music and all of sudden you get the chance to do something else.'[106]

An example of Bell's widening musical palette can be heard on the opening track, 'As Long as We're Together.' Written with Bell's brother, Anthony, and Jo Dee Omer, it starts with a whimsical baroque string intro that gives way to a deep midtempo orchestral groove, adding Caribbean flourishes from a marimba in the chorus.

LeRoy Bell takes over as Bell's songwriting partner on the following four tracks. 'Lullaby of Love' is a take on a classic Mathis ballad without rhythmical surprises. With the basic melody played on Fender Rhodes, there are rich textures from xylophone and harp with a melodramatic touch in the opulent strings and Mathis's soaring vocal. Things turn on a plate with the next track, 'Loving You – Losing You.' Phyllis Hyman had a hit with her version, the same year as Mathis. Although his version didn't live up to the song's commercial potential, it's a stunning interpretation that deserves its place in the canon of pre-Disco anthems. Starting out with a rhythm reminiscent of a beating heart, supported by a spinet, a rare soul instrument Barry White also used in 'I'm Gonna Love You Just a Little More Baby,' the song quickly gets into gear as a funky bass sets in and the strings lift the chorus with Mathis pleading in an emotional chiasm: 'loving you / is it worth the pain of losing you? / losing you / is it worth the pain of loving you?' It's the ecstasy and pain of love caught in the light of a glittering disco ball.

The marimba returns on 'I'll Make You Happy', whose tropical rays of sunshine support the optimistic mood of the song. The sitar is another key instrument. It plays a prominent role on the ballad 'Heaven Must Have Sent You,' and as Charles Waring points out, there are echoes of Bell's previous work with Mathis. 'A twangy electric sitar states the melodic theme of the elegant 'Heaven Must Have Made You Just For Me,' a soulful romantic ballad that has echoes of the Stylistics' 'Betcha By Golly Wow' and 'I'm Stone In Love With You,' two well-known Bell tunes that Mathis has previously recorded.'[107]

The reference to Bell's work with iconic soul groups becomes complete when a cover of the Spinners' 'Sweet Love of Mine' closes the album, but before that, the pen of Bell and Bell deliver another deep ballad with 'I Don't Wan't To Say No.' Once again, Mathis shows himself capable of mining new emotional territory as he delves into a desperation seldom found in his songs. It's a raw kind of emotional catharsis that is common in soul and R&B, and as with so many types of music, Mathis also found resonance in this genre: 'I always loved rhythm & blues and Tommy had this wonderful sophistication and I was thrilled by it. I was absolutely thrilled that he even knew who I was. (…) That was one of the great surprises and one of the great happenstances that has happened to me in my career, meeting people like Thom Bell.'[108]

Bell would not be the only producer who took Mathis into soul territory. Johnny Bristol would take up the baton after *I'm Coming Home* and once again show how sophisticated a Johnny Mathis take on soul could be.

Singer, songwriter, and producer Johnny William Bristol was born in Morganton, North Carolina, February 3, 1939. He wrote about the experience of growing up in the city in the song 'Morganton, North Carolina' from the album *Feeling the Magic* (1974). Just the year before, Bristol had had one of his biggest hits with the title track from the album, *Hang on in There Baby*, released on MGM. While pursuing his solo career, he also joined Columbia Records as an in-house producer in 1973.

When he came to Columbia, Bristol had already established his name as a producer for Motown. His association with the label started in the early sixties after the demise of the vocal duo Johnny & Jackey. As a writer and producer, he worked with some of the biggest names in the label's roster, including The Supremes, Stevie Wonder, The Four Tops, Martha Reeves, and not least, Marvin Gaye and Tammi Terrell, whom Bristol and co-producer Harvey Fuqua paired for the smash-hit 'Ain't No Mountain High Enough.' Summing up Bristol's accomplishments at Motown, the writer Jeff Burger concludes: 'Outside of label president Berry Gordy himself, perhaps only Holland/Dozier/Holland and Smokey Robinson boast Motown resumes as wide-ranging and impressive as Bristol's.'[109]

As much as Bristol enjoyed being at Motown, he also relished the possibility of collaborating with other artists when he left the label. As he comments in an interview with Trudy Gallant: 'You were exclusive to Motown as a producer, so getting away really opened up the whole music industry for me, because it gave an opportunity to work with another variety of artists, even though Motown's stable was incredible.'[110]

At Columbia, Bristol got the chance to work with Boz Scaggs, Tom Jones and not least Johnny Mathis. Mathis was a perfect fit for Bristol, who was interested in branching out in terms of the songs he could present on an album. As he explained to Jeff Burger: 'I consider myself a versatile writer. And if there's ten different kinds of songs on the top ten, I think I can write that many different types of songs.'[111]

His project with Mathis, *The Heart of a Woman*, gave him a chance to prove that, and Mathis was naturally up for the task of singing different types of songs, something he had practiced his whole life and career. Mathis told Joe Marchese in the notes for the reissue of *The Heart of a Woman / Feelings* that he respected Bristol: 'Johnny Bristol was a wonderful singer, had a good voice, and gave me a free hand, though I respected his judgment on things,'[112]

The opener on the album, 'Woman, Woman,' immediately shows a new side of Mathis as a soul singer. Starting with a driving acoustic rhythm guitar, it quickly settles into a syncopated funk groove, lifted by strings, punchy brass and gospel-infused call and response patterns. It's a move from Motown to Chicago soul, with the maestro, Curtis Mayfield, echoed in Bristol's writing, and like many of Mayfield's songs, there's a message in the music. Here it's about women's liberation. Mathis sings about women 'locked up with the key of tradition' and concludes, 'hey people / tell me / can't you see / that women in her wisdom should be free.' In the chorus, the perspective shifts, and he sings directly to women, offering them encouragement: 'I talk about the women of the world / you're something special girl / you're not a tool for some damn fool / to break down.'

Women are a topic Bristol often returned to in his writing, as he says to Jeff Burger: 'You know, all my writing is basically about women in one way or another. Not necessarily about personal contacts; sometimes, I'm just singing about something I've observed. But women are the key.'[113]

The Heart of a Woman is an album about women and relationships that goes beyond standard boudoir-balladry and typical love songs. In the four songs Bristol contributes, he embraces different aspects of love, from the ode to women's liberation in 'Woman, Woman' to the dreamy declaration of love in the perfect pop song 'Sail On White Moon,' but even in his most romantic mood, there's also a bitter touch of realism in the lyrics: 'Girl you must realize / there will be a difference in our lives / Girl We're going to be rejected / that's to be expected.'

In 'Memories Don't Leave Like People Do' all there is left of love is a memory, but as Mathis sings carried by a swampy groove: 'I find joy in all the pain / though your body's gone / the soul remains.' This is true soul music. Love as a life lived and not a life idealized, and just as things can go wrong, happiness can also come again. This is the case in the song 'Strangers in Dark Corners.' It showed up on Bristol's own solo album *Strangers* (1978) four years later and is a proof that he only offered Mathis his very best writing. Taken at a slower tempo than Bristol's own version, and with the added sophistication of Paul Riser's delicate string arrangement, it's a deep cut of complicated love, up there with 'Me and Mrs. Jones' and 'Dark End of the Street.' Mathis sings about a moment's redemption that is the existential nexus of a love affair. His falsetto soars as he brings out all the different shades of joy and pain in a much lighter vocal register than Bristol, whose own voice brings Barry White's bass-baritone to mind.

Sticking to the territory of complicated love, 'Gone,' 'The Way We Planned It' and 'House for Sale,' are songs of breakup and divorce, with the latter standing out as the heir to Bacharach and David's 'A House is Not a Home,' describing the details of a neglected house with stark realism: 'nothing on the shelves but dust / and nothing in the pipes but rust/roses blooming on a broken fence / an empty house never makes much sense.'

Balancing the songs of emotional pain, 'Feel Like Makin' Love' is a sensual samba-flavoured piece, while 'Wendy' enters the canon of poignant portrait songs done by Mathis and has the same infatuation with a name as 'Maria.' Fittingly, there is also a thematic link to the previous songs with the line, 'my house is not a home if you're not here with me.'

The title track also follows a thematic thread as it is a homage to women in general and connects women with singing: 'The heart of a woman is a wonderful thing / so sad for a moment / then eager to sing.'

On the album, Mathis is also eager to sing, and he sings his praise of women, love, and music, so all these aspects melt together into a forceful expression. The ten songs on the album form a perfect unity. Jerry Fuller produced the closing track, penned by George Clinton, 'The Way We Planned It.' With its crass realism, describing the aftermath of love, it fits the rest of the album, where hope and disillusion exist side by side.

Unfortunately, Bristol would only get one chance to work with Mathis. The album that followed, *When Will I See You Again* (1975), was produced by John Florez. This didn't mean that the soul connection was entirely lost. As Charles Waring writes, 'Florez rose to fame as a fledgling producer at RCA records in the 1960s and early '70s, working mainly with R&B acts which included The Friends of Distinction ('Grazin In The Grass'), Willie Hutch and Hues Corporation ('Rock the Boat').'[114]

It was a session Florez did with soul singer Ronnie Dyson that resulted in Columbia offering him the chance to collaborate with Mathis, but as it turned out, his influence on the choice of material was limited. Most of it had already been pre-assigned by the New York office of the label. This was a recurring pattern for a long period in Mathis's career and something he also experienced while working with Robert Mersey.

The influence of the label in the choice of songs resulted in some clunkers, like the baffling recording of The Doors' 'Light My Fire,' but the material presented to Mathis for *When Will I See You Again* was actually spot on. Especially the melodramatic pop of 'Mandy', another portrait of a woman, and the wistful 'The Way We Were' were made for his ability to transmit emotional depth in songs bordering on sentimentality.

'Only You (And You Alone)' and 'Nice To Be Around' are sophisticated ballads with jazzy undertones that show the lush nuances of Mathis's voice. The latter is co-written by Paul Williams, whom Florez knew personally, and two other songs with Williams' signature also show up on the album, 'You And Me Against The World,' and the medley 'Let Me Be The One / I Won't Last A Day Without You.'

Florez also made sure that Mathis's success with soul wasn't forgotten and his first-rate readings of the Philly soul songs, 'You're As Right As Rain' and 'When Will I See You Again,' both written by Thom Bell and Linda Creed, are a reminder of the perfect match between Bell and Mathis.

In fact, there are no bad songs on the album. Neil Sedaka's 'Laughter in the Rain' underlines that Mathis can be just as comfortable with an upbeat ballad as his slow signature songs, but the crooning closer, the country-tinged ballad 'The Things I Might Have Been,' once again shows him as a master of romantic songs. The mood is enhanced by D'Arneill Pershing, a friend of Florez, who contributed string arrangements for the album and did the conducting. It was an orchestrator Mathis appreciated much: 'He was my conductor for six or seven years, and he wrote extraordinary arrangements. I always told him about certain aspects of what I wanted to do for my performance, and he would acknowledge it, say no more than what was necessary, and a month later, he would come back with a complete roadmap of what I had asked for, and a complete arrangement, and it was such a wonderful surprise because when you're singing some things come to mind and you want to take advantage of them right away and sometimes you're not able to because you don't have the right writer. To have those things come back and be a work of art – some of his arrangements became highlights in my career.'[115]

The arrangements Pershing did for *When Will I See You Again* belong among his most wonderful work and the album was a success. Despite the difficult circumstances surrounding the choice of songs, Florez helped Mathis deliver musically and the album also sold well, but it wasn't enough for Columbia. Florez had hoped for a longer association with him, but it was not meant to be. Instead, Mathis would return to a familiar acquaintance, Jack Gold, who brought him new inspiration with the help of a prominent arranger: Gene Page.

Disco Nights and Days: The Gene Page Recordings

Born in Los Angeles, Eugene Edgar Page Jr. (1938-1998) was one of the great arrangers of popular music. He was taught piano by his father and educated at Brooklyn Conservatory after winning a four-year scholarship. In the early sixties, he was hired as in-house arranger for Reprise Records, but he was also a prolific arranger for Motown Records. Early on, he wrote pop history when he did the grandiose arrangement for The Righteous Brothers' 'You've Lost that Lovin' Feeling.' The song was produced by Phil Spector and Page followed his vision of a wall of sound. In contrast, the signature sound that he would create himself was much lighter and connected to a new wave of early disco music embodied by Barry White. In fact, Page was a mentor for White and took him into the studio to see how the musicians worked. Later, Page helped White realize his own musical visions, but it was a matter of mutual inspiration with Page admiring White's autodidactic orchestral skills, which he translated into proper charts. White had a complex understanding of sound that led him to use as many as five different guitars on a song, all playing different parts.

The sound Page and White created together on their iconic hit albums from the 70s was rhythmically direct and insisting and yet lush and sophisticated. The instruments were both grounded in tight rhythmical patterns and used in airy musical flights. The band White used was called Love Unlimited Orchestra and their instrumental hit 'Love's Theme' (1973) is considered the blueprint of the early disco sound together with another instrumental from the same year, 'TSOP (The Sound of Philadelphia),' recorded by MFSB, the legendary studio band of Philadelphia International Records (PIR).

The earthy, funky feeling with prominent use of wah-wah-guitar and syncopation is balanced by the light orchestral sweep of strings and subtle horns. Listen to 'Love's Theme' and it's all there. There's no better way of understanding the way Page and White changed the use of strings than listening to the opening with its almost endless spiraling movement of the strings. Barry White is considered the master of romantic music, but his use of strings isn't romantic in the sense much classic pop is. The strings were often used as a heavy coat of paint to emphasize subjective emotions, but the light and dynamic approach of Page and White is more playful, at times almost whimsical, and closer to Mozart than Mahler. Consequently, the focus also shifted from the aching subject of the song to the listener, or as White pointed out in an interview with David Ritz: 'Disco deserved a better name. It deserved a beautiful name because it was a beautiful art form. It was beautiful, you see, because it made the consumer beautiful. The consumer was the star.'[116]

Gene Page was at the forefront of propelling the sound of disco and the 70s were perhaps his most prolific period. Not only did he work intensely with Barry White, but he also recorded solo albums and soundtracks and found time to work with other artists, among them Johnny Mathis.

Page worked with producer Jack Gold on a series of albums that include *Feelings* (1975), *I Only Have Eyes For You* (1976), *Hold Me, Thrill Me, Kiss Me* (1977), *You Light Up My Life* (1978), *That's What Friends Are For* (1978), *The Best Days of My Life* (1979) and *Mathis Magic* (1979). They were all eclectic collections, including new compositions, contemporary pop material, standards and songs from movies and musicals. The Gene Page touch is immediately felt on the first track on *Feelings*: 'One Day In Your Life.' It's a pop ballad in medium tempo that was first recorded by Michael Jackson and Page's arrangement is a notable improvement of the song with moderate use of slinky strings, revealing the imprint of an orchestral auteur.

Mathis also recorded songs with a sound closer to the disco aesthetic Page was promoting. 'Till Love Touches Life' from *You Light Up My Life* and 'My Body Keeps Changing My Mind' from *Mathis Magic* are both superb examples of Mathis embracing the disco genre, with the latter examining a common trope in disco lyrics, the search for bodily redemption on the dancefloor. In fact, *Mathis Magic* is one of his most convincing explorations of the genre, starting out with an original co-written by Jack Gold, 'No One But The One You Love,' with an immediately recognizable Gene Page string intro that gives way to Mathis crooning majestically to a groovy midtempo-ballad.

The light of the mirror ball shines even stronger on 'Night and Day' that combines the past and the present. Mathis had already translated Cole Porter into the disco idiom on 'Begin the Beguine' from *The Best Days of My Life* and here he does it again. As Charles Waring writes, 'Mathis' decision to put a throbbing disco beat under such a classic tune could have resulted in a kitsch musical nightmare, but thanks to Gene Page's classy and imaginative arrangement, the song is tastefully transformed. At first, on the intro and first verse, where Mathis' smooth vocals are underpinned by Michael Boddicker's sequenced synthesizer and a percussive bass line, the song is almost unrecognisable, but when the chorus kicks in, there's no disguising Cole Porter's original melody and chords. As radical deconstructions go, Mathis' surprising take on 'Night and Day' is a triumph.'[117]

A reason why Mathis' interpretations of old songs in new settings are so successful is his ability to adapt his voice to the sound of the music. Instead of trying to squeeze a particular style of singing into every song, he lets the style grow naturally out of the sound and while keeping his musical elegance as a trademark, he can change style at the drop of a hat from the sweet soul of 'Do Me Wrong But Do Me' on *I Only Have Eyes For You* to the frolicsome vaudeville vocal on the Broadway tune 'One' from *Hold Me, Thrill Me, Kiss Me*.

Gene Page gave him a sound and Mathis showed he could use it, but they didn't record a fully-fledged disco album together. Instead, there are various disco songs scattered across his albums from the 70s. At one time, it seemed that Mathis would record the definitive disco album when Columbia enlisted Bernard Edwards and Nile Rodgers of the Chic Organization to produce an album for him. Chic had shown both the artistic and commercial potential of disco with hits like 'Le Freak,' 'Good Times' and 'Upside Down' and it was about time that the songwriting team of Edwards and Rodgers spread their stardust on a Mathis album.

The name of the project was *I Love My Lady*. It was recorded between December 1980 and January 1981 but was eventually abandoned by the label. Unfortunately, the album was made at a time when the disco tide had turned, and the genre was becoming offensive in the public eye, at least among certain listeners. The infamous destruction of disco records, Disco Demolition Night, had taken place in 1979 on July 12 at Comiskey Park baseball stadium, the home of Chicago White Sox. It was an act of musical intolerance with unfortunate undertones of racism and homophobia, and to this day, the event remains controversial. At that time, it had an immediate impact on the music business, and as a result, Chic started moving in new musical directions and this also affected their collaboration with Mathis. Instead of relying on a tried and tested formula of the past, they threw themselves into musical experiments in the studio. Mathis recalled the process of recording the album in an interview with Christian John Wikane for *PopMatters*: 'They were making up melodies as we went along in the studio. It was a process that was different from the recordings I had done up to that time. There was a lot of stopping and starting and stopping and starting. Conversations would be, 'maybe we would like to say this in the song, maybe we would like to say that in the song', and they would change the song right there and then. It was not like anything I'd done before. On-the-spot improvisation. It was fun. I'm thrilled when I listen to it with what was accomplished.'[118]

Interestingly, the process was like making jazz, something that Mathis would appreciate, with jazz being his first musical love, but the genre was pop, the artful, funky kind. Edwards and Rodgers avoided the elements that Mathis had made key components in most of his career: melodies and strings. The melodies were not completely shunned, but they were not essential for the music, as Mathis says: 'There wasn't too much of a concern about melody. If a melody came along, then fine, if it didn't, then the other elements of the song would hold up. A lot of it happened by accident. I would try to sing the melody that they would sing for me, and I would get it right maybe 85% of the time. The rest of the time, they said, 'Oh, well, we'll use that, it's OK.' It was fun. I had all these wonderful opportunities because I was in New York all by myself. I had nobody telling me what I had to do and what I didn't have to do. I just made sure that I was on time at the studio. I wasn't a musical snob in any way. I was young and interested in everything. I was so grateful to meet Bernard and Nile, who were excited about what they were doing and wanted to work with me. Now I listen to it and I really like it a lot. It's not very melodic, but the rhythms and the effect of singing the same thing over and over again is interesting. It has a child-like quality, not to say that it's not a grownup recording, but it does have a very youthful excitement about it.'[119]

The youthful excitement Mathis talks about might be the link to disco music, which always had a very positive and youthful vibe about it. Like the disco music Chic made, the album is both progressive and danceable, but Chic has moved beyond disco into post-disco mode, and the strings, an important element of disco music, are almost gone. As string arranger and conductor on the album, Nile Rodgers had very little to do. The lush string intro on the opening track, 'Fall in Love (I Want To)', isn't an indication of the rest of the album, as strings only show up sporadically on 'I Love My Lady' and 'Take Me.' The strings are used effectively, but it's the use of the choir that lifts the music. Present on almost every track, the choir, consisting of Alfa Anderson, Luci Martin, Fonzi Thornton, and Michelle Cobbs, is very far from the usual easy listening pop sweetening. The gospel power of the voices has a rhythmical drive that pushes the music forward, but at the same time, it's a very sophisticated take on the blending of voices. Singers Fonzi Thornton and Alfa Anderson elaborated on the approach to Joe Marchese in the notes he prepared for the first standalone release of the album in 2019: 'Part of the uniqueness of the Chic sound,' Thornton acknowledges, 'was how subtly my voice was folded into the unison with Alfa, Luci, and Michelle. Many people are not even aware there is a male vocalist in the group sound unless they read the liner credits. Normally Nile and Nard would have me lay down several tracks by myself, then bring in the ladies to sing with me. My voice also blended easily on group leads with Alfa and Luci. Along with Michelle, alto extraordinaire, my second tenor tone added vocal depth to the precise but lush staccato, group sound Chic was known for. All the backing vocals you hear on Johnny's album are the core group only: Alfa, Fonzi, Luci, and Michelle. We were so excited for the opportunity and had such fun singing the vocal parts. Alfa's clear soprano voice, Luci's middle, Michelle's solid alto adding body and soul, and Fonzi's second tenor adds shading and subtle overtones as male vocalist. Nile and Nard taught us the vocal parts but looked to me as section leader to oversee the blend in the studio and onstage, keep the vocals well-rehearsed, and make sure correct parts were being sung. It was Heaven!' Anderson concurs. 'I remember how incredibly happy we were and how tight the vocal sound was. This unit had worked together for quite a few projects, so we were used to singing and vibing together. And we all knew it when we nailed it.'[120]

Generally, the focus is on the rhythm and texture, or one should perhaps say the texture of rhythm, an element Mathis rarely indulged in. Here, he gets to be immersed in rhythm. Tony Thompson, who played on the album, did a March 1985 interview with the magazine *Echoes* and was quoted by Joe Marchese: 'You never heard Johnny Mathis sing like this. No one has. He grooves to death with this album, grooves to death. It was serious.'[121]

Mathis's clipped melodic phrases are as much a part of the texture as the sophisticated funk guitar of Nile Rodgers. Adding transposed layers of rhythm, it is a deconstruction of metric funk where elements like waves of classical piano on 'It's Alright to Love Me' play counterpoint to the tight funk of a thick, creamy bass and Rodgers' guitar.

Throughout the album, different genres are merged in a postmodern collage that includes everything from the rock trope of a double-kick drum break in 'Take Me' to blues licks and Curtis Mayfield guitar ornaments in 'Stay with Me' and Brazilian samba flavor on 'I Love My Lady.' Mathis's past as a painter of female portraits is also referenced in the superb synthesizer-heavy funk of 'Judy.' Like so many of Mathis's other portraits, there's an infatuation with the sound of the name itself, but 'Judy' takes this approach to the limit. It finds joy in repetition and singing in the same way as 'Something to Sing About' is just as much an ode to singing itself as it is a generic love song.

In the end, the album is wrapped up with a potent dance anthem, 'Love and Be Loved.' Introduced by advanced funky guitar chords, it settles into a deep groove with slap bass, organ and choir and Mathis pleading: 'love /love / and be loved.' It's essentially the message of disco revitalized in new musical clothes.

As irresistibly shiny, sensually glamorous, and artfully funky as the best moves on a dance floor, *I Love My Lady* was a musical answer to the bullies at Disco Demolition Night, showing that love and love to music cannot be held down. It's a cut-and-paste pop masterpiece worthy of Teo Macero's studio experiments with Miles Davis. Interestingly, the link between Davis and Chic can also be found on Chic's *Take It Off* that was released in 1981, the same year as *I Love My Lady* was recorded. Look at the cover of the album and spot the reference to Davis' album *On the Corner*. Chic was experimenting with a new sound, breaking free of the disco genre. Perhaps that album's failure to reach the pop charts scared Columbia away. At least the reaction from Mathis's manager, Ray Haughn, gives an indication of how the music was received by the people on top: 'My jaw dropped when I saw the material; the longest note was a quarter. I couldn't believe it. I think there was just one piece which could be termed a Johnny song. I think if the album was released in the States, it would have killed off Johnny; there might be more response in the UK. At least I feel a release there would not do the same amount of damage.'[122]

One thing is certain; the label didn't understand the merits of *I Love My Lady* at the time it was recorded. As a result, it was cancelled but finally released in 2017 as part of the massive Mathis box set, *The Voice of Romance*, and later as a standalone release in 2019. To this day, the album has not gotten the due it deserves as a key album in the aftermath of disco. It showed that Edwards and Rodgers were not burnt out, but perhaps more vital and playful than ever, and Mathis, as the curious artist he is, played along. Nile Rodgers still remembers the album and the process of recording it as something special, as he told Joe Marchese: 'Working with Johnny was one of the happiest times Bernard and I ever spent with an artist. When he walked into the Power Station for the first time, the reaction was incredible. This is a place I brought everyone from Bowie to Jagger and that was used to seeing Springsteen on a daily basis but no one ever caused the tumult that accompanied Johnny walking through the doors. Everyone was in awe. His singing on this album is brilliant and amongst the finest ever. There's a note on 'Fall in Love (I Want To)' that I'm quite certain is the longest note ever held on a recording by a vocalist. I've actually researched this extensively and I don't think anyone has ever beat what he does with the word LOVE. There's only one Johnny Mathis and I'm delighted you can finally experience how sublime he is on these songs.'[123]

With Nile Rodgers, Mathis experienced a process of artists working together without the interference of producers because the producers were also artists, focusing as much on making art as making hits. This collaborative space between artists was something he enjoyed immensely, and he also found it in another way when he sang duets.

The Art of Singing Together: The Duets

For a long time, Mathis has enjoyed singing duets and he has mentioned the opportunity of collaborating with other gifted singers as one of the highlights of his career. It seems natural that a singer so interested in texture as Mathis would embrace the possibility of exploring what different voices can do, but the idea of singing together with another artist didn't come from himself but Jack Gold. 'He had that wonderful insight about working in tandem with the girls' voices and I was thrilled when I got the opportunity, because, from the time I was a little kid, I was always singing with somebody, you know, singing in choirs, and what have you, and to sing with a pretty girl like that, I loved it.'[124]

The pretty girl was Deniece Williams, a rising star, whom Mathis already knew before he started singing with her, looking back at their relationship, he recalls: 'Deniece and I are pals all our lives and I first heard her sing at an early age, and I couldn't wait to meet her, and all of a sudden, we became pals, and we did some pretty successful things together and I took her to England with me. We had a wonderful time.'[125]

Pairing Mathis and Williams was a game-changer, both artistically and commercially. Their first duets together on the album, *You Light Up My Life* (1978), 'Emotion' and 'Too Much, Too Little, Too Late,' immediately proved the success of the format. Especially, 'Too Much, Too Little, Too Late' was in a class of its own, reaching number one on the pop, R&B and Adult Contemporary charts, a rare feat.[126]

Sporting Gene Page's featherlight string arrangement with bells and a deep bass groove, it's a silky medium tempo ballad with a serious topic, the breakup of a marriage after 'the kids are gone.' Williams takes care of the light and airy notes while Mathis stays a bit lower in the register, with his voice displaying a rougher edge, but they both rise forcefully together in vocal crescendos, soaring voices intertwined in a last desperate dance.

According to Tom Breihan of *Stereogum*, the album included a backing band with many Motown veterans and top session players, among them bassist Scott Edwards and drummer Ed Greene.[127] Together they craft a contemporary soul song that marries the best elements of the Motown and Philly sounds. Fortunately, Mathis and Williams would get a chance to flesh this aesthetic out on a whole album and an old friend would show up to help them: Thom Bell.

Following the success of 'Too Much, Too Little, Too Late,' it was a given to capitalize on the chemistry between Williams and Mathis and the result, *That's What Friends Are For* (1978), live up to the high expectations set by the single. With the exception of the title track, that was arranged and conducted by Glen Spreen, Gene Page was the arranger-conductor on the album. Picking up on the Motown vibe, it begins with 'You're All I Need To Get By,' a hit for Marvin Gaye and Tammi Terrell in 1968. Williams and Mathis lift each other in vocal exuberance and Mathis shows that he is comfortable singing soul music with a strong rhythmical drive. The deep bass ostinato is matched by Gene Page's string arrangement, where the tension and release of love is reflected by suspended strings redeemed in spiraling curves.

The Motown connection continues with 'Until You Come Back to Me (That's What I'm Gonna Do),' a song penned and recorded by Stevie Wonder. Before striking out on her own, Williams had sung backing vocals for Wonder, but here she takes center stage and reveals a wealth of vocal nuances and finely shaped ornaments. Together with Mathis, she brings out the sophistication in the laidback groove, supported by the elegant string arrangement.

While Page's arrangements form a vibrant and varied musical background, the focus is on the intertwining voices, singing everything from the slightly discofied funk of 'Ready Or Not' to ballads like Billy Joel's 'Just the Way You Are' where the contrast between Mathis's dark bass notes and Williams' high-pitched voice is pure bliss. Like Williams, Mathis isn't forced to stay in one register and the trading of subtle falsetto flights is a highlight on 'Me For You, You For Me,' but he can also be slow, deep and pleading. The proof is the cover of Holland-Dozier-Holland's classic 'Heaven Must Have Sent You.'

Speaking about the special chemistry between them and their way of complimenting each other, Mathis said to Tony Jasper: 'I sorta give a beautiful cushion and she penetrates like a thunderbolt, bringing up all the nuances and just making it happen. We're like racehorses when it comes to doing things; we work very quickly together and things get popping real fast.'[128]

There isn't a weak track on the album, the repertoire combines catchy rhythms and memorable hooks and an emotional trajectory that covers the ecstasy and agony of love. It's all wrapped in Page's intricate arrangements with a sound that references Motown and Philly, and in the middle of it all, the pure wonder of Mathis's and Williams's voices effortlessly playing and melting together with lush textures that rival the spectrum of a symphony orchestra. Additionally, the album has a unified mood. One need only listen to the giddy outtake 'Comme ci Comme ca' to be convinced that all the right choices were made when the album was put together and so it is with masterpieces.

Surprisingly, it would take some time before Mathis released an album of pure duets again. His collaboration with Natalie Cole on *Unforgettable: A Musical Tribute to Nat King Cole* (1983), the soundtrack to a BBC Television Special, didn't take full advantage of the meeting. Instead, it follows a dramaturgy with Mathis solo on the first section of the record, followed by a section with Natalie Cole. Then Mathis sings solo again before they unite in the grand finale, singing two of Cole's signature songs, 'Let There Be Love' and 'When I Fall in Love.' The former finds the two swinging with smoking sensuality while the latter is a poignant reading of the classic ballad, equally lush and subdued. Mathis's strong solo reading of 'Unforgettable' ends the program.

Mathis and Natalie Cole, both artists indebted to Nat King Cole in their own way, step forward as personal singers, and yet Cole's relaxed vocal deliverance with underlying emotional currents come across in the music. The album is a good example of how Mathis and the artists he sings with find their way into the music, depending on what they sing. Mathis tells about the process of recording duets:'It worked all kinds of ways. I was being interested in what they liked, and they would be interested in what I liked. According to their vocal qualities, that had a lot to depend on what we chose to sing, how big their vocal range was, whether it was a thin voice or a big voice, a small intimate voice, or a big loud voice. All of that came into play as far as who I sang with and who I was attracted to vocally. So by the time I first met up with the ladies I chose to sing with, Streisand, Deniece Williams and on and on, I was fascinated by what they wanted to sing and I would give them my ideas and somehow along the way we would all come to an agreement.'[129]

One of the best ways of sampling Mathis's different approaches to duets is the album *Better Together*. Released in 1991, it's a compilation of duets scattered across Mathis's albums, supplemented by three new songs, including the title track, a contemporary R&B ballad sung with Regina Belle and a duet with Patti Austin, 'You Brought Me Love,' which reunited Mathis with Thom Bell, who produced and arranged the song.

Although Mathis has done duets with male artists, including Ray Charles on the album *Isn't It Romantic: The Standards Album* (2005), the list of vocal partners on *Better Together* reveals that Mathis mostly sings with women. It's a conservative pattern in pop music that he tried to question without much success: 'I said, why don't two guys sing together. I listened to some of my operatic singers, you know, and some of the great tenors sang with one another, but as far as popular music is concerned, you know, girl and boy, not boy and boy.'[130]

On the other hand, the influence of women on Mathis's vocal style has been overlooked. Nat King Cole is often mentioned, but Mathis himself has highlighted both male and female influences, including Sarah Vaughan and Ella Fitzgerald, and as he points out: 'Mostly, I like facility as far as a vocal quality is concerned and the ladies always have this facility over the men, even though I grew up worshipping at the footsteps of Nat King Cole and Billy Eckstine, all those wonderful popular singers of the day.'[131]

Facility, meaning the physical capability of what you are able to sing, is important to Mathis, but it's not a matter of pure vocal power, but rather a question of range and texture. 'Ladies have a much bigger voice range than men, except occasionally I would listen to some of the Italian singers, from the time they were little, they actually had doctors who would fix their vocal cords so they can sing like a woman, incredible things.'[132]

This blurring of the boundary between a male and female vocal range is characteristic of Mathis himself. His is a pure musicality that stretches across gender and genres. His duets are much more interesting musically than the average vocal role play between a woman and a man. What you get in a Mathis duet is the thoughtful play between voices in the music. The voice is an instrument to Mathis and duets are his chance of riffing with another musician.

One of his most interesting vocal partners is Dionne Warwick. Like Mathis, she has the voice of a classically trained singer but sings popular music, and she moves effortlessly between genres. It is not a coincidence that both Warwick and Mathis are superb interpreters of Burt Bacharach, whose sophisticated songs are a suitable match for their vocal capabilities. So far, a complete album of duets between Mathis and Warwick has not become a reality, but one of their scattered duets shows up on *Better Together*. It's a song from Mathis's lost album *The Island*. Recorded in 1989, it was eventually released for the first time in 2017 as part of the box *The Voice of Romance*. The album, produced by Brazilian maestro Sergio Mendes, is a rare chance for Mathis to indulge his love of Latin music. Vincent L. Stephens gives an accurate description of the album when he writes, 'Contemporary listeners may find the sleek keyboard-laden production a bit retro, but the vocal performances on these mostly Brazilian classics are some of Mathis's best. The lithe nature of his voice is well suited to the gentle melodies and slinking rhythms. He also makes true lyric poetry out of the best lyrics here. In terms of the quality of the material, especially on wistful songs like 'Photograph,' 'Your Smile,' and 'Flower of Bahia,' and the passion in his voice, this is easily one of his most cohesive and enjoyable recordings.'[133]

Among the songs, the duet 'Who's Counting Heartaches' stands out musically. Written by Ina and Peter Wolf, the song is a melodramatic Disney-style ballad that Warwick and Mathis somehow manage to pull off musically and emotionally as their voices soar to a starlit sky. Its undiminished pathos is best summed up by the line 'heaven smiles at what we do', and the joy of singing together shines through in the song.

Since they were introduced in his repertoire by Jack Gold, duets would show up regularly on Mathis's albums and most of the producers he worked with since Gold included at least one duet among their productions. This was also the case with the producer who took over after Jack Gold: Denny Diante.

Part Six: The Late Styles of Johnny Mathis

Mature Mathis: The Denny Diante Productions

Born in New Kensington on July 21, 1943, producer, arranger, engineer and songwriter Denny Diante, entered the music business in the sixties as a singer and drummer in surf bands, The Sentinels and The Cornels. He then found his way into music publishing and was eventually headhunted for a job in the A&R department of United Artists Records, which gave him the chance of producing some of their biggest artists, including Paul Anka, Ike & Tina Turner, and the Grateful Dead. He then moved on to April/Blackwood Music that he helped change into CBS Songs. His success at CBS Songs, Columbia's publishing imprint, gave him the chance of working for the mother company. He was promoted to Vice President of A&R of Columbia Records and that way he became Mathis's producer.

Diante produced five records for Mathis: Three studio albums, a live album, and a collection of Christmas songs: *Christmas Eve with Johnny Mathis* (1986). Diante didn't change Mathis's sound significantly, but he refined and updated the things Mathis had already done, adding new nuances to his take on classic and contemporary pop and soul and R&B. In other words, he helped present a musical picture of a mature Mathis.

While the cover of *A Special Part of Me* (1984) shows an image of a composed Mathis sitting down and wearing a white suit, the album was released in the aftermath of a turbulent period in his life, as Charles Waring writes, 'There had been several bumps in the road – among them, his coming out as gay in 1982 – which brought him death threats – and drug and alcohol addiction, which he overcame by a three-week stint in rehab in 1984.'[134]

Always focused and hard-working, Mathis found a way back and the visual elegance of the cover is reflected in the sophisticated soul/pop repertoire. Starting with the funky shuffle 'Simple,' the album moves on with the ballad 'Love Won't Let Me Wait' that reunites Mathis with Deniece Williams in one of their best efforts as they melt androgynously together in a wealth of tonal textures. 'You're a Special Part of Me,' a midtempo ballad carried by a subtle bass groove and synthesizers, is another successful vocal pairing, this time with Angela Bofill. Both duets are also included on the compilation *Better Together* (1991).

The luxury soul sound of the album is indebted to Leon Ware. Mathis's congenial reading of Ware's composition, 'Priceless,' is a taste of what it might have sounded like had the two collaborated on a full album like

Mathis did with another former Motown associate, Johnny Bristol. On the song, Mathis gets to bask in Ware's lush harmonies as he unfolds a sensual love song that revels in the pleasure of sound.

Propelled by some of the best session musicians in Los Angeles, the album is soft and sleek, but the string arrangements are gone and replaced by horn arrangements and there's a heightened emphasis on rhythm. This tendency would be even more pronounced on *Right from the Heart* (1985) that added drum machines into the mix and brought Mathis closer to eighties pop.

Diante had already used songwriter and arranger Michel Colombier on *A Special Part of Me* and with his songwriting partner, lyricist Kathleen Wakefield, Colombier contributed the song 'Lead Me To Your Love.' The partnership of Colombier and Wakefield would form the core of *Right from the Heart,* with four of the eleven songs written by the pair, three of which were co-written with Diante. Besides that, Wakefield also showed up as a co-writer on two other songs, including the title track, a shimmering synth-adorned ballad that was featured in the soap opera *Ryan's Hope*. The slowed-down tempo suits Mathis and gives him a chance to unfold his subtle emotional vibrato in a contemporary pop setting.

Right from the Heart found Mathis returning to a concept with original songs written for him, but unlike his collaborations with Thom Bell and Rodgers and Edwards, he wasn't closely involved with the songwriters this time, as Kathleen Wakefield recalls: 'Michel and I were busy with many artists then, and I'm not sure we spent a lot of actual time with Mr. Mathis– or were at all needed, really.'[135]

This didn't prevent Wakefield and Colombier from doing a good job with the songs and Wakefield has fond memories of working on the album. 'Working with a couple of my cowriters on most of these songs, was lovely – especially my dear friends Michel Colombier, and Brian Fairweather, not to forget all of the wonderful players, including Robbie Buchanan.'[136]

There's a strong rhythmical edge on most of the tracks and this direct way of communicating is reflected in a lyric like 'Love Shock' where the sensation of love becomes physical. However, the highlight is a song that challenges this direct sound. The meditative 'I Need you (The Journey)' is both romantic and spiritual and the ethereal interplay between Mathis and Lynn Davis pure vocal bliss.

While 'I Need you (The Journey)' takes full advantage of Mathis's vocal range, the catchy upbeat pop of 'Step by Step' does little to challenge him vocally. 'Hold On' is the most interesting of the rhythmically inclined songs.

It's an anthem to identity and the process of finding and holding on to yourself, but it also becomes a celebration of life and love where love is seen as difference rather than likeness. Funky guitar, a vibrant choir and lively percussion carry the positive message of the song.

A Special Part of Me and *Right from the Heart* once again showed that Mathis could take on the pop sounds of the time successfully, but as a mature artist, he didn't forget his past. His collaboration with Henry Mancini, *The Hollywood Musicals* (1986), plays on his strengths as a singer of immense complexity and Mancini gives him a musical background that matches his musicality. Mathis first encountered the music of Mancini when he contributed the title track for his Global album *The Sweetheart Tree* (1965). It is a moment that he still remembers: 'The Sweetheart Tree' was written by Henry Mancini for the film The Great Race, and Natalie Wood sang it. Little did I know at the time what a great friend and influence Henry Mancini would be in my life.'[137]

The Hollywood Musicals could be considered the culmination of Mathis's association with Mancini. Although he contributes two wonderful songs, 'Whistling the Dark Away' and 'Crazy World,' his major contribution to the album is as an arranger and conductor. In an interview, he has commented on his role as a conductor. 'My function is one of dynamics, of shading, kind of building climaxes when I need them, getting the boys down. But it's not one of time-beating. They can do that for themselves. So many times when I start a piece and there's a solo involved, I'll step off the podium and I'll just listen.'[138]

Like a true musical friend, you get the feeling that Mancini listens to Mathis as the consistent solo voice of the album. While the arrangements are lush and layered, filled with instrumental details, the sound is also spacious and the balance between orchestra and voice carefully calibrated.

Mancini uses a 45-piece orchestra and a chorus of 12 voices, but there's a complex relationship between small and big musical settings as when 'True Love' starts with Mathis's gentle crooning supported by sparse electric guitar and bass before the big orchestra enters in a waltzing embrace. Skeletal passages of guitar also adorn 'Whistling Away the Dark' and 'Time After Time' and provide a counterpoint to the opulent strings.

'Taking A Chance On Love' is another example of the interplay between intimacy and orchestral richness that sees Mancini himself swinging at the piano. On the other hand, the full strength of the orchestra comes to the fore on 'It Might As Well Be Spring', where swirling strings reflect the singer who is 'as restless as a willow in a windstorm.'

Indeed, every song has a perfect musical choreography and the three outtakes. 'I'll Take Romance,' 'Baia (No Baixa do Sapateiro)' and 'Brazil (Aquarela do Brasil)' are all top-shelf songs, but it is understandable why they are left out. Especially the two Latin-flavored compositions break the mood of the album, which has the feeling of a classic Mathis album in the tradition of Percy Faith, Glenn Osser and Don Costa.

Mathis found the ideal way of combining past and present on his second live album, simply titled *Johnny Mathis Live* (1984). It practically moves through every genre he has covered from classic pop, jazz, Latin music and soul to singer/songwriter country and religious music. Early iconic hits like 'Chances Are' and 'Misty' are included as well as the Gene Page-arranged versions of Cole Porter's 'Begin the Beguine' and 'When A Child Is Born.' The latter is an example of Mathis expressing his opinion about the notion of race. This was also the case when he played in South Africa in 1978 during Apartheid. He had thirty-two performances in twenty-one days, with three out of four concerts played for a mixed audience. As Tony Jasper points out: 'Johnny closed his concerts with 'When A Child Is Born' and made it quite clear that the key line in the song is one which says that colour of skin, black, white or yellow, is irrelevant.'[139]

Three songs arranged for guitar by Gil Reigers are also noteworthy; the country-tinged 'Try To Win A Friend,' '99 Miles From L.A.' and a duet version of the early hit 'The Twelfth of Never' whose warm acoustic feeling recalls *Open Fire, Two Guitars*. The latter came into the repertoire by a happy coincidence, as Gil Reigers tells: 'Twelfth of Never had an interesting beginning. I had only been with John for a few years at the time and there were no duets of any kind at that time. We were somewhere in the northeast US and in the middle of the concert, someone yelled out for John to sing 'The Twelfth of Never'. John jokingly turned around and asked if anyone knew it. I sort of did, so I just started playing it on the electric guitar in his correct key. It wasn't flawless, but it got the job done, John really liked it as did the audience. I had a few laughs with the other musicians after the show and didn't give it another thought. The next night, he called me into the dressing prior to the show and wanted to run it some more. I asked him if I could drop the key a half step so that it would work better on guitar. John graciously accommodated me and he seemed to be very happy with the lower key. We switched it from electric to acoustic guitar as John preferred the acoustic. I did also as my style of playing had always lent itself to finger-style guitar on the nylon string acoustic. We continued to make changes over a couple of tours and 'The Twelfth of Never' has continued to be in the show ever since.'[140]

'Try to Win a Friend' made its way into the repertoire through Mathis's connection with country artist Larry Gatlin. 'John had been friends with Larry Gatlin for some time as they were both Columbia Artists. Larry and his brothers Steve and Rudy were also friends with John and the staff. Larry is an excellent songwriter as well as a singer. The folks at the table had suggested that John record a few of Larry's songs which he did. They were never released for whatever reasons but were still very nice. At some point, John had suggested that we try another duet, adding Try To Win A Friend to the show. We fussed with it in dressing rooms and hotel rooms for a bit and in a very short time, it was in the show. John would always explain what it was that he was looking for and as an accompanist, I would try to accommodate him. Sometimes I would make suggestions and he would give me his input. It was the same for most all of the duets. Most of the time, John knew what he wanted. On the times when he didn't, I would try to take up the slack by making suggestions of giving him alternatives from my vantage point. We did Try To Win A Friend for quite a few years and it is a beautiful song.'[141]

Another beautiful song is '99 Miles From LA' whose wistful feeling lends itself perfectly to the lyrical interplay between Mathis and Reigers. '99 Miles From LA was a gift to me. John had already recorded the song, but it was not the approach that he was looking for in a live performance. For someone that played finger-style acoustic guitar, it was a dream to play. John has always loved singing it, it was easy for him to sing and the song just flows nicely. It was a rather up-tempo song, so it was a great addition to a show that could tend to get ballad-heavy. It took very little to get the song up and running and we were initially able to use the string parts from the album version. John changed the ending several times over the years, but for the most part, it remained maintenance-free. The audience has always loved that song which is interesting considering it was not one of John's hits.'[142]

To this day, the song still remains in the repertoire along with 'The Twelfth of Never' while 'Try To Win a Friend' belongs to an era that has passed. Fortunately, the song is preserved on the live album and Reigers still recalls documenting the live experience and the effort it took for Mathis: 'One of the most difficult issues to making an album such as that is that it was done in the middle of or near the end of a tour that could be 36-48 shows over a period of 4-6 weeks. People have no idea of the amount of stamina that it took for John to be able to achieve such a feat while singing at such a high level. While John was only about 50 years old at the time, the touring schedule was brutal for anyone at any age.

I can't imagine a 30-year-old accomplishing such a difficult task. Mostly, we did two shows a night, six days a week, while traveling almost every day. Imagine having to do that for several weeks and then go directly to a recorded performance. In spite of it all, the energy for the show was up and I believe that a fair amount of it comes through on the recording. There were very few dubs after returning home. The producer did a great job and it was very well recorded, especially for the time.'[143]

Johnny Mathis Live proved that Mathis was still on top vocally and that he could sing a wide variety of songs and deliver them convincingly, but it also tells a particular narrative where Mathis steps into character as a ballad singer with his classic pop past. It is a narrative that Diante did little to disturb. He recast him as a singer of classic pop with Mancini and emphasized the rhythmical aspects in his contemporary material. It would be up to other producers to solve the conundrum of holding on to Mathis's special talent as a ballad singer in a contemporary pop setting.

Set the Night to Music: The Phil Ramone and Humberto Gatica Productions

Engineer and producer Phil Ramone, only worked with Mathis on one project, *All About Love* (1996), but the album was an important step in developing a contemporary ballad sound that would fit a singer of his capacity. At the time, Ramone had proven his worth as a legendary producer. He had already won Grammy Awards and worked with Burt Bacharach, Quincy Jones, Paul Simon, Billy Joel, and Frank Sinatra.

Ramone enlisted Mark Portmann as the arranger on the album. Portmann still recalls being contacted by Ramone whom he had worked with before: 'After working with David Foster and Barbra Streisand, I was working as session musician and arranger in LA. Phil's contractor contacted me and he was looking for a West Coast arranger/musician such as myself. We made several records together and Johnny Mathis was one of those. Phil had a list of songs that he had been in discussion with the record label and Johnny Mathis. He sent me that list and we made a meeting with Johnny at his house to see if this 'team' all connected with each other. That meeting was unforgettable in many ways.'[144]

The chemistry between Mathis, Ramone and Portmann turned out to be very special and he remembers Ramone's dedication and ability to promote a creative environment that was not just limited to the studio. 'Every producer has their style and way of working. It's up to me to quickly adapt and learn how to give them exactly what they are searching for. I spent a great deal of time with Phil when he came to Los Angeles. Typical days we would start 10 am, and I wouldn't go home until nearly midnight. He always invited me out to dinner and drinks after the session. And this is where the really valuable info and wisdom came. At the studio, it was all about work. Off hours, we would share his wisdom, experience, stories, personal views on everything. Phil can come across reserved at times, but that is only by appearance. He watches and studies before commenting and reacting. That was new for me to experience in the studio. Everybody loved Phil. His energy was contagious and magnetic in many places we would go. Phil was courageous, meaning he would always embrace technology, whether proven or not, we had the best equipment, best studios, best musicians, he had no limitations to achieving the results he was looking for.'[145]

Modern technology played an important role on the album. Without using a string orchestra, Portmann, who also played keyboards, achieved the same depth and detail found on the classic pop records. By focusing on the layered sounds of the keyboard supplied by rhythm machines, guitars, and choir, he created a lush modern background for Mathis's voice: 'That was the idea to bring Mathis into a contemporary setting while remaining true to his artistry and style. I did not have any specific musical references. I did spend time learning about Mathis's voice from older recordings. His tendencies, phrasing, spacing of interments and arrangements around his voice. But I did not spend much time here because I wanted to stay completely open to bringing in fresh and original ideas. My three years previous with David Foster taught me so much. David always had an element of surprise in the arrangements/production and his instincts guided him 100%. He taught me how to develop and trust my musical instincts. That's important. Those initial instincts can lead you to new and unexpected places. This was the state of mind I was in. And absorbing what was current on the radio or pop market during the time I was making that record. You want to make the music sound current while retaining the core elements of the artist (Mathis). It was an awesome challenge to take on. Phil and Johnny trusted me 100% to go with my instincts. And that's exactly what happened. Everyone was happy with the process and results.'[146]

The delicate modern pop sound Portmann created is introduced from the beginning on 'Let Your Heart Remember' that marries ambient keyboard sounds and a ticking drum machine with the warmth of an organ, a bluesy electric guitar, and waves of choir. The combination of earthy soulfulness and ethereal elegance is reflected by Mathis's voice, that is both pleading and soaring lightly.

Portmann also understood the importance of unfolding dramatic curves in time. 'I Will Walk Away' is a fine example of how the arrangement gradually builds the climax of the chorus, that is realized by Mathis's prolonged tonal flight. On the other hand, 'Every Beat of My Heart' has a relatively flat curve where the beauty is found in the soft touch and the blending of Mathis and the choir.

The album reunited Mathis and one of his greatest songwriters, Burt Bacharach. Bacharach had been an important part of Mathis's story from the early years. Mathis recorded Bacharach's 'Warm and Tender' in 1957, but his most important contribution came when Bacharach helped Mathis bridge the gap between classic pop and the new rhythm-oriented pop sound of the sixties and seventies. On *All About Love*, the Bacharach sound is updated to a contemporary pop sound without strings. However, 'Like No One In The World' and 'Let Me Be the One' both have the Bacharach touch that can be felt in the harmonies and use of choir. Having a producer of Ramone's stature involved meant that Portmann had direct access to the songwriters and so he recalls getting input from Bacharach himself. 'Phil would bring in the songwriters to A&M recording studios as I was working on and tracking the arrangements. This was amazing and very intense for me. For example, Burt Bacharach came in one day to hear his song. Being an incredible arranger himself, well there was some feedback. More importantly, he shared some insights with me on music creating in general.'[147]

As it turned out, the Bacharach songs would provide the biggest challenge for Portmann's focus on modern technology. 'The Bacharach songs were the most difficult for me. His songs may not sound intricate or involved, but they are very intricate and involved. Lots of odd meters, interesting and unexpected chords, melodies. This works better with live musicians as they can move tempos and rhythms more easily as a group playing live together. To get computers and machines to do this? That took some effort but again, what wonder full challenge for me. Also, my experience with arranging and recording with Streisand and Foster gave me that knowledge and experience. That was key to my learning how to use technology creatively and without limitations. I think that was a key to making this project and probably why I was selected to work with Phil and Johnny. That became a path forward for me, working with so many talented artists. Not everyone accepts technology as being musical. Phil did! He taught me to always be cutting edge and use technology to experiment with and find ways to make them 'musical'.'[148]

If Bacharach represented Mathis's musical past, Diane Warren's song 'Why Goodbye' offered a peek into the future. Mathis liked the song and later decided to do a whole album of Warren songs. Portmann also felt comfortable with the song since he had worked with Warren before. 'I knew Diane from working with David Foster in the studio with Celine and Michael Bolton sessions. So I was familiar with Diane's songwriting style and how to adapt those to an elegant pop ballad. Johnny can only sing his way and is a world-class song interpreter with his unique signature vocals. It was just my job to surround him with music and arrangement to support and leave space for his artistry. Watching him record vocals was incredible. It always flowed out perfect. Johnny approached this song gently as with all of them. Once he was comfortable, then it all flowed.'[149]

The song has an orchestral intro with layers of keyboard strings that sound organic and warm despite coming from a string sample: 'That specific string sound was from a custom string sample library that a few of us had in Los Angeles. What makes these sample strings so realistic is that the floor, room, ceiling of the iconic recording studio noises were in the samples. You can hear the slight shuffling of chairs, feet, little creaks in the room (which are all normal for live orchestra recordings), the noise floor below 60hz also in there. Most sample libraries record in a sterile and isolated environment and eliminate sounds like these. The orchestra musicians, studio, mics, engineers were all top-notch. This kind of technology was groundbreaking at the time.'[150]

The orchestral intro is followed by the pared-down beauty of piano and voice, with Mathis rising in a dramatic chorus. The interplay between keyboards and voice is distilled even more on the final track, 'Could It Be Love This Time,' a close collaboration with just Mathis and Portmann.

'I would play piano with him singing to get the key/tempo. Once you have that, creating the arrangement comes very naturally. I started it as a solo piano performance with Mathis. Then added pad colors and orchestration, building little by little. I had to learn Johnny's style, when to pull back, when to support and give him more foundation to lift him higher.'[151]

Portmann changes between the lush ambient layers of the keyboard and a sparse acoustic sound. It matches the tension between intimacy and dramatic grandeur that Mathis brings out vocally. It's a beautiful ballad that underlines that Mathis had found a way of translating his classic pop style into a contemporary pop sound and the perfect way of ending the record.

Mathis would take this contemporary pop ballad style a step further when he decided to do a modern songbook of compositions penned by

Diane Warren. Born in 1956 in Van Nuys, California, Diane Warren grew up listening to famous songwriters like Carole King, Leiber and Stoller and Burt Bacharach, but she wasn't satisfied just by listening. Early on, she had an interest in writing herself and as a child she got a guitar and from then on, worked tirelessly at becoming an established songwriter. Her breakthrough came with the song 'Solitaire' (1982), performed by Laura Branigan, but things really started happening when she wrote 'Rhythm of the Night' for DeBarge three years later. From then on, her reputation just grew, and she became one of the most important songwriters of the 1990s, penning two of the greatest hits of the decade, 'Because You Loved Me' (1996) and 'Un-Break My Heart' (1996), sung by Celine Dion and Tony Braxton respectively. Besides placing hits on the charts, Warren's songs also showed up in different movies, including *Coyote Ugly*, *Gone In Sixty Seconds* and *Bounce*.[152]

A dedicated songwriter with cinematic ties and a penchant for writing songs for singers with big voices, it would be hard to find a better match for Mathis and Warren's affinity for ballads underlined this: 'I just love writing a great ballad, something so essential that it reaches across genres. You could almost say the best songs are genre-transcendent. They translate well into a variety of styles sung by different artists.'[153]

A songwriter who loves writing genre-transcendent ballads and a singer who loves singing them. Warren and Mathis were certainly made for each other, and so it seemed like a good idea to record the book of songs that became *Because You Loved Me* (1998). Unfortunately, Warren did not write new songs for Mathis. Instead, a program of previously recorded hits were chosen. In terms of sound, producer Humberto Gatico continued the contemporary pop sound aesthetic that had been sketched by Phil Ramone, but he added a Latin touch that can be felt in the use of Spanish guitar throughout the album.

Mathis covers Warren's signature hits, 'Un-Break My Heart' and the title track, 'Because You Loved Me,' but they don't fit his voice particularly well. While he has an impressive vocal range, he falls short compared to the sheer vocal power of Braxton and Dion, and these songs are essentially power ballads. Fortunately, the rest of the program plays to Mathis's strength and on 'Love Will Lead You Back,' he gets to exhibit his impressive vocal range on his own terms in an emotional ballad.

Things get more upbeat on 'Don't Take Away My Heaven' and 'All I Want Is Forever' that are sensually groovy and tuneful. In fact, the chaste romantic love expressed on the classic albums is replaced by a more bodily sense of redemption. In many ways, 'Set the Night to Music' is a quintessential Mathis ballad, starting out with an emulation of crickets and an ambient keyboard intro, the lyric mentions moonlight and romantic fantasy, but the difference is quite explicit this time: 'We could be making love / and with the slightest touch / we could set the night to music.'

The direct erotic reference to the rhythm of love is continued on the closing track, 'Missing You Now', where Mathis sings: 'I talk to you / but it's not the same / as touching you / and every time you whisper my name / I want to run to you.' It's another nuance added to Mathis's expression of longing.

At this point, Mathis was singing songs of real bodily love and Warren's biggest achievement is perhaps that she brings flesh to his musical daydreams in a way that feels more daring than what he had done before. Despite this, there is no doubt that Mathis's muse is music itself and he wasn't satisfied singing one type of songs. Other singers might have settled into the late style of the contemporary pop ballad that he developed so successfully with *All About Love* and *Because You Loved Me*, but Mathis couldn't be contained in one style. Instead, it would be the job of his executive producer, Jay Landers, to help him realize and revisit a cornucopia of musical genres.

Let It Be Me: The Jay Landers Productions

Born in Los Angeles, California, A&R man, songwriter, song publisher and producer Jay Landers, is one of the heavyweights of the music industry. His work spans movies and music in several genres and he has collaborated with a wide range of artists, but the one that stands out is Barbra Streisand. Streisand and Mathis have expressed admiration for each other and it's easy to see them as kindred spirits. Both are supreme vocalists, stylistically curious and not afraid of occasionally incorporating a dramatic element in their music. It's the balance between high art and popular music that Landers helped Streisand realize, and he did the same thing for Mathis. In other words, Landers supported Mathis in the belief that there is no wrong music, no high or low art, just music delivered the right way with the right songs and the right sound.

Landers' collaboration with Mathis covers 12 albums that he either Executive Produced, co-produced or A&R'd and spans a period of 28 years, making it one of Mathis's longest-lasting musical associations. To this day, Landers still recalls the beginning of their collaboration: 'I was working as a song publisher for a legendary music executive named Charles Koppelman (Executive Producer for Barbra Streisand, Dolly Parton, Diana Ross, etc.)

He'd been asked to oversee a few songs on John's next album *Friends In Love*. I'd recently found a song titled 'When The Lovin' Goes Out Of The Lovin'' by two writers I knew named Bobby Whiteside and Richard Wold (aka Richard Parker.)Charles loved the song and generously invited me to the session to hear John record it. This was in 1982 and I can still remember it like it was yesterday. I walked into the control room just as John was beginning to record his vocal. He was in an isolated sound booth, so I couldn't see him, but I could hear his signature voice coming through those giant overhead studio speakers. I turned to Charles and said, 'My God, he sounds exactly like Johnny Mathis!'"[154]

Landers helped Mathis flesh out the full potential of his voice in many different genres. Mathis has always been curious musically and Landers both encouraged him to revisit past genres and suggested new musical vistas. Elaborating on his own role on the albums, he says, 'Generally speaking, on the albums we've done together, I came up with the concepts – movie songs, country songs, '50s era songs, Christmas songs, duets, etc. Then I came up with song suggestions, suggested a producer and various arrangers. Then I worked closely with John, the producer and arranger, to discuss how each song should be approached. Once we're actually in the studio, the producer is like the pilot, and I'm like the co-pilot / sounding board.'[155]

Landers' first album as an Executive Producer, *Once in a While* (1988), was also the most uneven in terms of aesthetic direction. The reason was that it involved a patchwork of different producers. Peter Bunetta and Rick Chudacoff produced the first side of the LP, while Preston Glass and Robert Kraft took care of the other side. In the end, the irresistibly jazzy synth-pop of 'Daydreamin'' didn't win. This time, Mathis was more inclined to explore the possibilities of the past rather than the present and the producer pair Peter Bunetta and Rick Chudacoff opened his eyes for the potential of doo-wop with the Anthony and the Imperials hit 'I'm on the Outside Looking In.' 'Little Anthony and the Imperials. That was group singers' kind of material. I was singing other stuff. It wasn't in the picture of the lone crooner standing in the spotlight. That's what I was doing when all this other stuff was going on. I never listened to it until it was brought to my attention by Peter Bunetta and Rick Chudacoff.'[156]

It was clear that Peter Bunetta and Rick Chudacoff were onto something and so they took over completely for the next album, *In the Still of the Night* (1989), that perfected the use of doo-wop by enlisting the renowned vocal group, Take 6, on two tracks. On the title track, Mathis is bathed in lush, swinging harmonies and there's a pleasing contrast between deep bass and light falsetto. 'It's All in the Game' follows with a lazy walking bass and keyboards and the exquisite harmonies of Take 6 residing in the background as Mathis sings of love and longing. Carl Sigman wrote the lyrics to a melody by Charles G. Dawes and Tommy Edwards made it a hit in 1958. The song is seen from the perspective of a woman telling of the joys and sorrows of love, but it's also a rare occasion where Mathis's own biography adds another layer to the lyrics as he sings: 'Once in a while he won't call, but it's all in the game / Soon he'll be there at your side with a sweet bouquet / And he'll kiss your lips and caress your waiting fingertips / And your hearts will fly away.'

Never ashamed of his sexuality but protective of his private life, Mathis had decided to take a stance by coming out as gay in 1982. The song can be heard as a way of challenging the conservative patterns of pop, where it isn't unusual to change the pronouns of a love lyric, depending on whether it is a man or woman singing. Here the lyric shines in its ambiguity. The song is about the emotional games of love that every human experiences.

The strength of the album is not only the careful selection of songs that revive a repertoire of doo-wop and early rock and pop from the fifties and sixties but also the intimacy of the recording. A song like the bluesy 'Then You Can Tell Me Goodbye,' supported by bubbling organ and brass, could easily have been recorded in an old club if it wasn't for the modern glossy keyboard sheen that also permeates the rest of the record. Somehow Bunetta and Chudacoff manage to find the balance between past and present, so the album neither sounds anachronistic nor nostalgic. It's simply great music and although they only collaborated on two albums, Mathis's reverence for the producers says something about what they achieved together. Commenting on the songs 'You Belong to Me' and 'All Alone Am I,' two other ballads from the album, he says: 'Sometimes you don't know how to describe people who are so very talented and special, but Peter Bunetta and Rick Chudacoff, the producers of these songs, are two such rare people.'[157]

In the Still of the Night was followed by an ambitious project titled *The Island* that paired Mathis with Sergio Mendes to explore a program of Dori Caymmi's music. It sounded promising, but turned out to be a complicated affair, and to this day, Landers still have mixed feelings about the album as he recalls the circumstances: 'I'd played John an album by the legendary Brazilian composer Dori Caymmi. He instantly fell in love with Dori's music and would listen to it in his dressing room before every concert. Dori's album was produced by the legendary Sergio Mendes. Fast forward,

I hired Sergio to produce a Brazilian-influenced album with John. We got together to pick out the songs and select the keys. We were at Sergio's house, having a great time, and he kept pouring wine for himself from a seemingly bottomless bottle! He appeared to be totally coherent and not even slightly tipsy. As each key was established, we both wrote it down in our respective notebooks. A few weeks later, Sergio went into the studio to record the tracks with a stellar group of musicians. Everything sounded great. In hindsight, I should have confirmed that each song was being recorded was in the key we'd all agreed upon! A few days later, though, John came into the studio to record his vocals, and to my shock, every song was in the completely wrong key!! I was mortified! I looked at Sergio, who sheepishly admitted that he'd lost his notes and simply cut each song by guessing Johnny's key! Needless to say, we had to scrap all the songs that he'd so meticulously recorded…in the wrong key! We quickly reassembled the musicians and recut the songs, but the budget had been so stretched that we had to work really fast. Then, there was a change of management at Columbia Records and the new bosses decided John should make a different kind of record altogether, so the so-called 'Brazilian' album was shelved. Many years later, it was reissued as part of a career retrospective box set. There's actually some nice moments on it, but it's not even close to the album I'd envisioned.'[158]

Mathis himself is more positive about the album. In the notes Joe Marchese penned for the standalone release of the album in 2019, he is quoted as saying: 'I've seen Sergio on two or three occasions [since *The Island*] and we have great memories of this something that we've done together. It was one of the golden moments of my career to work with Sergio and Dori and Dionne, and honor the people of Brazil.'[159]

After the aborted Brazilian album, Mathis returned to an old favorite: Duke Ellington. It was a project he was very excited about. 'I was so glad for the opportunity to pay tribute to Duke Ellington. We went to England and Mike Berniker produced it in a church. Mike was delicious to work with. I so love Ellington's music.'[160]

In a Sentimental Mood (1990) mostly focuses on the lyrical aspect of Ellington's music while the element of swing shows up in truncated instrumental versions of 'Things Ain't What They Used to Be,' 'Perdido,' 'Satin Doll' and 'Caravan.' Mathis had, in fact, cut a swinging vocal version of 'Caravan' on his debut and he also revisits 'Prelude to a Kiss.' The two versions make up a timeline from the youthful symphony of the debut to the intimate chamber music of a mature Mathis accompanied by the soliloquy of a violin. There's no dramatic lift, in the end, this time, only a softly sung crescendo.

'Lush Life' and 'Solitude' are two other essential ballads delivered with the poignancy of a Schubert lied. This doesn't mean that Mathis completely shuns the element of swing. 'Something To Live For,' 'In A Mellow Tone,' 'Don't Get Around Much Anymore' and 'Do Nothing 'Till You Hear From Me' all have a swinging pulse and the big band occasionally packs a punch, but the musicians are not in focus. The most important participants are trumpeter Bill Barry and baritone saxophonist Ronny Ross, who both get solos and not least pianist Fred Hersch whose lyrical presence can be felt on the instrumental 'I Got It Bad And That Ain't Good.' His piano chords also grace the closer 'Day Dream.' Accompanied by strings, Mathis brings Ellington's music into the concert hall or into the church on the spiritual 'Come Sunday,' bolstered by a wave of choir. The only place that's really missing is the spontaneity and vibrancy of a jazz club. Mathis portrays another Ellington: The composer of timeless songs.

After a compilation of duets, *Better Together* (1991), mostly consisting of previously released songs, Mathis made another songbook focusing on a single composer. This time it was Michel Legrand. He had already cut a Legrand composition, 'I Will Wait For You,' for the album *So Nice* (1966) while he was at Global, but he started recording his songs more extensively at Columbia in the early Jack Gold era. Speaking of the meeting with Legrand's music, Mathis says: 'I find that I fall in love with a lyricist and composer and want to sing everything they've written. That's the way I feel about Michel Legrand and Alan and Marilyn Bergman. I didn't know who Alan and Marilyn were at first, but I found out.'[161]

Alan and Marilyn Bergman provided the lyrics for many of Legrand's greatest songs and when Mathis did get around to record a complete album of Legrand's music, all the songs included the Bergmans. The result turned out great, according to Jay Landers: 'How Do You Keep The Music Playing? was a collection of brilliant songs by composer Michel Legrand and lyricist Alan & Marilyn Bergman, that was so musically satisfying.'[162]

There are several reasons why the album works so well. One of them is that it was a rare occasion where the composer also orchestrated the songs and worked in tandem with Mathis in sculpting the perfect sound for his voice. Henry Mancini and Mathis had also collaborated closely together, but the material wasn't just his. In fact, only a few of Mancini's songs were included on *The Hollywood Musicals* (1986). This time the album only consisted of carefully selected songs written by Legrand and the Bergmans.

Another reason was that Mathis had rarely found a collaborator so compatible in terms of aesthetic approach. Speaking of his work as a film composer, Michel Legrand has said: 'The great advantage of writing for the cinema is that I can achieve a synthesis of my different musical cultures and express myself in any style possible with no limits. Each film is a different game, a different bet. Music scores like Les Demoiselles de Rochefort or Yentl were each conceived in a totally different spirit. And inside a single film, you can explore quite varied directions. Take Castle Keep, for example: in order to keep the enchantment there, the colour of the score oscillates between baroque, jazz and modern music... Which actually suits me because I've always tried not to carry a label. They did once try to stick a 'romantic composer' label on me, though.'[163]

Replace composer with singer and you have a description of Mathis. An artist interested in expressing himself freely, who was nevertheless pigeonholed as a romantic singer. Unlike Legrand, one could argue that Mathis has never escaped the image of a romantic artist, just think of the title that was chosen for his monumental career retrospective: *The Voice of Romance*. Mathis himself has been skeptical of this epithet, as expressed in a profile in the New Yorker. As Johnny Green writes: 'It occurred to me that, unlike Sinatra, he was not really a romantic at all but a classicist, one concerned less with personal expression than with vocal production, breath control, enunciation, color. 'I don't understand why I'm called a romantic,' he said after the show. 'My romantic feelings are about beaches and sunsets. They're not very big or dark or serious, which is what I think people mean by 'romance.''[164]

Unfortunately, the image of Mathis as a romantic has hurt his critical reception in parts of the musical press. To some critics, it seems like there is not enough *sturm und drang* in his music that is perceived as light and shallow, like the beaches and sunsets he talks about. Nevertheless, Mathis has remained cutting edge in his own quiet way through his insistence on a fluid musicality without the burden of biography. His romanticism doesn't center around a staged biographical subject, but the emotions found in the music and the space left for the listener and he is open to every turn the music takes through his constant questioning of genres and style. His music is always in process and never fixed. This is also a quality that the Bergmans have noticed about Legrand's music: 'Michel hates to see anything end, so his melodies have a tendency to begin again under the last note – like mirrors reflecting into eternity.'[165]

The mirror image is the structural principle of the album that is bookended by the title track. It was included on the score for the movie

Best Friends (1982) and director Norman Jewison still remembers the moment of hearing the song: 'The combination of the Bergmans and Legrand is like a great marriage. They again blew me away with Michel at the piano singing the Bergmans' lyrics to 'How Do You Keep the Music Playing?'[166]

The song is carried by a lyrical conceit that compares music with a relationship: 'How do you keep the music playing? / How do you make it last? / How do you keep the song from fading / Too fast? / How do you lose yourself to someone / And never lose your way? / How do you not run out of new things / To say?'

Here is the perfect song for Mathis, whose songs are also declarations of love to music itself. The song is captured nakedly with Legrand at the piano and is a proof that he is one of the orchestrators and producers who has understood that Mathis shines in a sparse setting. Even when the strings appear in the jazzy reading of 'Summer Knows,' they do so as a breeze drifting away just as quickly as it came. The same lightness of the strings grace 'Something New In My Life' and 'What Are You Doing The Rest Of Your Life.' The strings are only colors on a palette that also include the celestial spinet and harp of 'The Windmills Of Your Mind.'

Vocally, lyrically and musically, *How Do You Keep The Music Playing?* is about the beauty of texture. It's an intimate musical painting consisting of timeless melodies and words transmitted through the human voice. There isn't really a musical hierarchy: the words, the sounds, and the voice exist on the same level. Only a singer of Mathis' stature could disappear so sweetly into the compositions of Legrand and the Bergmans. These are celluloid interpretations worthy of supreme musical cinema.

Jay Lander's next project with Mathis was a collection of Broadway songs, *On Broadway* (2000). It turned out to be another special album, according to Landers: 'I have a particular fondness for Mathis On Broadway, which I co-produced with my good friend and colleague Richard Jay-Alexander. Richard was the Executive Producer of the Broadway musicals Miss Saigon, Les Miserables and many other distinguished productions. His wealth of experience was invaluable to the project.'[167]

In 1964, Mathis had already recorded a shelved project of Broadway songs while he was at Global, but this was the first time he truly caught the theatrical spirit of Broadway on a complete album. Since his lush interpretation of Bernstein and Sondheim's 'Maria' from *West Side Story* on *Faithfully* (1959), there was a promise of what Mathis could do with Broadway songs and now he finally fulfilled it.

In terms of genres, Mathis is as curious as ever. He embraces everything from the jazzy organ groove of the title track to a string of strong sentimental ballads like 'Loving You,' 'Bring Him Home' and 'All I Ask of You' that are delivered profoundly. There is also a duet with Betty Buckley on a marvelous medley of 'Children Will Listen / Our Children' while the rhythmically vibrant 'They Live In You' and 'Seasons of Love' add a welcome contrast to the ballads.

On Broadway is the antidote to the understated beauty of *How Do You Keep The Music Playing?* Here, Mathis surrenders completely to the majestic melodramatic potential of Broadway tunes in operatic excursions that never seem mannered but somehow speak directly from the heart. Play the two albums side by side and it becomes clear what a complete singer Mathis is. He masters the full theatrical flights of emotion and the rippling tensions found in a slight accentuation or a pause. It would be easy to make the critical conclusion that the artful interpretations on *How Do You Keep The Music Playing?* are most worthy of praise, but Mathis's way of interpreting Broadway material is just as impressive. He is never condescending to the songs and respects their inherent sentimentality, so it becomes a strength rather than a weakness. He doesn't sing from a distance but throws himself into the deep end without a sign of pretense.

On Broadway was followed by one of Mathis's greatest Christmas albums, *The Christmas Album* (2002) and then he returned to the songbook format. Once again, he didn't focus on a particular composer but made an album of romantic standards. The result *Isn't It Romantic: The Standards Album* (2005) is one of his most mellow efforts. It was produced and arranged by Jorge Calandrelli and the seed for the collaboration was sown when Calandrelli did an arrangement of a song for Mathis. 'I had already worked with Jay Landers on several projects like Barbra Streisand and Neil Diamond, one of those projects was the album On Broadway that Johnny Mathis recorded in 2000 – I wrote an arrangement of 'Life is Just a Bowl of Cherries' for that album in the style of a 'Standard' with a vocal quartet (with a 'Hi Lo's' feel) and an orchestra... it seems they liked what I wrote and so when they decided to do the album of 'Standards' they called me to arrange and co-produce Isn't It Romantic.'[168]

As it turned out, Mathis hadn't forgotten about the arrangement Calandrelli wrote for him. 'A fun part of the story is that Jay called me first and told me about the project, the next thing that happened was a meeting between the three of us at Johnny Mathis's lovely home in Beverly Hills – as soon as I arrived at the house, the first thing I noticed sitting on top of the piano was 'a bowl of cherries'!... that was a great moment I will never forget and it set the tone for a great team effort!'[169]

It was clear from the beginning that Landers and the record company had confidence in Calandrelli and wanted him to do the album with his own sound. 'The references they gave me were primarily of work I had done previously. At that point, I had recorded around 13 albums with Tony Bennett, so I imagine they had heard a lot of arrangements of mine in that style and they said they wanted that kind of approach for the album. No outside references from other arrangers at all, so what I had to work from were the songs, the format, and the piano that I recorded for myself at our meetings. I like writing like that, so it was refreshing and a lot of fun.'[170]

The fun started with Mathis and Calandrelli working closely together, discussing the songs and how to approach them. 'We started talking about the project and from that moment on, we had several meetings in his house, and we discussed repertoire, keys etc., and then on the piano I started playing the tunes that we had selected and as we went along, recording it on a cassette with a reference vocal of Johnny with me playing the idea of the arrangement. I would work out the introductions, then do the structure, and he would sing, and the things we liked we recorded for our reference only.'[171]

When it was time to record the project, Calandrelli had a specific sound in mind. 'I suggested an intimate setup with the strings, woodwinds, and French horns, so once I had the cassette with the ten tunes, I started working on the orchestrations and planning the project. We decided to do it in O'Henry's Sound Studios, which I loved, and when we did it, in order to get that intimacy, we decided to record everything live. So it was Johnny in a booth, the strings in the studio, and the piano, bass and drums isolated in a booth, too, all at that same time with me conducting. That was the whole deal and Don Murray was the engineer who got a great sound. That's the way we recorded it. We did everything in three days, but then I had to do postproduction, like fixing little things here and there, but basically, the whole thing was done live in three days of three sessions a day or something like that.'[172]

Structured around the intimate sound of a small piano group, the lush strings and soft horn arrangements add warmth and depth to the songs, but there is little drama. The music is closer to chamber jazz than a symphony. Unlike his previous vocal flights, Mathis stays solidly in the middle register and unfolds the many nuances of a vocal whisper and swings sensually on 'Day By Day' and the Brazilian standard 'Dindi.' It was a deliberate choice from the singer and producer. As Calandrelli reveals: 'The reason for which we used Johnny's vocals in the mid-range instead of high notes, it was precisely to keep that intimacy in the sound – like a chamber ensemble rather than a big orchestra.'[173]

There are many wonderful readings of timeless ballads, but the climax is the inclusion of two rainbow songs that come near the end of the album. 'Jay and Johnny were the ones that decided to do the sequence of the songs with the rainbow concept, which I thought was fantastic, but I wasn't the one that came up with that idea. The whole concept of the album in terms of picking tunes was very much done by Jay. Jay is a great Executive Producer and Johnny had a very clear idea of what he wanted, and I went with that. Of course, I gave my opinion, with respect to the tunes and selection of the songs, based on which I liked the best, and we were all in agreement when we decided to go with that list.'[174]

'The Rainbow Connection' is a classic Mathis song about 'the lovers, the dreamers and me' whose understated emotional trajectory unfolds the dramatic curves of a Mathis song in miniature. On the closer, 'Over the Rainbow,' the orchestral grandeur, so familiar in Mathis's oeuvre, is revisited in a duet with Ray Charles, which still has an air of intimacy about it. It's a song of experience that has old age as the subtext for a timeless articulation of longing. In fact, it was a song that was not even recorded for the album.'The duet with Ray Charles was a completely different thing and it came from another album that Ray had done for Concord Records. At that time, I was the Musical Director of Concord Records, so we were able to get the licence to use that track in our album. The duet wasn't recorded together because Ray was very sick at that time, so Johnny recorded and overdubbed the duet to that track.'[175]

It doesn't really matter that the song wasn't recorded for the album because it fits perfectly with the arc of the work and Calandrelli has no regrets about the choices that were made. 'I totally think of it as a unified work and love the album the way it is. I wouldn't change anything. I believe It's one of the most beautiful albums Johnny has ever done.'[176]

After returning to his jazz roots, Mathis made another attempt at modern pop with *A Night to Remember* (2008). Unlike *All About Love* (1996) and *Because You Loved Me* (1998), there isn't any ambition of translating his classic ballad style into a contemporary sound this time. Throughout the album, Mathis stays in the middle register and Walter Afanasieff's soft pop-soul production places him in a luxurious setting with notable guest spots from smooth saxophonists Kenny G and Dave Koz. Vocal contributions come from Yolanda Adams, Mone't and most prominently, Gladys Knight, who sings a duet with Mathis on the title track penned by Afanasieff and Jay Landers.

The album mixes old and new songwriters. Thom Bell and Linda Creed show up again on the ballad, 'You Make Me Feel Brand New,' featuring Bell's signature use of sitar, while Carole King's 'Hey Girl' and Burt Bacharach's 'Walk On By' get a modern makeover. The best songs are some sweet pop soul ballads: 'Always and Forever', 'Closer I Get to You,' 'We're In This Love Together' and the slick, jazzy funk of 'Where Is This Love.' Whether in slow, medium, or up tempo, Mathis's silky phrasing caresses the melodies on an exquisite collection of pop songs spanning three decades from the 60s to the 80s.

At this point, it was difficult to imagine that Mathis could do anything new. He had successfully reintroduced himself as a contemporary pop artist and it was just a matter of following the template Afanasieff had presented: a smooth take on a modern pop sound that seemed the perfect solution for adapting Mathis to the current pop climate.

Fortunately, Jay Landers had other plans. It was an album that would take Mathis back to the very beginning of his life and the place he was born. Before San Francisco, there was Texas, and before jazz, classical and pop, there was country music. Early on, Mathis was exposed to country music through his father and his relationship with the genre deepened when he started recording for Columbia, the home of some of country music's greatest stars. 'My father grew up in Texas and he sang country music and I laughed at it and then when I got to Columbia records, I met a lot of really great country artists and I hung out with them and loved that stuff. I love all kinds of music. It's only the occasion when you can hear it and then get to know it a little bit better and my goodness, some of my best buddies are country music singers. Larry Gatlin. Larry and I are golfing buddies, and he is one of the best country singers in the world.'[177]

Charles Waring, who has followed Mathis's career closely and penned notes for many of his albums, has also noticed the country connection in Mathis's discography: 'Johnny Mathis' inclination to record country songs should not be surprising. After all, he was born in Texas, the famous Lone Star State, one of country and western music's principal strongholds and heard it on the radio when he was growing up. Country songs can be found dotted throughout Mathis's long discography; and in 2010, he devoted a whole album to the music when he travelled to Tennessee to record *Let It Be Me: Mathis in Nashville*.'[178]

Nominated for a Grammy in the category Best Traditional Pop Vocal, the album was the culmination of Mathis's relationship with country music. Fred Mollin, the producer, still remembers getting the call from Landers and the process of recording the album: 'When I got the call from Jay Landers, I was in my home in Martha's Vineyard, Massachusetts, which was a summer home for myself. I was thrilled to be asked to produce this project and initially, apparently, Johnny wasn't that interested in doing a country album, but once he saw the song choices that Jay had put together, we were able to put together a wonderful list of songs that Johnny could not help but want to do. We assembled everything to be recorded in Nashville and Johnny was very much in favor of that because he knew the musicians would be the right musicians to record classic country. There weren't many discussions with him, I just wound up meeting him in Los Angeles and going over some ideas and the next thing you know, we were in the studio in Nashville.'[179]

According to Jay Landers, making the album was a memorable experience, especially recording with Mollin's Nashville musicians: '*Let It Be Me: Mathis In Nashville* was so much fun to record with producer Fred Mollin. The Nashville musicians work in an entirely different way than in any other city in the world!'[180]

Mollin elaborates on the qualities of his musicians and the feeling in the studio during the sessions: 'My Nashville musicians are the best in the world, and they are lovely people as well, so besides being the most virtuosic musicians in the studio I have ever worked in the studio, it was very obvious to me that they were thrilled to have the chance to play for Johnny. So it was a tremendous feeling in the studio. We recorded about 16 songs in three days, and they were just like rolling off a log, so easy.'[181]

13 songs ended up on the album that is bookended by two different versions of 'What a Wonderful World,' a standard and a Christmas version. Made famous by Louis Armstrong, Mathis matches Armstrong's sincere sentimentalism with the country touch coming from pedal steel, banjo, and cosmopolitan strings.

Preferring to stay in the light mood, Mathis mostly shuns the doom and gloom of the genre, although he touches the painful aspects of emotion in the country standards 'Crazy,' 'I Can't Stop Loving You' and 'Make the World Go Away.' The latter is Mathis's most traditional take on the country genre on an album that isn't a country album for purists. As Vincent Stephens points out: 'Despite the rural cover art and the song selection, this is more of a country-flavoured pop set–strings with pedal steel accents-- than a true country album.'[182] Stephen Thomas Erlewine of *AllMusic* agrees and concludes his review by writing that: 'Mathis sounds as silky as his surroundings, but that may be because he wound up having Nashville accept his terms instead of bending to the rules of the Music City.'[183]

'Shenandoah' is a fine example of a song that does not seem like the most obvious choice for a selection of country standards, but the song's solemn beauty is the ideal vehicle for Mathis. The arrangement was done by Mollin with help from Jay Landers, with room for two eloquent solos from pedal steel and acoustic guitar. 'The arrangement of 'Shenandoah' was one that I worked on and Jay then put his two cents into because the song is public domain. We did do an arrangement of that song and I did include a beautiful segment for a steel guitar for a guitar solo as well. And that was just some song that I felt would be perfect for Johnny to sing and also beautiful for strings for Matt McCauley and for some of our solo musicians.'[184]

Throughout the album, Mollin's musicians create a relaxed and yet tight country sound. Valuing the contributions of all the musicians, Mollin highlights the importance of two specific musicians who also play an important role on 'Shenandoah': 'There were some musicians that I would say added tremendous contributions: Paul Franklin on steel, especially on his exquisite solo on our version of 'Shenandoah.' As well, we had Brian Sutton, who is probably the world's greatest acoustic guitar player and his playing is beautiful on the album, as well as his one song, 'Love Me Tender,' where it's just pretty well Brian and Johnny, it's just an exquisite moment.'[185]

The album is made up of many memorable moments and Mollin's work was acknowledged when he was enlisted to produce Mathis's next album, *Sending You a Little Christmas* (2013). Guitarist Gil Reigers was involved on both records and especially recalls the recording process on the albums: 'The part that was most interesting about the two of them is the manner in which they were recorded. The producer, engineer and most of the players would first gather in the control room and listen to the song by one or sometimes more than one other artist. There would be some discussion at that point initiated by the producer where they would discuss how similar or different the song would be approached. The total of this initial group of musicians was generally between four and seven. Piano, usually a couple of guitars, occasionally a second keyboard, bass and drums. For the Nashville-only album, there was occasionally an extra instrument like a fiddle or maybe even a third guitar. The music was typically written out in the Nashville style, that is, with numbers and not in typical music manuscript.

This gave the players a lot of latitude in how and what they played. This style is less confining than the typical method of players playing their individual parts, just as written. They are an amazing group of individuals who play together unbelievably well with great regard for each other musically. They almost never got in each other's way, maybe because they work together often and have done so for so long. Here was a group of musicians playing from a piece of paper with mostly just numbers on it, who almost always played the right thing at the right time. There seemed to be no ego issues at all. John would usually be in an isolated booth, singing a guide vocal for the players which also gave him an opportunity to fine-tune his approach to the song. Any strings or blowing instruments would be added after the fact at a future session. Very often, they would keep parts of John's initial vocals if they were particularly good and then he would complete his vocals at a later time, often back in Los Angeles. The Nashville process was very exhilarating, to say the least.'[186]

Mollin agrees about the special feeling of the Nashville album and the album that followed. 'The Christmas album was a dream come true again and this one we recorded in Nashville and then like the last album, the Nashville album, all the final vocal overdubs were done in Los Angeles to be closer to Johnny's home.'[187]

At this point, Jay Landers was out of the picture as Executive Producer, but he still had an important role to play on Mathis's next album, a collection of contemporary songs with ambitions of being more than pop ephemera.

Right: A jazzy beginning. The cover for JM's self-titled debut. (*Columbia, 1956*)

Left: Alternative album cover for JM's self-titled debut. (*Columbia, 1956*)

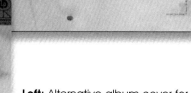

Right: In a spiritual mood. JM delved into religious songs on *Good Night, Dear Lord*. (*Columbia, 1958*)

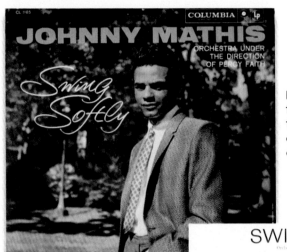

Left: Percy Faith and JM found the perfect swing formula when they began to *Swing Softly*, as their album from 1958 was called. (*Columbia, 1958*)

Right: Alternative US album cover for JM's *Swing Softly*. (*Columbia, 1958*)

Left: French album cover for JM's *Swing Softly*. (*Fontana, 1959*)

Right: One greatest hits collection to rule them all. JM's *Greatest Hits.* (*Columbia, 1958*)

CL 1133

JOHNNY'S
GREATEST HITS
JOHNNY MATHIS

Chances Are · All the Time · The Twelfth of Never
When Sunny Gets Blue · When I Am with You
Wonderful! Wonderful! · It's Not for Me to Say
Come to Me · Wild Is the Wind
Love · I Look at You

COLUMBIA ● lp

Faithfully
JOHNNY MATHIS

arranged and conducted by Glenn Osser
Faithfully·Tonight·Nobody Knows·One Starry Night·Follow Me·You
Maria·Where Do You Think You're Going·And This Is My Beloved·W

COLUMBIA ● lp
CL 1113

Left: *Heavenly.* One of JM's most iconic albums and a fan favorite. (*Columbia, 1959*)

STEREO ◄═══► FIDELITY   COLUMBIA ● lp

HEAVENLY

HEAVENLY · MOONLIGHT BECOMES YOU · THEY SAY IT'S WONDERFUL · MORE THAN YOU KNOW · HELLO YOUNG LOVERS · STRANGER IN PARADISE
A LOVELY WAY TO SPEND AN EVENING · A RIDE ON A RAINBOW · I'LL BE EASY TO FIND · MISTY · THAT'S ALL · SOMETHING I DREAMED LAST NIGHT

JOHNNY MATHIS

ORCHESTRA UNDER THE DIRECTION OF GLENN OSSER

Right: Mathis followed *Heavenly* with *Faithfully.* It was released the same year as the previous album, with titles echoing each other. (*Columbia, 1959*)

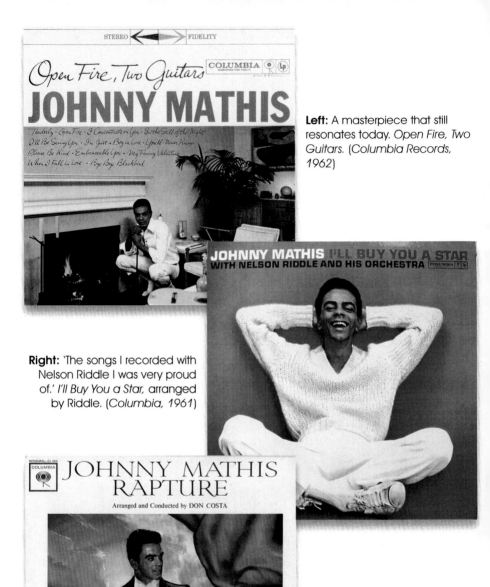

Left: A masterpiece that still resonates today. *Open Fire, Two Guitars.* (*Columbia Records, 1962*)

Right: 'The songs I recorded with Nelson Riddle I was very proud of.' *I'll Buy You a Star,* arranged by Riddle. (*Columbia, 1961*)

Left: The cover painting of the first Mathis-Costa collaboration, *Rapture,* was done by Ralph Wolfe Cowan. He also painted the *Heavenly* cover. (*Label?*)

Right: The most intriguing Mathis release during the Global years the Latin-flavored *Olé*. (*Mercury Records/Global, 1964*)

Left: Finding a new pop sound with Robert Mersey, *Love Is Blue*. (*Columbia Records, 1968*)

Right: *Mathis Sings the Music of Bert Kaempfert* has the honor of being Mathis's first songbook album. (*Columbia Records, 1968*)

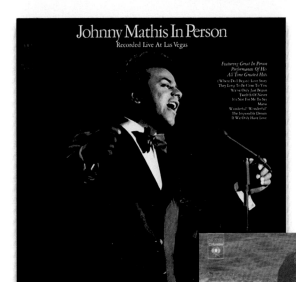

Left: JM's first live album, *JM in Person*. (*Columbia Records, 1972*)

Right: JM sat down with Thom Bell and Linda Creed. His musings became the inspiration for *I'm Coming Home*. (*Columbia Records, 1973*)

Left: *The Heart of a Woman* is an album about women and relationships that goes beyond standard boudoir-balladry. (*Columbia Records, 1973*)

Right: *Me and Mrs. Jones* was produced by Jerry Fuller, who introduced soul songs into Mathis' repertoire. (*Columbia Records, 1975*)

Left: *Mathis Is* was the second collaboration between JM and Thom Bell. (*Columbia Records, 1977*)

Right: Game changer. Produced by Jack Gold, *You Light Up My Life* brought JM back to the top. (*Columbia Records, 1978*)

Left: The first album of duets produced by Jack Gold, *That's What Friends are For*, with Deniece Williams. (*Columbia Records, 1978*)

Right: JM found the ideal way of combining the past and present on *Johnny Mathis Live*. (*Columbia Records, 1984*)

Left: *The Hollywood Musicals* could be considered the culmination of Mathis's association with Mancini. (*Columbia Records, 1986*)

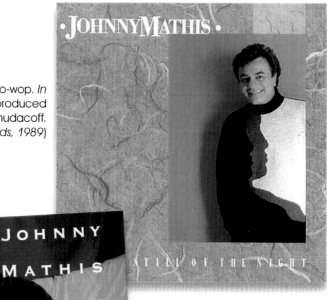

Right: In love with doo-wop. *In the Still of the Night,* produced by Bunetta and Chudacoff. (*Columbia Records, 1989*)

Left: The art of singing together. *Better Together* collected some of JM's many duets. (*Columbia Records, 1991*)

Right: The songbook masterpiece, *How Do You Keep the Music Playing? The Songs of Michel Legrand and Alan and Marilyn Bergman.* (*Columbia Records, 1993*)

Left: Old ballad style in a new sound. *All About Love.* (*Columbia Records, 1996*)

Right: Jay Landers: 'I have a particular fondness for *Mathis on Broadway*.' (*Columbia Records, 2000*)

Left: Jorge Calandrelli: 'It's one of the most beautiful albums Johnny has ever done.' *Isn't It Romantic.* (*Columbia Records, 2005*)

Right: JM devoted a whole album to country music when he travelled to Nashville to record *Let It Be Me*. *(Columbia Records, 2010)*

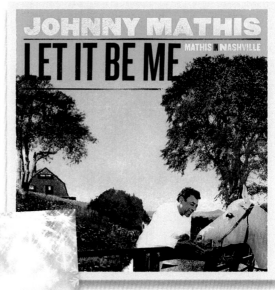

Left: Christmas in Nashville. *Sending You a Little Christmas.* *(Columbia Records, 2013)*

Right: To the rescue. Jay Landers saved the recording of *Sings the Great New American Songbook*. *(Columbia Records, 2017).*

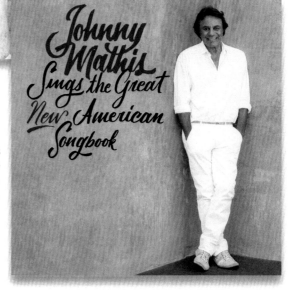

Left: The Christmas classic. *Merry Christmas.* (Columbia Records, 1958)

Right: Alternative cover for *Merry Christmas.* (Columbia Records, 1958)

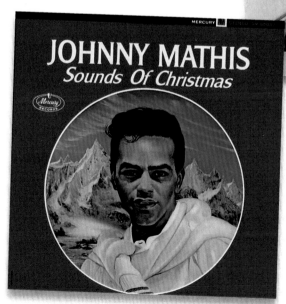

Left: Dream team. Don Costa, Glenn Osser and Jack Feierman together on *Sounds of Christmas.* (Mercury Records / Global, 1963)

Right: *Give Me Your Love for Christmas* emphasized the secular side of the holiday season. *(Columbia Records, 1969)*

Left: Overall, *Christmas Eve with Johnny Mathis* is Mathis's smoothest festive album. *(Columbia Records, 1986)*

Right: A late seasonal masterpiece. *The Christmas Album.* *(Columbia Records, 2002)*

Left: Instant hits. 'Chances Are' b/w 'Twelfth of Never.' (*Columbia Records, 1957*)

Right: Signature song. The cover for the famous 'Misty' single. (*Columbia Records, 1958*)

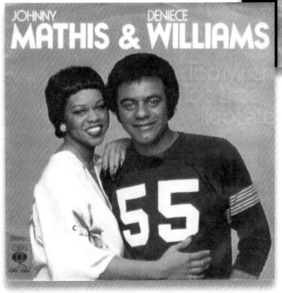

Left: Things really started happening commercially and artistically with the single, 'Too Much, Too Little, Too Late.' (*Columbia Records, 1978*)

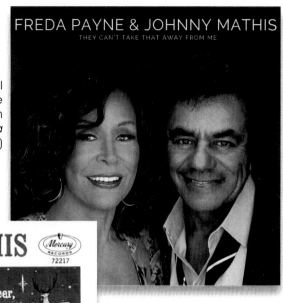

Right: Still swinging after all these years. 'They Can't Take That Away From Me' with Freda Payne. (*Columbia Records, 2020*)

Left: 'The Little Drummer Boy' b/w 'Have Reindeer Will Travel.' An early festive single. (*Mercury Records/Global, 1963*)

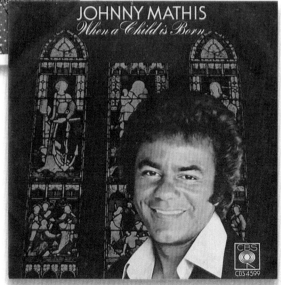

Right: 'When a Child is Born' b/w 'Every Time You Touch Me I Get High.' The Christmas single was a massive hit in the UK. (*CBS, 1976*)

Left: Lost album *Broadway*. It was planned for release on Global Records in 1964, but it was shelved until it materialized in 2012. (*Real Gone Music / Sony Music Entertainment, 2012*)

Right: *I Love My Lady*. This cancelled post-disco masterpiece produced by Bernard Edwards & Nile Rodgers was released for the first time in 2017. (*Sony Music Entertainment, 2017*)

Left: Take two. Mathis's lost album *The Island* was recorded twice. It was released for the first time in 2017. (*Sony Music Entertainment, 2017*)

Johnny Mathis

JOHNNY MATHIS

Epilogue: Always Another Song to Sing: The New and Old American Songbook

Johnny Mathis Sings the New American Songbook (2017) found Mathis returning to recording contemporary pop. It was a concept he had tried many times before, his latest modern pop offering being *A Night to Remember* (2008), but this time the process of making an album would be a bit more difficult. Eventually, Jay Landers had to step in to help, although he was not directly involved as Executive Producer. 'I worked on an album called *Mathis Sings The New American Songbook*. The legendary music executive Clive Davis had invited John to sing at his annual Grammy party, which features musical performances by an array of contemporary stars. John hands-down stole the show! So Clive approached him to record an album… and his concept was focusing the repertoire on contemporary pop hits. The only problem was that much of contemporary music is sort of 'R-Rated' with language that John would never be comfortable with. Also, many of the hits we hear today are studio concoctions as opposed to traditional songs with beginnings, middles and ends! Clive had hired a producer who Johnny ultimately didn't really connect with, so the project sort of stalled. I was surprised when I heard this, because John is so adaptable and open to working with new people. Nevertheless, Clive called me to step into the breach, which I did by asking Kenny 'Babyface' Edmonds to produce. Kenny is a brilliant record maker, and some of the album works, but I was never fully onboard with the concept in the first place. In theory, it was a better album title than an actual album!!'[188]

Hearing the album, it's hard not to agree with Landers' assessment. In fact, *Mathis Sings The New American Songbook* is one of his least accomplished albums. There are many reasons for this. One is that the concept doesn't work. The title promises a new American songbook, but few of them, although finely crafted songs, have the quality of standards; the opening, Leonard Cohen's 'Hallelujah', is a notable exception.

Another problem is the sound. It simply lacks intimacy and space. There's a feeling of *horror vacui*, which leaves little room for the delicacy of Mathis's phrasings and it doesn't help that pitch correction is used, adding to the clinical feeling of the sound. The song choices are also hit-and-miss. Diane Warren's power ballads never worked especially well for Mathis and so it's not a surprise that the closer 'Run to You' misses the mark. Written by Jud Friedman and Allan Rich, the song became a hit for Whitney Houston and is tailor-made for her forceful vocal, but not for Mathis. Fortunately, some of the other songs fit him better, as Vincent L. Stephens points out: 'He is at his best on Peter Allen's classic 'Once Before I Go' and country singer Keith Urban's charming 2016 hit 'Blue Ain't Your Color' where he can sing the story without competing with the original versions or production effects.'[189]

Overall, the album doesn't play on Mathis's strengths as a singer and the repertoire isn't particularly inspiring, but once again, he underlines that he can sing almost everything.

Although the possibility of recording another album has come up from time to time, Mathis hasn't released an album since *Johnny Mathis Sings the New American Songbook (2017)*. These days, his focus is mostly on doing concerts. After many years of working intensely in the studio, the priority has understandably shifted to singing live. Still, it came as a pleasant surprise when a duet with Freda Payne was released in 2020.

The standard 'They Can't Take That Away From Me' is a wonderful return to Mathis's jazz roots. It starts with an orchestral intro and Mathis singing: 'There are many, many crazy things / That will keep me loving you.' It's an example of how he can still sculpt a line perfectly, using pauses, vibrato, and vocal emphasis. Payne responds with: 'And with your permission / May I list a few' and then they are off to swing land, supported by walking bass, trumpet and drums played with brushes. As their voices intertwine in tight harmony and gentle banter, the orchestra wraps itself around them and it all ends with Mathis exclaiming: 'yeah!'

In October 2021, under the guidance of Executive Producer Jay Landers, Mathis released another duet, this time with his old idol and friend, the late Nat King Cole, available on the album *A Sentimental Christmas with Nat King Cole and Friends: Cole Classics Reimagined*. Through the technical wizardry of recording engineer and mixer David Reitzas, Mathis is able to sing a medley of 'Deck the Hall' and 'Joy To The World' with King Cole, who originally recorded them as solo songs. Thanks to the vocal arrangement by Tim Davis and the orchestral arrangement by Jorge Calandrelli, it's a completely fresh musical setting with new players, but it wouldn't work without Mathis, who is in his element singing classic Christmas songs. There is a present feeling of joy in Mathis's vocal that makes the fiction of a real-time duet convincing. It's a Christmas dream come true.

86 years old, Mathis still sounds zestful and elegant and, at this point, he has nothing left to prove. His musical legacy is established, and he can concentrate on the things he loves best: singing and golf. He also keeps himself fit and is known to be a connoisseur of food; a great cook who once wrote a cookbook.

In the end, it's the music that matters most. To Mathis, there will always be another song to sing, and his voice teacher made sure that he got the tools to preserve his instrument, the voice. Throughout the years, his music has changed constantly and even though the fans require the old songs and hits, and Mathis is glad to sing them, he isn't a sentimentalist when it comes to music. He treasures the memory of his parents, especially his father, whose importance he keeps coming back to, but he isn't stuck in the past. In a sense, he is the musical embodiment of the American frontier, always moving forward. He isn't interested in the boxes that genres provide and when it comes to other boxes like fixed gender roles, race and the concept of high art and low art, he is also critical. Instead, he prefers to improve and refine his craft. Thinking of him as a pure technician focused on *l'art pour l'art* would also be a mistake. Although it's true that Mathis has shunned the role of the outgoing entertainer, he is very much interested in communicating with his music, but it's the music itself he wants to convey on its own premises, and not a show or a projected biographical image.

Mathis is cutting edge when it comes to the blurring of genres and musical stereotypes connected to gender and identity. His voice is fluid, as elusive and light as a midsummer night's dream. In contrast, he is demystifying the romantic role of the suffering artist. He is emphasizing craft over originality and statements from family, friends and fellow musicians point out his friendliness, warmth, professionalism, and consideration. Far from being isolated in his own world, he has generously made himself available to the press in several interviews. At the same time, he has also maintained the right to privacy.

In a world where presence and appearances on social media has become an integral part of the music industry, independent or not, Mathis has insisted on giving his music to the public instead of himself. He has served his fans faithfully as an artist and not as an imaginary friend. It's an admirable choice that many artists could learn from and perhaps one of the reasons why he hasn't been destroyed by fame.

Listening to the music as a complete story, unfolded through countless singles and albums, you don't get closer to the biographical essence of John Royce Mathis, but you do get a sense of the historical transformation of genres and the personal devotion to music that has carried Mathis through his impressive career. Somehow, he has always found new ways to keep the music playing while other legends have been frozen in their own image. For those who want to listen, Mathis will keep singing as long as his voice allows him. The mystery and love of music will float as notes in the air, discs and cassettes in players and songs streamed in the digital sea.

Appendix One: Discography

Johnny Mathis Album Discography with acknowledgements to Joe Marchese

The following album discography excludes compilations, except Johnny Mathis's first iconic compilation of singles, *Johnny's Greatest Hits*. Although *Johnny Mathis Sings the Music of Bacharach & Kaempfert* and *Better Together: The Duet Album* include previously released material, they are both concept albums. The discography contains the original track order of the albums and doesn't list bonus tracks from reissues of albums.

Columbia Albums

1956
CL 887 **Johnny Mathis**

A: 01 'Autumn in Rome' (Sammy Cahn, Alessandro Cicognini, Paul Weston) – 3:56; 02 'Easy to Love' from *Born to Dance* (Cole Porter) – 2:29; 03 'Street of Dreams' (Victor Young, Sam M. Lewis) – 2:15; 04 'Love, Your Magic Spell is Everywhere' from *The Trespasser* (Edmund Goulding, Elsie Janis) – 2:59; 05 'Prelude to a Kiss' (Duke Ellington, Irving Mills, Irving Gordon) – 4:26; 06 'Babalu' (Margarita Lecuona). B: 01 'Caravan' (Juan Tizol, Duke Ellington, Irving Mills) – 3:59; 02 'In Other Words (Fly Me to the Moon)' (Bart Howard) – 3:52; 03 'Star Eyes' from I Dood It (Don Raye, Gene DePaul) – 2:48; 04 'It Might as Well Be Spring' from *State Fair* (Richard Rodgers, Oscar Hammerstein II) – 4:47; 05 'Cabin in the Sky' from *Cabin in the Sky* (Vernon Duke, John LaTouche) – 2:57; 06 'Angel Eyes' from Jennifer (Matt Dennis, Earl Brent) – 4:19.
Produced by George Avakian. Arranged and conducted by Manny Albam, Gil Evans, Teo Macero, John Lewis & Bob Prince.
Recorded: March 14, 1956 – April 6, 1956. Released: July 16, 1956.

1957
CL 2028 **Wonderful, Wonderful**

A: 01 'Will I Find My Love Today?' (Alex Fogarty, Sydney Shaw) – 3:32; 02 'Looking at You' (Cole Porter) – 2:16; 03 'Let Me Love You' (Bart Howard) – 3:47; 04 'All Through the Night' from *Anything Goes* (Porter) – 2:56; 05 'It Could Happen to You' from *And the Angels Sing* (Johnny Burke, Jimmy Van Heusen) – 3:47; 05 'That Old Black Magic' (Harold Arlen, Johnny Mercer) – 2:51. B: 01 'Too Close for Comfort' from *Mr. Wonderful* (Jerry Bock, George David Weiss, Larry Holofcener) – 2:34; 02 'In the Wee Small Hours of the Morning' (David Mann, Bob Hilliard) – 3:13; 03 'Year After Year' (Howard) – 3:12; 04 'Early Autumn' (Ralph Burns, Woody Herman, Johnny Mercer) –

3:38; 05 'You Stepped Out of a Dream' from *Ziegfeld Girl* (Nacio Herb Brown, Gus Kahn) – 2:44; 06 'Day In, Day Out' (Rube Bloom, Mercer) – 2:08.

Produced by George Avakian. Arranged and conducted by Percy Faith.

Recorded: March 27, 1957, March 28, 1957, April 1, 1957. Released: July 8, 1957.

CL 1078 **Warm**

A: 01 'Warm' (Sid Jacobson, Jimmy Krondes) – 3:24; 02 'My One and Only Love' (Robert Mellin, Guy Wood) – 3:37; 03 'Baby, Baby, Baby' (Mack David, Jerry Livingston) – 3:00; 04 'A Handful of Stars' (Jack Lawrence, Ted Shapiro) – 3:20; 05 'By Myself' (Howard Dietz, Arthur Schwartz) – 4:09; 06 'I've Grown Accustomed to Her Face' from *My Fair Lady* (Frederick Loewe, Alan Jay Lerner) – 3:29. B: 01 'Then I'll Be Tired of You' (E.Y. Harburg, Arthur Schwartz) – 4:07; 02 'I'm Glad There Is You' (Jimmy Dorsey, Paul Madeira) – 4:04; 03 'What'll I Do' (Irving Berlin) – 2:55; 04 'The Lovely Things You Do' (Alex Fogarty) – 3:18; 05 'There Goes My Heart' (Benny Davies, Abner Silver) – 3:40; 06 'While We're Young' (William Engvick, Alec Wilder, Morty Palitz) – 2:42.

Produced by Mitch Miller. Arranged and conducted by Percy Faith.

Recorded: October 22–24, 1957. Released: November 11, 1957. Gold, RIAA certified on May 5, 1960.

1958
CL 1119 **Good Night, Dear Lord**

A: 01 'Good Night, Dear Lord' (Paul Tripp, Ray Carter) – 3:30; 02 'Swing Low, Sweet Chariot' (traditional) – 3:48; 03 'May the Good Lord Bless and Keep You' (Meredith Willson) – 3:47; 04 'I Heard a Forest Praying' (Sam M. Lewis, Peter De Rose) – 3:10; 05 'The Rosary' (Ethelbert Nevin, Robert Cameron Rogers) –2:21; 6 'One God' (Ervin Drake, Jimmy Shirl) – 3:48. B: 01 'Deep River' (traditional) – 2:49; 02 'Where Can I Go?' (Sonny Miller, Leo Fuld, Sigmunt Berland) – 3:36; 03 'Eli Eli' (traditional) – 4:29; 04 'Kol Nidre' (traditional) – 2:56; 05 'Ave Maria' (Franz Schubert) – 4:34; 06 'Ave Maria' (Johann Sebastian Bach, Charles Gounod) – 2:59.

Produced by Mitch Miller & Al Ham. Arranged and conducted by Percy Faith.

Recorded: January 1–2, January 6, 1958. Released: March 3, 1958.

CL 1133 **Johnny's Greatest Hits**

A: 01 'Chances Are' performed with Ray Conniff & His Orchestra (Robert Allen, Al Stillman) – 3:03; 02 'All the Time' from the Broadway musical *Oh, Captain!* (1958); performed with Ray Ellis & His Orchestra (Jay Livingston, Ray Evans) – 2:44; 03 'The Twelfth of Never' performed with Ray Conniff & His Orchestra (Livingston, Paul Francis Webster) – 2:28; 04 'When Sunny Gets Blue' performed with Ray Conniff & His

Orchestra (Marvin Fisher, Jack Segal) – 2:41; 05 'When I Am with You' performed with Ray Ellis & His Orchestra (Stillman, Ben Weisman) – 2:58; 06 'Wonderful! Wonderful!' performed with Ray Conniff & His Orchestra & Chorus (Sherman Edwards, Ben Raleigh) – 2:49. B: 01 'It's Not for Me to Say' from *Lizzie* (1957); performed with Ray Conniff & His Orchestra (Allen, Stillman) – 3:05; 02 'Come to Me' from the Kraft Television Theatre episode 'Come to Me' (1957) (Allen, Peter Lind Hayes) – 3:05; 03 'Wild Is the Wind' from *Wild Is the Wind* (1957); performed with Ray Ellis & His Orchestra (Dimitri Tiomkin, Ned Washington) – 2:27; 04 'Warm and Tender' from *Lizzie* (1957); performed with Ray Conniff & His Orchestra (Burt Bacharach, Hal David) – 2:25; 05 'No Love (But Your Love)' performed with Ray Conniff & His Orchestra (Billy Myles) – 2:19; 06 'I Look at You' performed with Ray Ellis & His Orchestra [13] (Johnny Mathis, Jessie Mae Robinson) – 2:43.

Produced by Mitch Miller & Al Ham. Arranged and conducted by Ray Ellis & Ray Conniff.

Compilation of singles. Recorded: September 20, 1956, June 16, 1957, October 1, 1957, October 31, 1957, January 7, 1958. Released: March 17, 1958. Gold, RIAA certified on June, 1959. Platinum on November 21, 1986. 3x Multi-Platinum on November 1, 1999.

CL 1165 **Swing Softly**
A: 01 'You Hit the Spot' from Collegiate (Mack Gordon, Harry Revel) – 2:52; 02 'It's De-Lovely' from *Red Hot and Blue* (Cole Porter) – 2:47; 03 'Get Me to the Church on Time' from *My Fair Lady* (Alan Jay Lerner, Frederick Loewe) – 1:45; 04 'Like Someone in Love' from *Belle of the Yukon* (Johnny Burke, Jimmy Van Heusen) – 2:40; 05 'You'd Be So Nice to Come Home To' from *Something to Shout About* (Porter) – 2:12; 06 'Love Walked In' from *The Goldwyn Follies* (George Gershwin, Ira Gershwin) – 2:38. B: 01 'This Heart of Mine' from *Ziegfeld Follies* (Arthur Freed, Harry Warren) – 2:31; 02 'To Be in Love' (Bart Howard) – 3:01; 03 'Sweet Lorraine' (Clifford Burrell, Mitchell Parish) – 2:24; 04 'Can't Get Out of This Mood' from *Seven Days' Leave* (Frank Loesser, Jimmy McHugh) – 3:08; 05 'I've Got the World on a String' (Harold Arlen, Ted Koehler) – 3:11; 06 'Easy to Say (But So Hard to Do)' (Marvin Fisher, Jack Segal) – 2:44.

Produced by Mitch Miller & Al Ham. Arranged and conducted by Percy Faith. Recorded: May 15–16, 1958, June 17, 1958. Released: July 28, 1958. Gold, RIAA certified on December 4, 1962.

CL 1195 **Merry Christmas**
A: 01 'Winter Wonderland' (Richard B. Smith, Felix Bernard) – 3:19; 02 'The Christmas Song' (Mel Tormé, Robert Wells) – 4:18; 03 'Sleigh Ride' (Leroy Anderson, Mitchell Parish) – 2:58; 04 'Blue Christmas' (Billy Hayes, Jay W. Johnson) – 3:02; 05 'I'll Be Home

for Christmas' (Buck Ram, Kim Gannon, Walter Kent) – 4:04; 06 'White Christmas' from *Holiday Inn* (Irving Berlin) – 3:32. B: 01 'O Holy Night' (Adolphe Adam) – 4:35; 02 'What Child Is This? (Greensleeves)' (William Chatterton Dix) – 3:58; 03 'The First Noel' (Traditional) – 3:49; 04 'Silver Bells' from *The Lemon Drop Kid* (Jay Livingston, Ray Evans) – 3:34; 05 'It Came Upon the Midnight Clear' (Richard Storrs Willis, Edmund Sears) – 3:08; 06 'Silent Night, Holy Night' (Franz Xaver Gruber, Joseph Mohr) – 3:51.

Produced by Mitch Miller & Al Ham. Arranged and conducted by Percy Faith. Recorded: June 16, 18, and 20, 1958. Released: October 6, 1958. Gold, RIAA certified on December 7, 1960. Platinum on November 21, 1986. 2x Multi-Platinum on November 10, 1989. 5x Multi-Platinum on November 1, 1999.

1959
CL 1270 **Open Fire, Two Guitars**
A: 01 'An Open Fire' (Jerry Leiber, Mike Stoller) – 3:52; 02 'Bye Bye Blackbird' (Mort Dixon, Ray Henderson) – 4:07; 03 'In the Still of the Night' from *Rosalie* (Cole Porter) – 2:35; 04 'Embraceable You' from *Girl Crazy* (George Gershwin, Ira Gershwin) – 3:28; 05 'I'll Be Seeing You' from *Right This Way* (Irving Kahal, Sammy Fain) – 4:26; 06 'Tenderly' (Jack Lawrence, Walter Gross) – 2:58. B: 01 'When I Fall in Love' (Edward Heyman, Victor Young) – 4:31 02 'I Concentrate on You' from *Broadway Melody of 1940* (Cole Porter) – 3:16 03 'Please Be Kind' (Sammy Cahn, Saul Chaplin) – 3:24 04 'You'll Never Know' from *Hello, Frisco, Hello* (Mack Gordon, Harry Warren) – 4:07 05 'I'm Just a Boy in Love' (Shirley Cowell) – 2:44 06 'My Funny Valentine' from *Babes in Arms* (Richard Rodgers, Lorenz Hart) – 3:37.

Produced by Mitch Miller. Recorded: October 2–3, 1958. Released: January 5, 1959.

CL 1351 **Heavenly**
A: 01 'Heavenly' (Burt Bacharach, Sydney Shaw) – 3:23; 02 'Hello, Young Lovers' from *The King and I* (Richard Rodgers, Oscar Hammerstein) – 4:18; 03 'A Lovely Way to Spend an Evening' (Harold Adamson, Jimmy McHugh) – 4:04; 04 'A Ride on a Rainbow' from the *Producers' Showcase* episode 'Ruggles of Red Gap' (Leo Robin, Jule Styne) – 4:11; 05 'More Than You Know' from *Great Day* (Vincent Youmans, Edward Eliscu, Billy Rose) – 4:18; 06 'Something I Dreamed Last Night' (Sammy Fain, Herbert Magidson, Jack Yellen) – 4:32. B: 01 'Misty' (Erroll Garner, Johnny Burke) – 3:38; 02 'Stranger in Paradise' from *Kismet* (George Forrest, Robert Wright) – 4:06; 03 'Moonlight Becomes You' from *Road to Morocco* (Johnny Burke, Jimmy Van Heusen) – 4:06; 04 'They Say It's Wonderful' from *Annie Get Your Gun* (Irving Berlin) – 3:33; 05 'I'll Be Easy to Find' (Bart Howard)– 4:04; 06 'That's All' (Alan Brandt, Bob Haymes) – 3:50.

Produced by Al Ham. Arranged and conducted by Glenn Osser.
Recorded: April 16, 1959, April 20–21, 1959. Released: August 10, 1959. Gold, RIAA certified on April 21, 1960. Platinum on November 21, 1986. GRAMMY Nomination for 'Misty' in 1960 for Best Male Vocal Performance (Single Record or Track) and induction into GRAMMY Hall of Fame in 2002.

CL 1422 **Faithfully**

A: 01 'Faithfully' (Burt Bacharach, Sydney Shaw) – 2:37; 02 'Tonight' from *West Side Story* (Leonard Bernstein, Stephen Sondheim) – 3:15; 03 'Nobody Knows (How Much I Love You)' (Bart Howard) – 4:14; 04 'One Starry Night' (Abner Silver, Sid Wayne) – 4:23; 05 'Follow Me' (Kay Thompson) – 3:24; 06 'You Better Go Now' (Irvin Graham, Bickley Reichner) – 4:14. B: 01 'Secret Love' from *Calamity Jane* (Paul Francis Webster, Sammy Fain) – 3:33; 02 'Maria' from *West Side Story* (Bernstein, Sondheim) – 3:50; 03 'Where Do You Think You're Going' (Bart Howard) – 4:04; 04 'And This Is My Beloved' from *Kismet* (Bob Wright, George Forrest) – 4:01; 05 'Where Are You' from *Top of the Town* (Harold Adamson, Jimmy McHugh) – 3:31; 06 'Blue Gardenia' from *The Blue Gardenia* (Lester Lee, Bob Russell) – 4:27.
Produced by Mitch Miller. Arranged and conducted by Glenn Osser.
Recorded: November 4–6, 1959.Released: December 21, 1959. Gold, RIAA certified on December 4, 1962.

1960
CL 1506 **Ballads of Broadway**

A: 01 'Moanin' Low' from *The Little Show* (Howard Dietz, Ralph Rainger) – 3:56; 02 'Fun to Be Fooled' from *Life Begins at 8:40* (Harold Arlen, Ira Gershwin, E. Y. Harburg) – 4:02; 03 'I Have Dreamed' from *The King And I* (Oscar Hammerstein II, Richard Rodgers) – 4:04; 04 'On the Sunny Side of the Street' from *Lew Leslie's International Revue* (Dorothy Fields, Jimmy McHugh) – 3:57; 05 'My Romance' from *Jumbo* (Lorenz Hart, Rodgers) – 3:10; 06 'Dancing on the Ceiling' from *Ever Green* (Hart, Rodgers) – 3:54. B: 01 'I Married an Angel' from *I Married an Angel* (Hart, Rodgers) – 3:48; 02 'Isn't It a Pity?' from *Pardon My English* (George Gershwin, I. Gershwin) – 3:55; 03 'Spring Is Here' from *I Married an Angel* (Hart, Rodgers) – 3:48; 04 'Don't Blame Me' from *Clowns in Clover* (Fields, McHugh) – 4:38; 05 'Taking a Chance on Love' from *Cabin in the Sky* (Vernon Duke, Ted Fetter, John LaTouche) – 3:33; 06 'The Party's Over' from *Bells Are Ringing* (Betty Comden, Adolph Green, Jule Styne) – 4:01.
Produced by Mitch Miller. Arranged and conducted by Glenn Osser.
Recorded: April 4, 1960, April 7-8, 1960, May 19, 1960. Released: June 20, 1960.

CS 8326 **Johnny's Mood**

A: 01 'I'm Gonna Laugh You Right Out of My Life' (Cy Coleman, Joseph McCarthy) – 3:35; 02 'Stay Warm' (Buddy Greco) – 3:13; 03 'There's No You' (Tom Adair, George Durgom, Hal Hopper) – 3:55; 04 'How High the Moon' from *Two for the Show* (Nancy Hamilton, Morgan Lewis) – 3:22; 05 'I'm So Lost' (Shirley Cowell) – 3:52; 06 'Once' (Otis G. Clements, Sydney Shaw) – 3:47. B: 01 'Goodnight My Love' from *Stowaway* (Mack Gordon, Harry Revel) – 3:42; 02 'The Folks Who Live On the Hill' from *High, Wide, and Handsome* (Jerome Kern, Oscar Hammerstein II) – 3:50; 03 'April in Paris' from *Walk a Little Faster* (Vernon Duke E. Y. Harburg) – 3:35; 04 'Corner to Corner' (Robert Marcus, Harold Mott) – 3:05; 05 'In Return' (Leon Carr, Paul Vance) – 3:27; 06 'I'm in the Mood for Love' from *Every Night at Eight* (Jimmy McHugh, Dorothy Fields) – 5:00.

Produced by Mitch Miller. Arranged and conducted by Glenn Osser.

Recorded: September 8, 1959, May 24–26, 1960. Released: July 18, 1960.

CL 1507 **The Rhythms of Broadway**

A: 01 'Everything's Coming Up Roses' from *Gypsy: A Musical Fable* (Stephen Sondheim, Jule Styne) – 2:51; 02 'Guys and Dolls' from *Guys and Dolls* (Frank Loesser) – 3:00; 03 'I Wish I Were in Love Again' from *Babes in Arms* (Hart, Rodgers) – 3:36, 04 'You Do Something to Me' from *Fifty Million Frenchmen* (Cole Porter) – 3:05; 05 'Let's Misbehave' from *You Never Know* (Porter) – 2:46; 06 'I Could Have Danced All Night' from *My Fair Lady* (Alan Jay Lerner, Frederick Loewe) – 3:01. B: 01 'A Cock-Eyed Optimist' from *South Pacific* (Hammerstein, Rodgers) – 2:33; 02 'I Just Found Out About Love' from *Strip for Action* (Harold Adamson, McHugh) – 3:12; 03 'Let's Do It (Let's Fall in Love)' from *Paris* (Porter) – 3:50; 04 'I Am in Love' from *Can-Can* (Porter) – 4:15; 05 'Love Eyes' from *Whoop-Up* (Moose Charlap, Norman Gimbel) – 2:32; 06 'Love Is a Gamble' from *American Motors Industrial Show* (Sydney Shaw, Jane Douglas White) – 2:35.

Produced by Mitch Miller. Arranged and conducted by Ralph Burns.

Recorded: May 17, 1960, May 19-20, 1960, May 23, 1960. Released: August 15, 1960.

1961
CS 8423 **I'll Buy You a Star**

A: 01 'I'll Buy You a Star' from *A Tree Grows in Brooklyn* (Dorothy Fields, Arthur Schwartz) – 3:20; 02 'Stairway to the Stars' (Matty Malneck, Mitchell Parish, Frank Signorelli) – 4:51; 03 'When My Sugar Walks Down the Street' (Gene Austin, Jimmy McHugh, Irving Mills) – 3:30; 04 'Magic Garden' (Alan Bergman, Marilyn Keith, Lew Spence) – 3:58; 05 'Smile' (Charlie Chaplin, Geoffrey Parsons, John Turner) – 3:15; 06 'Oh, How I Try' (Roy Alfred, Marvin Fisher) – 3:40. B: 01 'Ring the Bell' (Johnny Burke, Jimmy Van

Heusen) – 1:57; 02 'Love Look Away' from *Flower Drum Song* (Oscar Hammerstein II, Richard Rodgers) – 3:28; 03 'Sudden Love' (Arthur Hamilton) – 3:28; 04 'The Best Is Yet to Come' (Cy Coleman, Carolyn Leigh) – 3:42; 05 'Warm and Willing' from *A Private's Affair*[8] (Jay Livingston, Ray Evans, McHugh) – 3:13; 06 'My Heart and I' (Allyn Ferguson, Donald Sargent) – 3:29.

Produced by Irving Townsend. Arranged and conducted by Nelson Riddle.

Recorded: February 7, 1961, February 10, 1961, February 13, 1961. Released: February 27, 1961.

CS 8511 **Live It Up!**

A: 01 'Live It Up' (Alan Bergman, Marilyn Bergman) – 3:28; 02 'Just Friends' (John Klenner, Sam M. Lewis) – 4:01; 03 'Ace in the Hole' from *Let's Face It!* (Cole Porter) – 2:46; 04 'On a Cold and Rainy Day' (Lee Pockriss, Paul Vance) – 3:06; 05 'Why Not' (Otis G. Clements, Sydney Shaw) – 2:08; 06 'I Won't Dance' from *Roberta* (Dorothy Fields, Oscar Hammerstein II, Otto Harbach, Jerome Kern, Jimmy McHugh) – 3:58. B: 01 'Johnny One Note' from *Babes in Arms* (Lorenz Hart, Richard Rodgers) – 2:39; 02 'Too Much Too Soon' (Marvin Fisher, Jack Segal) – 2:51; 03 'The Riviera' (Cy Coleman, Joseph Allen McCarthy) – 3:03; 04 'Crazy in the Heart' (William Engvick, Alec Wilder) – 3:55; 05 'Hey, Look Me Over' from *Wildcat* (Coleman, Carolyn Leigh) – 1:48; 06 'Love' from *Ziegfeld Follies* (Ralph Blane, Hugh Martin) – 3:46.

Produced by Irving Townsend. Arranged and conducted by Nelson Riddle.

Recorded: April 24–25, 1961. Released: December 11, 1961.

1962
CS 8715 **Rapture**

A: 01 'Rapture' (Marian Kennedy) – 3:20; 02 'Love Me as Though There Were No Tomorrow' from the musical *Strip for Action* (Harold Adamson, Jimmy McHugh) – 3:08; 03 'Moments Like This' from *College Swing* (Burton Lane, Frank Loesser) – 2:50; 04 'You've Come Home' from *Wildcat* (Cy Coleman, Carolyn Leigh) – 3:58; 05 'Here I'll Stay' from *Love Life* (Alan Jay Lerner, Kurt Weill)– 4:20; 06 'My Darling, My Darling' from *Where's Charley?* (Loesser) – 3:45. B: 01 'Stars Fell on Alabama' (Mitchell Parish, Frank Perkins) – 3:24; 02 'I Was Telling Her About You' (Moose Charlap, Don George) – 3:38; 03 'Lament (Love, I Found You Gone)' (Joe Bailey, Morris Levy, Dinah Washington) – 3:20; 04 'The Love Nest' from the musical *Mary* (Otto Harbach, Louis Hirsch) – 3:05; 05 'Lost in Loveliness' from *The Girl in Pink Tights* (Leo Robin, Sigmund Romberg) – 4:19; 06 'Stella by Starlight' (Ned Washington, Victor Young) – 3:33.

Produced by Ernie Altschuler. Arranged and conducted by Don Costa.

Recorded: August 1, 1962, August 6, 1962, August 8-9, 1962. Released: September 17, 1962.

1963
CS 8844 **Johnny**

A: 01 'Easy Does It' (Kenny Jacobson, Rhoda Roberts) – 2:08; 02 'The Most Beautiful Girl in the World' from *Jumbo* (Lorenz Hart, Richard Rodgers) – 3:45; 03 'Miracles' (Bart Howard) – 2:51; 04 '(Ah, the Apple Trees) When the World Was Young' (M. Phillippe-Gérard, Johnny Mercer) – 3:47; 05 'Never Never Land' from *Peter Pan* (Betty Comden, Adolph Green, Jule Styne) – 4:01; 06 'Poor Butterfly' from the musical *The Big Show* (John Golden, Raymond Hubbell) – 4:15. B: 01 'Jump for Joy' (Duke Ellington, Sid Kuller, Paul Francis Webster) – 2:15; 02 'Joey, Joey, Joey' from *The Most Happy Fella* (Frank Loesser) – 3:56; 03 'I Can't Believe That You're in Love with Me' (Clarence Gaskill, Jimmy McHugh) – 3:00; 04 'I Love You' from *Mexican Hayride* (Cole Porter) – 3:27; 05 'Weaver of Dreams' (Jack Elliott, Victor Young) – 3:13; 06 'No Man Can Stand Alone' (Jack Segal, Paul Vance) – 2:35. Produced by Ernie Altschuler. Arranged and conducted by Don Costa.
Recorded: January 3, 1963, January 7–8, 1963, April 23-25, 1963. Released: July 15, 1963.

CS 8898 **Romantically**

A: 01 'Getting to Know You' from *The King and I* (Oscar Hammerstein II, Richard Rodgers) – 3:11; 02 'Moonlight in Vermont' (John Blackburn, Karl Suessdorf) – 3:40; 03 'Hi-Lili, Hi-Lo' from *Lili* (Helen Deutsch, Bronislaw Kaper)– 3:30; 04 'Friendly Persuasion (Thee I Love)' from *Friendly Persuasion* (Dimitri Tiomkin, Paul Francis Webster) – 3:51; 05 'Autumn in New York' from *Thumbs Up!* (Vernon Duke) – 4:50; 06 'In Wisconsin' (Calvin Bostick) – 3:15. B: 01 'All That Is Missing' (Eddie Snyder, Paul Vance) – 2:58; 02 'The Sound of Music' from *The Sound of Music* (Oscar Hammerstein II, Richard Rodgers) – 3:22; 03 'Theme from 'Carnival!'' from *Carnival!* (Bob Merrill) – 2:33; 04 'Too Young to Go Steady' from the musical *Strip for Action* (Harold Adamson, Jimmy McHugh) – 3:42; 05 'It's Only a Paper Moon' from *The Great Magoo* (Harold Arlen, E. Y. Harburg, Billy Rose) – 3:53; 06 'September Song' from *Knickerbocker Holiday* (Maxwell Anderson, Kurt Weill) – 4:07. Produced by Ernie Altschuler. Arranged and conducted by Don Costa.
Recorded: February 26–28, 1963, April 23-25, 1963. Released: November 18, 1963.

Global Albums

1963
MG 20837 **Sounds of Christmas**

A: 01 'The Sounds of Christmas' (Jerry Livingston, Paul Francis Webster) – 2:35; 02 'Have Yourself a Merry Little Christmas' from *Meet Me in St. Louis* (Ralph Blane, Hugh

Martin) – 3:34; 03 'A Marshmallow World' (Peter DeRose, Carl Sigman) – 2:37; 04 'God Rest Ye Merry, Gentlemen' (traditional) – 3:19; 05 'Let It Snow! Let It Snow! Let It Snow!' (Sammy Cahn, Jule Styne) – 4:12; 06 'The Little Drummer Boy' (Katherine Davis, Henry Onorati, Harry Simeone) – 3:32. B: 01 'Have Reindeer, Will Travel' (Livingston, Webster) – 3:31; 02 'The Secret of Christmas' from *Say One for Me* (Cahn, Jimmy Van Heusen) – 4:12; 03 'Rudolph the Red-Nosed Reindeer' (Johnny Marks) – 2:20; 04 'Carol of the Bells' (Mykola Leontovych, Peter J. Wilhousky) – 1:22; 05 'Christmas Is a Feeling in Your Heart' (Joe Darion, Joe Kleinsinger) – 3:03; 06 'Hallelujah Chorus' from the oratorio *Messiah* (George Frederick Handel) – 4:02.
Produced by Don Costa. Arranged by Glenn Osser and conducted by Jack Feierman.
Recorded: July 12, 1963, July 16, 1963, July 17, 1963, July 25, 1963. Released: October 4, 1963.

1964
MG 20890 **Tender Is the Night**
A: 01 'Tender Is the Night' from *Tender Is the Night* (Sammy Fain, Paul Francis Webster) – 3:44; 02 'Laura' from *Laura* (David Raksin, Johnny Mercer) – 4:38; 03 'No Strings' from *No Strings* (Richard Rodgers) – 3:13; 04 'I Can't Give You Anything But Love' from *Blackbirds of 1928* (Jimmy McHugh, Dorothy Fields) – 2:46; 05 'April Love' from *April Love* (Sammy Fain, Paul Francis Webster)- 2:58; 06 'Call Me Irresponsible' from *Papa's Delicate Condition* (Sammy Cahn, Jimmy Van Heusen) – 3:42. B: 01 'A Dream Is a Wish Your Heart Makes' from *Cinderella* (Mack David, Al Hoffman, Jerry Livingston) – 3:01; 02 'A Ship Without a Sail' from *Heads Up!* (Richard Rodgers, Lorenz Hart) – 4:08; 03 'Forget Me Not' (Bart Howard) – 2:33; 04 'Where Is Love?' from *Oliver!* (Lionel Bart) – 2:26; 05 'Somewhere' from *West Side Story* (Leonard Bernstein, Stephen Sondheim) – 4:32; 06 'Tomorrow Song' (Bart Howard)- 3:06.
Produced by Johnny Mathis. Arranged and conducted by Don Costa.
Recorded: October 1963, November 1963. Released: January 23, 1964.

MG 20913 **The Wonderful World of Make Believe**
A: 01 'Camelot' from *Camelot* (Alan Jay Lerner, Frederick Loewe) – 2:50: 02 'I'm Always Chasing Rainbows' from *Oh, Look!* (Harry Carroll, Joseph McCarthy) – 3:37; 03 'House of Flowers' from *House of Flowers* (Harold Arlen, Truman Capote) – 3:36; 04 'Beyond the Sea' (Jack Lawrence, Charles Trenet) – 3:25; 05 'Sky Full of Rainbows' (Bart Howard) – 3:09; 06 'Sands of Time' from *Kismet* (George Forrest, Robert Wright) – 3:11. B: 01 'Shangri-La' (Matty Malneck, Robert Maxwell, Carl Sigman) – 3:30; 02 'Alice in Wonderland' from *Alice in Wonderland* (Bob Hilliard, Sammy Fain) –

2:46; 03 'Dream, Dream, Dream' (Jimmy McHugh, Mitchell Parish) – 3:09; 04 'The World of Make-Believe' (Jay Livingston, Paul Francis Webster) – 2:43; 05 'When You Wish Upon a Star' from *Pinocchio* (Leigh Harline, Ned Washington) – 4:21; 06 'Beyond the Blue Horizon' from *Monte Carlo* (Leo Robin, Richard Whiting) – 2:57.

Produced by Johnny Mathis. Arranged by Allyn Ferguson and conducted by Jack Feierman.

Recorded: February 7, 1964, February 10, 1964. Released: July 10, 1964.

MG 20942 **This Is Love**

A: 01 'Put On a Happy Face' from *Bye Bye Birdie* (Charles Strouse, Lee Adams) – 3:15; 02 'Poinciana (Song of the Tree)' (Buddy Bernier, Nat Simon) – 4:07; 03 'The Touch of Your Lips' (Ray Noble) – 3:28; 04 'Just Move Along, Meadow Lark' (Eddie Snyder, Paul Vance) – 2:43; 05 'Under a Blanket of Blue' (Jerry Livingston, Al J. Neiburg, Marty Symes) – 3:45; 06 'Over the Weekend' (John Benson Brooks, Joseph McCarthy) – 3:52. B: 01 'More' from *Mondo Cane* (Norman Newell, Nino Oliviero, Riz Ortolani) – 2:56; 02 'You Love Me' from *Tovarich* (Anne Croswell, Lee Pockriss) – 3:47; 03 'Limehouse Blues' (Philip Braham, Douglas Furber) – 4:23, 04 'What Do You Feel in Your Heart' (Bart Howard) – 3:12; 05 'The End of a Love Affair' (Edward Redding) – 3:32; 06 'Fantastic' (Bart Howard) – 3:57.

Produced by Johnny Mathis. Arranged by Allyn Ferguson and conducted by Jack Feierman.

Recorded: March 12, 1964, March 17, 1964, March 19, 1964. Released: September 18, 1964.

MG 20988 **Olé**

A: 01 'Granada' (Agustín Lara) – 3:11; 02 'Without You (Tres Palabras)' (Osvaldo Farrés, Ray Gilbert) – 2:45; 03 Medley a. 'Generique' (Antônio Carlos Jobim, Vinicius De Moraes) b. 'Felicidade' (Antônio Carlos Jobim, Vinicius De Moraes) – 4:20; 04 'Manhã de Carnaval (Morning of the Carnival)' from '*Orfeu Negro (Black Orpheus)*' (Luiz Bonfá) – 3:12; 05 'Samba de Orfeu' from '*Orfeu Negro (Black Orpheus)*' (Luiz Bonfá, Antônio Maria) – 2:23. B: 01 'La Montaña' (Augusto Alguero) – 3:35; 02 'Babalu' (Margarita Lecuana, Bob Russell) – 2:45; 03 'Serenata' (Leroy Anderson, Mitchell Parish) – 3:37; 04 'Bachianas Brasileiras, Pts. 1–3' (Heitor Villa-Lobos) – 7:01.

Produced by Johnny Mathis. Arranged by Allyn Ferguson and conducted by Jack Feierman.

Recorded: March 30, 1964, April 2, 1964, April 9, 1964. Released: November 1964.

1965
Broadway

01 'Ain't It de Truth' from *Jamaica* (Harold Arlen, E.Y. Harburg) – 3:47; 02 'Get Out of Town' from *Leave It to Me!* (Cole Porter) – 3:16; 03 'Independent (On My Own)' from *Bells Are Ringing* (Betty Comden, Adolph Green, Jule Styne) – 2:54; 04 'Hello, Dolly!' from *Hello, Dolly!* (Jerry Herman) – 3:28; 05 'Manhattan' from *The Garrick Gaieties* (Lorenz Hart, Richard Rodgers) – 3:40; 06 'Once in a Lifetime' from *Stop the World – I Want to Get Off* (Leslie Bricusse, Anthony Newley) – 2:22; 07 'You'd Better Love Me' from *High Spirits* (Timothy Gray, Hugh Martin) – 3:13; 08 'Don't Rain on My Parade' from *Funny Girl* (Bob Merrill, Jule Styne) – 2:55; 09 'Of Thee I Sing' from *Of Thee I Sing* (George Gershwin, Ira Gershwin) – 3:12; 10 'When I'm Not Near the Girl I Love' from *Finian's Rainbow* (E.Y. Harburg, Burton Lane) – 2:49; 11 'Ridin' High' from *Red, Hot and Blue* (Cole Porter) – 3:19; 12 'She Loves Me' from *She Loves Me* (Jerry Bock, Sheldon Harnick) – 2:44.

Produced by Johnny Mathis. Arranged and conducted by Allyn Ferguson.
Recorded: September 24, 1964, October 5, 1964, October 9, 1964. Released: August 28, 2012.

MG 20991 **Love Is Everything**

A: 01 'Never Let Me Go' from *The Scarlet Hour* (Jay Livingston, Ray Evans) – 2:31; 02 'People' from *Funny Girl* (Bob Merrill, Jule Styne) – 3:08; 03 'A Thousand Blue Bubbles' (Bart Howard, Carlo Rossi) – 2:40; 04 'Love Is Everything' (Edward Pola, George Wyle) – 2:56; 05 'Young and Foolish' from *Plain and Fancy* (Albert Hague, Arnold Horwitt) – 3:40; 06 'An Affair to Remember (Our Love Affair)' from *An Affair to Remember* (Harold Adamson, Leo McCarey, Harry Warren) – 2:42. B: 01 'Come Ride the Wind with Me' (Alfred Bartles, Bryan Lindsay) – 3:01; 02 'Go Away Little Girl' (Gerry Goffin, Carole King) – 3:19; 03 'Dancing in the Dark' from *The Band Wagon* (Arthur Schwartz, Howard Dietz) – 2:52; 04 'Long Ago (and Far Away)' from *Cover Girl* (Jerome Kern, Ira Gershwin) – 3:42; 05 'This Is All I Ask' (Gordon Jenkins) – 4:04; 06 'One More Mountain' (Eddie Snyder, Paul Vance) – 2:24.

Produced by Al Ham. Arranged and conducted by Glenn Osser.
Recorded: December 9, 1964, December 10, 1964, December 12, 1964. Released: March 5, 1965.

MG 21041 **The Sweetheart Tree**

A: 01 'A Wonderful Day Like Today' from *The Roar of the Greasepaint – The Smell of the Crowd* (Leslie Bricusse, Anthony Newley) – 2:42; 02 'Arrivederci Roma' from *Seven Hills of Rome* (Pietro Garinei, Sandro Giovannini, Renato Rascel, Carl Sigman) – 3:41; 03 'Clopin Clopant' (Bruno Coquatrix, Pierre Dundan, Alex Kramer, Joan

Whitney) – 3:40; 04 'This Is Love' (Norman Newell) – 3:23; 05 'I'll Close My Eyes' (Buddy Kaye, Billy Reid) – 3:53; 06 'The Very Thought of You' (Ray Noble) – 3:49. B: 01 'Danny Boy' (Frederick Weatherly) – 4:55; 02 'The Sweetheart Tree' from *The Great Race* (Henry Mancini, Johnny Mercer) – 2:15; 03 'Symphony' (Alex Alstone, Jack Lawrence, Andre Tabet) – 2:59; 04 'The Skye Boat Song' (traditional) – 3:50; 05 'Autumn Leaves' (Joseph Kosma, Johnny Mercer, Jacques Prevert) – 3:45; 06 'Mirage' from *Mirage* (Quincy Jones, Bob Russell) – 2:06.

Produced by Norman Newell. Alyn Ainsworth – arranger, conductor ('The Very Thought of You'); arranger ('Symphony'). Allyn Ferguson – arranger, conductor ('Autumn Leaves', 'The Skye Boat Song'); arranger ('I'll Close My Eyes'); conductor ('Danny Boy', 'This Is Love'). Geoff Love – arranger ('Danny Boy', 'This Is Love'). Lincoln Mayorga – arranger, conductor ('The Sweetheart Tree'). Tony Osborne – arranger, conductor ('Arrivederci Roma', 'Clopin Clopant', 'I'm in Love for the Very First Time', 'A Wonderful Day Like Today'); conductor ('I'll Close My Eyes', 'Symphony').

Recorded: May 6–8, 1965, June 15, 1965. Released: September 30, 1965.

1966
MG 21073 **The Shadow of Your Smile**

A: 01 'Moment to Moment' from *Moment to Moment* (Henry Mancini, Johnny Mercer) – 2:23; 02 'The Shadow of Your Smile' from *The Sandpiper* (Johnny Mandel, Paul Francis Webster) – 3:03; 03 'Michelle' (John Lennon, Paul McCartney) – 2:33; 04 'Yesterday' (Lennon, McCartney) – 3:04; 05 'Something's Coming' from *West Side Story* (Leonard Bernstein, Stephen Sondheim) – 2:50; 06 'A Taste of Honey' (Rick Marlow, Bobby Scott) – 3:09. B: 01 'I'm in Love for the Very First Time' from *An Alligator Named Daisy* (Paddy Roberts, Jack Woodman) – 3:15; 02 'Quiet Nights of Quiet Stars (Corcovado)' (Antonio Carlos Jobim, Gene Lees) – 2:26; 03 'I Left My Heart in San Francisco' (George Cory, Douglass Cross) – 2:59; 04 'On a Clear Day (You Can See Forever)' from *On a Clear Day You Can See Forever* (Alan Jay Lerner, Burton Lane) – 2:43; 05 'Melinda' from *On a Clear Day You Can See Forever* (Lerner, Lane) – 3:18; 06 'Come Back to Me' from *On a Clear Day You Can See Forever* (Lerner, Lane) – 2:16.

Produced by Don Reiber. Jack Elliott – arranger, conductor ('Moment to Moment', 'The Shadow of Your Smile'). Bryan Fahey – conductor ('Something's Coming'). Tony Osborne – arranger, conductor ('I Left My Heart in San Francisco', 'I'm in Love for the Very First Time'); arranger ('Something's Coming'). Glenn Osser – arranger, conductor ('Come Back to Me', 'Melinda', 'On a Clear Day You Can See Forever', 'Quiet Nights of Quiet Stars (Corcovado)', 'Yesterday'). John Pisano – arranger, conductor ('Michelle', 'A Taste of Honey').

Recorded: August 27, 1965, September 14, 1965, January 12–13, 1966. Released: March 1966.

MG 21091 **So Nice**

A: 01 'The Impossible Dream (The Quest)' from *Man of La Mancha* (Joe Darion, Mitch Leigh) – 3:44; 02 'I Will Wait for You' from *The Umbrellas of Cherbourg* (Jacques Demy, Norman Gimbel, Michel Legrand) – 3:01; 03 'What the World Needs Now Is Love' (Burt Bacharach, Hal David) – 2:37; 04 'Hurry! It's Lovely Up Here' from *On a Clear Day You Can See Forever* (Alan Jay Lerner, Burton Lane) – 2:47; 05 'Elusive Butterfly' (Bob Lind) – 2:08; 06 'So Nice (Samba de Verao)' (Gimbel, Marcos Valle, Paulo Sergio Valle) – 3:05. B: 01 'Dulcinea' from *Man of La Mancha* (Darion, Leigh) – 2:52; 02 'What Now My Love' (Gilbert Becaud, Carl Sigman) – 3:14; 03 'Man of La Mancha (I, Don Quixote)' from *Man of La Mancha* (Darion, Leigh) – 2:18; 04 'The Music That Makes Me Dance' from *Funny Girl* (Bob Merrill, Jule Styne) – 3:35; 05 'I Dream of You' (Marjorie Goetschius, Edna Osser) – 3:23; 06 'Baubles, Bangles & Beads' from *Kismet* (Robert Wright, George Forrest) – 3:32.

Produced by Johnny Mathis. Arranged and conducted by Glenn Osser, except Bryan Fahey – arranger, conductor ('Baubles, Bangles & Beads'), Jack Feierman – conductor ('Dulcinea', 'Man of La Mancha (I, Don Quixote)'), Mort Stevens – arranger, conductor ('So Nice (Samba de Verao)').

Recorded: May 31, 1966, June 23, 1966, July 7, 1966, July 11–12, 1966. Released: September 16, 1966.

1967
MG 21107 **Johnny Mathis Sings**

A: 01 'Saturday Sunshine' (Burt Bacharach, Hal David) – 2:36; 02 'Lovers in New York' (Jay Livingston, Ray Evans, Henry Mancini) – 3:03; 03 'Eleanor Rigby' (John Lennon, Paul McCartney) – 2:55; 04 'Sunny' (Bobby Hebb) – 4:19; 05 'Who Can I Turn To?' from *The Roar of the Greasepaint–the Smell of the Crowd* (Leslie Bricusse, Anthony Newley) – 2:40; 06 'Strangers in the Night' (Bert Kaempfert, Charles Singleton, Eddie Snyder) – 3:30. B: 01 '(There's) Always Something There to Remind Me' (Bacharach, David) – 2:42; 02 'Somewhere My Love' (Maurice Jarre, Paul Francis Webster) – 3:30; 03 'Who Can Say' (Norman Gimbel, Riz Ortolani) – 2:50; 04 'I Wish You Love' (Albert Beach, Charles Trenet) – 4:22; 05 'The Second Time Around' from *High Time* (Sammy Cahn, Jimmy Van Heusen) – 3:13; 06 'Wake the Town and Tell the People' (Jerry Livingston, Sammy Gallop) – 2:50.

Produced by Johnny Mathis.

Recorded: November 4, 1963, August 27, 1965, June 23, 1966, September 15, 1966, October 28, 1966, October 31, 1966. Released: March 10, 1967.

Columbia albums (1967-present)

1967
CS 9526 **Up, Up and Away**

A: 01 'Up, Up and Away' (Jimmy Webb) – 2:54; 02 'The More I See You' (Mack Gordon, Harry Warren) – 4:03; 03 'Where Are the Words' from *Doctor Dolittle* (Leslie Bricusse) – 2:50; 04 'Morning Side of the Mountain' (Dick Manning, Larry Stock) – 4:21; 05 'I Won't Cry Anymore' (Al Frisch, Fred Wise) – 3:30; 06 'Far Above Cayuga's Waters' (lyrics adapted by Sammy Cahn) – 3:37. B: 01 'Misty Roses' (Tim Hardin) – 2:43; 02 'Drifting' (Kim Gannon, Bronisław Kaper) – 3:27; 03 'At the Crossroads' from *Doctor Dolittle* (Leslie Bricusse) – 2:59; 04 'I Thought of You Last Night' (Ralph Freed) – 3:04; 05 'When I Look in Your Eyes' from *Doctor Dolittle* (Leslie Bricusse) – 3:26.
Produced by Robert Mersey. Arranged and conducted by Glenn Osser, except Robert Mersey – arranger, conductor ('Misty Roses').
Recorded: May 15, 1967, September 25–26, 1967, September 28, 1967. Released: October 23, 1967.

1968
CS 9637 **Love Is Blue**

A: 01 'I Say a Little Prayer' (Burt Bacharach, Hal David) – 2:17; 02 'By the Time I Get to Phoenix' (Jimmy Webb) – 3:18; 03 'The Look of Love' from *Casino Royale* (Burt Bacharach, Hal David) – 3:45; 04 'Don't Go Breakin' My Heart' (Burt Bacharach, Hal David) – 2:24; 05 'Here, There and Everywhere' (John Lennon, Paul McCartney) – 3:37. B: 01 'Never My Love' (Dick Addrisi, Don Addrisi) – 2:41; 02 'Moon River' from *Breakfast at Tiffany's* (Henry Mancini, Johnny Mercer) – 3:07; 03 'Walk On By' (Burt Bacharach, Hal David) – 3:03; 04 'Venus' (Ed Marshall) – 2:40; 05 'Love Is Blue' (Bryan Blackburn, Pierre Corr, Andre Popp) – 3:12.
Produced by Robert Mersey. Arranged and conducted by Robert Mersey.
Recorded: January 23–24, 1968, February 3, 1968. Released: March 6, 1968.
CS 9705 *Those Were the Days*
A: 01 'Those Were the Days' (Gene Raskin) – 3:59; 02 'Little Green Apples' (Bobby Russell) – 3:38; 03 'The End of the World' (Arthur Kent, Sylvia Dee) – 3:10; 04 'This Guy's In Love With You' (Hal David, Burt Bacharach) – 4:37; 05 'The 59th Street Bridge Song (Feelin' Groovy)' (Paul Simon) – 2:10. B: 01 'Light My Fire' (Jim Morrison, John Densmore, Ray Manzarek, Robby Krieger) – 3:48; 02 'Every Time I Dream of You' (Richard Ahlert, Bert Kaempfert, Herbert Rehbein) – 3:53; 03 'The World I Used to Know' (Rod McKuen) – 2:30; 04 'You Make Me Think About You' from *With Six You Get Eggroll* (Bob Hilliard, Robert Mersey) – 1:59: 05 'Turn Around Look at Me' (Jerry Capehart) – 2:50.

Produced by Robert Mersey. Arranged and conducted by Robert Mersey. Recorded: July 5, 1968, July 9, 1968, July 10, 1968, July 22, 1968, August 20, 1968, October 4, 1968. Released: November 6, 1968.

1969
63524 Sings the Music of Bert Kaempfert

A: 01 'Wonderland by Night' (Lincoln Chase, Klaus-Gunter Neumann) – 3:34; 02 'Spanish Eyes' (Bert Kaempfert, Charles Singleton, Eddie Snyder) – 3:00; 03 'The Lady Smiles' (Richard Ahlert, Kaempfert, Herbert Rehbein) – 3:06; 04 'Danke Schoen' (Milt Gabler, Kaempfert, Kurt Schwabach) – 2:56; 05 'The Times Will Change' (Kaempfert, Rehbein, Carl Sigman) – 3:09; 06 'Remember When (We Made These Memories)' (Kaempfert, Singleton, Snyder) – 2:58. B: 01 'Strangers in the Night' (Kaempfert, Singleton, Snyder) – 3:34; 02 'Don't Stay' (Ahlert, Kaempfert, Rehbein) – 2:51; 03 'If There's a Way' (Kaempfert, Jimmy Radcliffe, Rehbein, Buddy Scott) – 2:55; 04 'Lady' (Kaempfert, Larry Kusik, Rehbein, Singleton) – 3:00; 05 'L-O-V-E' (Gabler, Kaempfert) – 2:30; 06 'It Makes No Difference' (Gabler, Kaempfert, Rehbein) – 2:32.

Produced by Robert Mersey. Arranged and conducted by Herbert Rehbein. Recorded, October 21-23, 1968. Released: November 1969. Note: *Sings the Music of Bert Kaempfert* was first released as a standalone album in Germany in 1968. The track 'It Makes No Difference' was added for the UK release in 1969. When *Sings the Music of Bert Kaempfert* was released in the US in 1970, it was combined with a selection of Burt Bacharach songs on the double album *Sings the Music of Bacharach & Kaempfert*. The double album didn't include the UK bonus track 'It Makes No Difference.'

CS 9909 Love Theme from 'Romeo And Juliet' (A Time for Us)

A: 01 'Love Theme from 'Romeo and Juliet' (A Time for Us)' from *Romeo and Juliet* (Larry Kusik, Nino Rota, Eddie Snyder) – 2:58; 02 'Aquarius/Let the Sunshine In' from *Hair* (Galt MacDermot, Gerome Ragni) – 3:04; 03 'Without Her' (Harry Nilsson) – 3:01; 04 'I'll Never Fall in Love Again' from *Promises, Promises* (Burt Bacharach, Hal David) – 3:02; 05 'Live for Life' from *Live for Life* (Norman Gimbel, Francis Lai) – 2:59; 06 We' from *Me, Natalie* (Henry Mancini, Rod McKuen) – 3:03. B: 01 'Didn't We' (Jimmy Webb) – 2:49; 02 'Love Me Tonight' (Barry Mason, Daniele Pace, Mario Panzeri, Lorenzo Pilat) – 2:58; 03 'The Windmills of Your Mind' from *The Thomas Crown Affair* (Alan and Marilyn Bergman, Michel Legrand) – 3:33; 04 'The World I Threw Away' (Howard Greenfield, Neil Sedaka) – 3:18; 05 'Yesterday When I Was Young' (Charles Aznavour, Herbert Kretzmer) – 2:55.

Produced by Jack Gold. Arranged and conducted by Ernie Freeman.

Recorded: January 18, 1969, June 5, 1969, June 10, 1969, June 13, 1969. Released: July 30, 1969.

CS 9923 **Give Me Your Love for Christmas**

A: 01 'Jingle Bell Rock' (Joseph Carleton Beal, James Ross Boothe) – 2:11; 02 'Have Yourself a Merry Little Christmas' from *Meet Me in St. Louis* (Ralph Blane, Hugh Martin) – 3:29; 03 'My Favorite Things' from *The Sound of Music* (Richard Rodgers, Oscar Hammerstein II)– 2:37; 04 'Give Me Your Love for Christmas' (Jack Gold, Phyllis Stohn) – 2:37; 05 'Santa Claus Is Coming to Town' (J. Fred Coots, Haven Gillespie) – 2:19; 06 'What Are You Doing New Year's Eve?' (Frank Loesser) – 2:52. B: 01 'Do You Hear What I Hear?' (Gloria Shayne Baker, Noel Regney) – 3:21; 02 'Calypso Noel' (Gordon Krunnfusz) – 2:13; 03 'The Little Drummer Boy' (Katherine Davis, Henry Onorati, Harry Simeone) – 2:28; 04 'Christmas Day' from *Promises, Promises* (Burt Bacharach, Hal David) – 3:24; 05 'The Lord's Prayer' (Albert Hay Malotte) – 2:40.

Produced by Jack Gold. Arranged and conducted by Ernie Freeman.

Recorded: July 15, 1969, September 23, 1969. Released: October 13, 1969. Gold RIAA certified on December 26, 1979. Platinum on November 5, 2001.

1970
CS 1005 **Raindrops Keep Fallin' on My Head**

A: 01 'Raindrops Keep Fallin' on My Head' from *Butch Cassidy and the Sundance Kid* (Burt Bacharach, Hal David) – 2:36 02 'Honey Come Back' (Jimmy Webb) – 3:02 03 'Watch What Happens' from *The Umbrellas of Cherbourg* (Norman Gimbel, Michel Legrand) – 3:20 04 'Something' (George Harrison) – 2:34 05 'Alfie' from *Alfie* (Burt Bacharach, Hal David) – 3:15 06 'Midnight Cowboy' from *Midnight Cowboy* (John Barry, Jack Gold) – 2:49. B: 01 'A Man and a Woman' from *A Man and a Woman* (Pierre Barouh, Jerry Keller, Francis Lai) – 3:25; 02 'Odds and Ends' (Burt Bacharach, Hal David) – 3:04; 03 'Jean' from *The Prime of Miss Jean Brodie* (Rod McKuen) – 3:44; 04 'Everybody's Talkin'' from *Midnight Cowboy* (Fred Neil) – 3:02; 05 'Bridge Over Troubled Water' (Paul Simon, Art Garfunkel) – 4:37.

Produced by Jack Gold. Arranged and conducted by Ernie Freeman.

Recorded: October 14, 1969, January 6–7, 1970, January 22, 1970. Released: February 25, 1970.

C 30210 **Close to You**

A: 01 '(They Long to Be) Close to You' (Burt Bacharach, Hal David) – 3:26 02 'Evil Ways' (Sonny Henry) – 2:36 03 'Come Saturday Morning' from *The Sterile Cuckoo* (Fred Karlin, Dory Previn) – 2:10 04 'Yellow Days' (Alan Bernstein, Álvaro Carrillo) – 2:40

05 'Pieces of Dreams' from *Pieces of Dreams* (Alan Bergman, Marilyn Bergman, Michel Legrand) – 2:44 06 'Song of Joy (Himno a la Alegria)' (Ludwig van Beethoven, Waldo de los Rios) – 4:00. B: 01 'Everything Is Beautiful' (Ray Stevens) – 3:28; 02 'The Long and Winding Road' (John Lennon, Paul McCartney) – 3:25; 03 '(If You Let Me Make Love to You Then) Why Can't I Touch You?' from *Salvation* (Charles Courtney, Peter Link) – 3:15; 04 'Wave' (Antônio Carlos Jobim) – 3:30; 05 'Until It's Time for You to Go' (Buffy Sainte-Marie) – 3:55.

Produced by Jack Gold. Arranged and conducted by Ernie Freeman.

Recorded: May 27, 1970, July 10, 1970, July 13, 1970, July 15, 1970. Released: August 19, 1970.

C 30352 Johnny Mathis Sings the Music of Bacharach & Kaempfert

A: 01 'Wonderland by Night' (Lincoln Chase, Klaus-Gunter Neumann) – 3:34; 02 'Spanish Eyes' (Bert Kaempfert, Charles Singleton, Eddie Snyder) – 3:00; 03 'The Lady Smiles' (Richard Ahlert, Kaempfert, Herbert Rehbein) – 3:06; 04 'Danke Schoen' (Milt Gabler, Kaempfert, Kurt Schwabach) – 2:56; 05 'The Times Will Change' (Kaempfert, Rehbein, Carl Sigman) – 3:09; 06 'Remember When (We Made These Memories)' (Kaempfert, Singleton, Snyder) – 2:58. B: 01 'Strangers in the Night' (Kaempfert, Singleton, Snyder) – 3:34 02 'Don't Stay' (Ahlert, Kaempfert, Rehbein) – 2:51; 03 'If There's a Way' (Kaempfert, Jimmy Radcliffe, Rehbein, Buddy Scott) – 2:55; 04 'Lady' (Kaempfert, Larry Kusik, Rehbein, Singleton) – 3:00; 05 'L-O-V-E' (Gabler, Kaempfert) – 2:30. C: 01 'Walk On By' (Burt Bacharach, Hal David) – 3:00; 02 'The Look of Love' from *Casino Royale* (Bacharach, David) – 3:41; 03 'I Say a Little Prayer' (Bacharach, David) – 2:14 above three recorded and released in 1968 for the album *Love Is Blue*. 04 'Heavenly' (Bacharach, Sydney Shaw) – 3:19. rec. and rel. in 1959 for the album *Heavenly*; 05 'This Guy's in Love with You' (Bacharach, David) – 4:35 rec. and rel. in 1968 for the album *Those Were the Days*. D: 01 'I'll Never Fall in Love Again' from *Promises, Promises* (Bacharach, David) – 3:00 rec. and rel. in 1969 for the album *Love Theme from 'Romeo And Juliet' (A Time for Us)*; 02 'Alfie' from *Alfie* (Bacharach, David) – 3:13; 03 'Odds and Ends' (Bacharach, David) – 3:02 above two rec. and rel. in 1970 for the album *Raindrops Keep Fallin' on My Head*; 04 'Faithfully' (Bacharach, Shaw) – 2:32 rec. and rel. in 1959 for the album *Faithfully*; 05 'Don't Go Breakin' My Heart' (Bacharach, David) – 2:21 rec. and rel. in 1968 for the album *Love Is Blue*.

Produced by Robert Mersey except Jack Gold – producer ('Alfie', 'Odds and Ends'), Mitch Miller – producer ('Faithfully', 'Heavenly'), Al Ham – producer ('Heavenly'). Robert Mersey – arranger and conductor ('Don't Go Breakin' My Heart', 'I Say a Little Prayer', 'I'll Never Fall in Love Again', 'The Look of Love', 'Walk On By'). Herbert Rehbein – arranger and conductor (sides A and B). Ernie Freeman – arranger and conductor ('Alfie', 'Odds

and Ends'). Glenn Osser – arranger and conductor ('Faithfully', 'Heavenly'). D'Arneill Pershing – arranger and conductor ('This Guy's In Love With You').
Recorded: October 21–23, 1968 (sides A and B). 1959–1960, 1968–1970 (sides C and D). Released: Autumn 1970.

1971
C 30499 **Love Story**
A: 01 '(Where Do I Begin) Love Story' (Francis Lai, Carl Sigman) – 2:45; 02 'Rose Garden' (Joe South) – 2:51; 03 'Ten Times Forever More' (Burt Bacharach, Hal David) – 2:36; 04 'It's Impossible' (Armando Manzanero, Sid Wayne) – 3:00; 05 'I Was There' (Gerry Goffin, Carole King) – 2:26; 06 'What Are You Doing the Rest of Your Life?' from *The Happy Ending* (Alan Bergman, Marilyn Bergman, Michel Legrand) – 3:00. B: 01 'We've Only Just Begun' (Roger Nichols, Paul Williams) – 3:05; 02 'Traces' (Buddy Buie, J. R. Cobb, Emory Gordy Jr.) – 2:45; 03 'For the Good Times' (Kris Kristofferson) – 3:42; 04 'My Sweet Lord' (George Harrison) – 3:16; 05 'Loss of Love' (Henry Mancini, Bob Merrill) – 2:51.
Produced by Jack Gold. Arranged and conducted by Perry Botkin, Jr.
Recorded: January 18, 1969, July 15–August 14, 1970, December 16, 1970, December 23, 1970, January 4, 1971. Released: February 10, 1971.

C 30740 **Today's Great Hits You've Got a Friend**
A: 01 'You've Got a Friend' (Carole King) – 4:31; 02 'How Can You Mend a Broken Heart?' (Barry Gibb, Robin Gibb) – 3:16; 03 'Help Me Make It Through the Night' (Kris Kristofferson) – 3:16; 04 'If You Could Read My Mind' (Gordon Lightfoot) – 4:01; 05 'Never Can Say Goodbye' (Clifton Davis) – 3:07. B: 01 'It's Too Late' (Carole King) – 3:07; 02 'We Can Work It Out' (John Lennon, Paul McCartney) – 3:03; 03 'Long Ago and Far Away' (James Taylor) – 3:11; 04 'If' (David Gates) – 3:03; 05 'For All We Know' from *Lovers and Other Strangers* (Jimmy Griffin, Fred Karlin, Robb Royer) – 2:54; 06 'If We Only Have Love' (Eric Blau, Jacques Brel, Mort Shuman) – 3:16.
Produced by Richard Perry except Johnny Mathis – producer ('You've Got a Friend', 'How Can You Mend a Broken Heart?', 'It's Too Late', 'If We Only Have Love'). Jack Gold – producer ('If', 'For All We Know'). Arranged by D'Arneill Pershing and conducted by Roy M. Rogosin except Al Capps – arranger and conductor ('If', 'For All We Know').
Recorded: April 30, 1971, May 5, 1971, May 7, 1971, May 11, 1971, June 30, 1971, July 8, 1971. Released: August 11, 1971.

KG 30979 **Johnny Mathis in Person: Recorded Live at Las Vegas**
A: 01 'In the Morning' (Barry Gibb) – 3:22; 02 Medley a. '(They Long to Be) Close to You' (Burt Bacharach, Hal David) b. 'We've Only Just Begun' (Roger Nichols,

Paul Williams) – 4:40; 03 Medley a. 'Dreamy' (Erroll Garner, Sydney Shaw) b. 'Misty' (Johnny Burke, Garner) – 4:29; 04 'Come Runnin'' (Roc Hillman) – 2:20. B: 01 '(Where Do I Begin) Love Story' (Francis Lai, Carl Sigman) – 3:00; 02 'April in Paris' (Vernon Duke, E.Y. 'Yip' Harburg) – 3:32; 03 'Day In, Day Out' (Johnny Mercer, Rube Bloom) – 3:01. C: 01 Medley a. 'The Twelfth of Never' (Jerry Livingston, Paul Francis Webster) b. 'Wild Is the Wind' (Dimitri Tiomkin, Ned Washington) c. 'When Sunny Gets Blue' (Marvin Fisher, Jack Segal) d. 'It's Not for Me to Say' (Robert Allen, Al Stillman) e. 'Chances Are' (Allen, Stillman) f. 'Love Theme from Romeo and Juliet (A Time for Us)' (Larry Kusik, Nino Rota, Eddie Snyder) g. 'Tonight' (Leonard Bernstein, Stephen Sondheim) h. 'Dulcinea' (Joe Darion, Mitch Leigh) i. 'The Impossible Dream (The Quest)' (Darion, Leigh) j. 'Wonderful! Wonderful!' (Sherman Edwards, Ben Raleigh) – 8:52; 02 'And Her Mother Came Too' from A to Z (Ivor Novello, Dion Titheradge) – 2:49. D: 01 'I Got Love' from Purlie (Gary Geld, Peter Udell) – 3:34; 02 'Maria' (Bernstein, Sondheim) – 3:54; 03 'If We Only Have Love' (Eric Blau, Jacques Brel, Mort Shuman) – 5:05; 04 'If We Only Have Love' (instrumental) – 1:23.
Produced by Jack Gold and Sid Feller. Arranged by D'Arneill Pershing except Perry Botkin, Jr. – arranger ('(Where Do I Begin) Love Story'), Jack Elliott – arranger ('Day In, Day Out', 'I Got Love'), Allyn Ferguson – arranger ('Come Runnin''), David Rhodes – arranger ('Maria'). Conducted by Roy M. Rogosin.
Recorded: May 20–22, 1971. Released: December 22, 1971.

1972
KC 31342 The First Time Ever (I Saw Your Face)
A: 01 'The First Time Ever (I Saw Your Face)' (Ewan MacColl) – 3:36; 02 'Love Theme from 'The Godfather' (Speak Softly Love)' (Larry Kusik, Nino Rota) – 3:08; 03 'Theme from Summer of '42 (The Summer Knows)' (Alan Bergman, Marilyn Bergman, Michel Legrand) – 2:39; 04 'Brian's Song (The Hands of Time)' (A. Bergman, M. Bergman, Legrand) – 3:24; 05 'Since I Fell for You' (Buddy Johnson) – 3:17. B: 01 'Without You' (Tom Evans, Peter Ham) – 2:58; 02 'Betcha by Golly, Wow' (Thom Bell, Linda Creed) – 2:49; 03 'Life and Breath' (George S. Clinton) – 3:27; 04 'I Need You' (Gerry Beckley) – 2:36; 05 '(Last Night) I Didn't Get to Sleep at All' (Tony Macaulay) – 3:33; 06 'Life Is What You Make It' from Kotch (Marvin Hamlisch, Johnny Mercer) – 2:50.
Produced by Jerry Fuller. Al Capps – arranger and conductor ('The First Time Ever (I Saw Your Face)', 'Speak Softly Love (Love Theme from 'The Godfather')', 'Theme from 'Summer of 42'', 'Brian's Song', 'Without You'). D'Arneill Pershing – arranger and conductor ('Since I Fell for You', 'Betcha by Golly Wow', 'Life and Breath', 'I Need You', '(Last Night) I Didn't Get to Sleep at All', 'Life Is What You Make It').
Recorded: January 27, 1972, February 11, 1972, March 13, 1972, March 20, 1972, April 3, 1972. Released: May 10, 1972.

KC 31626 **Song Sung Blue**

A: 01 'Play Me' (Neil Diamond) – 3:49; 02 'Alone Again (Naturally)' (Gilbert O'Sullivan) – 4:20; 03 'Where Is the Love' (Ralph MacDonald, William Salter) – 2:32; 04 'Goodbye to Love' (John Bettis, Richard Carpenter) – 3:12; 05 'Too Young' (Sylvia Dee, Sidney Lippman) – 3:16. B: 01 'Make It Easy on Yourself' (Burt Bacharach, Hal David) – 3:29; 02 'Lean on Me' (Bill Withers) – 3:51; 03 'How Can I Be Sure' (Felix Cavaliere, Eddie Brigati) – 3:42; 04 'Run to Me' (Barry Gibb, Maurice Gibb, Robin Gibb) – 2:58; 05 'Song Sung Blue' (Neil Diamond) – 3:12; 06 'He Ain't Heavy, He's My Brother' (Bob Russell, Bobby Scott) – 3:16.

Produced by Jerry Fuller. Arranged and conducted by D'Arneill Pershing.

Recorded: April 3, 1972, June 7, 1972, June 21, 1972, July 24, 1972, July 28, 1972. Released: September 13, 1972.

1973
KC 32114 **Me and Mrs. Jones**

A: 01 'Me and Mrs. Jones' (Kenny Gamble, Cary Gilbert, Leon Huff) – 4:10; 02 'Sweet Surrender' (David Gates) – 2:35; 03 'Summer Breeze' (Dash Crofts, Jim Seals) – 4:02; 04 'Corner of the Sky' from *Pippin* (Stephen Schwartz) – 3:27; 05 'Happy (Love Theme from Lady Sings the Blues)' from *Lady Sings the Blues* (Michel Legrand, Smokey Robinson) – 3:36; 06 Medley a. 'Soul and Inspiration' (Barry Mann, Cynthia Weil) b. 'Just Once in My Life' (Gerry Goffin, Carole King, Phil Spector) – 3:33. B: 01 'Don't Let Me Be Lonely Tonight' (James Taylor) – 3:21; 02 'If I Could Reach You' (Randy McNeill) – 3:16; 03 'Remember' (Harry Nilsson) – 4:35; 04 'You're a Lady' (Peter Skellern) – 5:10; 05 Medley a. 'I Was Born in Love with You' from *Wuthering Heights* (1970) (Alan Bergman, Marilyn Bergman, Michel Legrand) b. 'Summer Me, Winter Me' (A. Bergman, M. Bergman, Legrand) – 3:38.

Produced by Jerry Fuller. Arranged and conducted by D'Arneill Pershing except Larry Muhoberac – arranger ('Corner of the Sky', 'You're a Lady'). Al Capps – arranger and conductor ('I Was Born In Love / Summer Me, Winter Me).

Recorded: June 30, 1971, September 28, 1972, December 5, 1972, December 12, 1972, December 21, 1972, January 3, 1973. Released: April 27, 1973.

KC 32258 **Killing Me Softly with Her Song**

A: 01 'Killing Me Softly with Her Song' (Charles Fox, Norman Gimbel) – 5:18; 02 'Aubrey' (David Gates) – 3:37; 03 'And I Love You So' (Don McLean) – 3:26; 04 'Break Up to Make Up' (Thom Bell, Linda Creed, Kenneth Gamble) – 3:50; 05 'Arianne' (Martin Charnin, Christian Roudey) – 3:29. B: 01 'Neither One of Us (Wants to Be the First to Say Goodbye)' (Jim Weatherly) – 4:26; 02 'Wildflower'

(Doug Edwards, David Richardson) – 4:21; 03 'You Are the Sunshine of My Life' (Stevie Wonder) – 2:41; 04 'Sing' from *Sesame Street* (Joe Raposo) – 3:04; 05 'Good Morning Heartache' (Ervin Drake, Dan Fisher, Irene Higginbotham) – 2:25; 06 'Show and Tell' (Jerry Fuller) – 3:12.
Produced by Jerry Fuller. Arranged and conducted by D'Arneill Pershing.
Recorded: March 1, 1973, March 29, 1973, April 2, 1973, April 25–26, 1973. Released: May 25,

1973
KC 32435 **I'm Coming Home**
A: 01 'I'm Coming Home' – 3:24; 02 'I'd Rather Be Here with You' – 3:47; 03 'Foolish' (Thom Bell, Linda Creed, Bruce Hawes, Joseph B. Jefferson) – 4:38; 04 'I'm Stone in Love with You' (Anthony Bell, T. Bell, Creed) – 3:30; 05 'And I Think That's What I'll Do' – 3:41. B: 01 'Life Is a Song Worth Singing' – 6:06; 02 'A Baby's Born' – 4:28; 03 'Sweet Child' – 4:02; 04 'Stop Look and Listen to Your Heart' – 4:18; 05 'I Just Wanted to Be Me' (Bruce Hawes, Joseph B. Jefferson) – 3:12.
Produced by Thom Bell. Arranged and conducted by Thom Bell.
Recorded: May 23–25, 1973. Released: September 21, 1973.

1974
KC 33251 **The Heart of a Woman**
A: 01 'Woman, Woman' (Johnny Bristol) – 3:16; 02 'Sail On White Moon' (Bristol) – 3:12; 03 'It's Gone' (Eliot Tucker) – 3:13; 04 'House for Sale' (Lawrence Howard Brown, Oleg Lopatin) – 3:18; 05 'Feel Like Makin' Love' (Eugene McDaniels) – 3:40. B: 01 'Memories Don't Leave like People Do' (Bristol, Jerry Butler, James Anthony Dean, John Henry Glover) – 4:23; 02 'Strangers in Dark Corners' (Bristol) – 3:50; 03 'Wendy' from *Three the Hard Way* (Lowrell Simon, Richard Tufo) – 3:36; 04 'The Heart of a Woman' (Lee Adams, Charles Strouse) – 2:57; 05 'The Way We Planned It' (George S. Clinton) – 3:35.
Produced by Johnny Bristol except Jerry Fuller – producer ('The Way We Planned It'). Arranged by Paul Riser except H. B. Barnum – arranger ('The Way We Planned It'). James C. Barnett – arranger ('I Feel Like Makin' Love,' 'The Heart Of A Woman'). Recorded: June 28, 1974, September 2–7, 1974. Released: November 22, 1974.

1975
PC 33420 **When Will I See You Again**
A: 01 'Mandy' (Scott English, Richard Kerr) – 3:31; 02 'Nice to Be Around' (John Williams, Paul Williams) – 3:52; 03 'You're As Right As Rain' (Thom Bell, Linda Creed) – 3:02; 04 'When Will I See You Again' (Kenny Gamble, Leon Huff) – 2:35; 05 'Only

You (And You Alone)' (Buck Ram) – 2:50. B: 01 Medley a. 'Let Me Be the One' (Roger Nichols, Paul Williams) b. 'I Won't Last a Day Without You' (Nichols, Paul Williams) – 4:06; 02 'The Way We Were' from *The Way We Were* (Alan Bergman, Marilyn Bergman, Marvin Hamlisch) – 3:49; 03 'Laughter in the Rain' (Neil Sedaka, Phil Cody) – 2:31; 04 'You and Me Against the World' (Kenny Ascher, Paul Williams) – 3:59; 05 'The Things I Might Have Been' (Richard M. Sherman, Robert B. Sherman) – 3:27.

Produced by John Florez. Arranged and conducted by D'Arneill Pershing.

Recorded: January 13, 1975, January 20, 1975, January 23, 1975. Released: March 1975.

PC 33887 **Feelings**

A: 01 'One Day in Your Life' (Renée Armand, Samuel F. Brown III) – 4:14; 02 'Stardust' (Hoagy Carmichael, Mitchell Parish) – 3:27; 03 'What I Did for Love' from *A Chorus Line* (Marvin Hamlisch, Edward Kleban) – 2:44; 04 'Midnight Blue' (Melissa Manchester, Carole Bayer Sager) – 3:34; 05 'The Greatest Gift' from *The Return of the Pink Panther* (Hal David, Henry Mancini) – 2:49. B: 01 '99 Miles from L.A.' (Hal David, Albert Hammond) – 3:35; 02 'Hurry Mother Nature' (Jerry Fuller) – 3:24; 03 'Feelings' (Morris Albert, Loulou Gasté) – 3:28; 04 'That's All She Wrote' (Jerry Fuller) – 3:38; 05 'Solitaire' (Neil Sedaka, Phil Cody) – 4:33.

Produced by Jack Gold. Arranged and conducted by Gene Page.

Recorded: March 25, 1975, May 5, 1975, June 16, 1975, August 2, 1975, August 9, 1975, August 29, 1975. Released: October 20, 1975. Gold, RIAA certified on December 30, 1980.

1976
PC 34117 **I Only Have Eyes for You**

A: 01 'I Write the Songs' (Bruce Johnston) – 3:57; 02 'Do Me Wrong, but Do Me' (Alan O'Day) – 3:17; 03 'The Hungry Years' (Howard Greenfield, Neil Sedaka) – 4:35; 04 'I Only Have Eyes for You' from *Dames* (Al Dubin, Harry Warren) – 3:33; 05 'Yellow Roses on Her Gown' (Michael Moore) – 4:33. B: 01 '(Do You Know Where You're Going To) Theme from Mahogany' from *Mahogany* (Gerry Goffin, Michael Masser) – 3:47; 02 'Ooh What We Do' (Harriet Schock) – 3:25; 03 'Send in the Clowns' from *A Little Night Music* (Stephen Sondheim) – 3:35; 04 'Every Time You Touch Me (I Get High)' (Charlie Rich, Billy Sherrill) – 2:52; 05 'When a Child Is Born' (Ciro Dammicco, Fred Jay) – 3:41.

Produced by Jack Gold. Arranged and conducted by Gene Page.

Recorded: June 16, 1975, January 20–21, 1976, February 23–March 5, 1976, March 12, 1976. Released: May 10, 1976.

1977
PC 34441 **Mathis Is...**

A: 01 'As Long As We're Together' (Anthony Bell, Thom Bell, Jo Dee Omer) – 4:59; 02 'Lullaby of Love' – 3:43; 03 'Loving You-Losing You' – 4:33; 04 'I'll Make You Happy' – 4:57. B: 01 'Heaven Must Have Made You Just for Me' – 4:09; 02 'Hung Up in the Middle of Love' (T. Bell, Sherman Marshall) – 4:22; 03 'World of Laughter' (T. Bell, Casey James) – 3:23; 04 'I Don't Want to Say No' – 5:16; 05 'Sweet Love of Mine' (Vinnie Barrett, Bobby Eli) – 3:47.

Produced by Thom Bell. Arranged and conducted by Thom Bell except Tony Bell Sr. – arranger ('I'll Make You Happy', 'Sweet Love of Mine').

Recorded: October 4–6, 1976. Released: February 21, 1977.

PC 34872 *Hold Me, Thrill Me, Kiss Me*

A: 01 'Hold Me, Thrill Me, Kiss Me' (Harry Noble) – 2:56; 02 'We're All Alone' (Boz Scaggs) – 3:22; 03 'All the Things You Are' from *Very Warm for May* (Oscar Hammerstein II, Jerome Kern) – 3:33; 04 'One' from *A Chorus Line* (Marvin Hamlisch, Edward Kleban) – 2:26; 05 'When I Need You' (Albert Hammond, Carole Bayer Sager) – 3:26. B: 01 'The Most Beautiful Girl' (Rory Michael Bourke, Billy Sherrill, Norris Wilson) – 2:30; 02 'Tomorrow' from *Annie* (Martin Charnin, Charles Strouse) – 2:29; 03 'Evergreen (Love Theme from A Star Is Born)' from *A Star Is Born* (Barbra Streisand, Paul Williams) – 3:15; 04 'I Always Knew I Had It in Me' from The Greatest (Gerry Goffin, Michael Masser) – 3:02; 05 'Don't Give Up on Us' (Tony Macaulay) – 3:57.

Produced by Jack Gold. Arranged and conducted by Gene Page.

Recorded: April 20, 1977, May 31, 1977, June 9, 1977, June 13, 1977. Released: August 15, 1977.

1978
JC 35259 **You Light Up My Life**

A: 01 'You Light Up My Life' from *You Light Up My Life* (Joe Brooks) – 3:55; 02 'Emotion' (Barry Gibb, Robin Gibb) duet with Deniece Williams – 3:16; 03 'All I Ever Need' (Jacques Sawyer) – 3:12; 04 'Where or When' from *Babes in Arms* (Lorenz Hart, Richard Rodgers) – 2:35; 05 'If You Believe' (a.k.a. 'Believe in Yourself' (reprise)) from *The Wiz* (Charlie Smalls) – 3:31. B: 01 'Too Much, Too Little, Too Late (Nat Kipner, John Vallins) duet with Deniece Williams – 2:59; 02 'How Deep Is Your Love' from *Saturday Night Fever* (Barry Gibb, Maurice Gibb, Robin Gibb) – 3:42; 03 'Till Love Touches Your Life' from *Madron* (Arthur Hamilton, Riz Ortolani) – 4:00; 04 'I Wrote a Symphony on My Guitar' (Arthur Hamilton, LeRoy Holmes) – 3:05; 05 'It Was Almost Like a Song' (Hal David, Archie Jordan) – 3:49.

Produced by Jack Gold. Arranged and conducted by Gene Page.

Recorded: December 19–21, 1977. Released: March 13, 1978. Album Gold

RIAA certified on May 2, 1978. Platinum on July 6, 1978. The single 'Too Much, Too Little, Too Late' with Deniece Williams Gold RIAA certified on May 2, 1978.

JC 35435 **That's What Friends Are For**

A: 01 'You're All I Need to Get By' (Nickolas Ashford, Valerie Simpson) duet with Deniece Williams – 2:40; 02 'Until You Come Back to Me (That's What I'm Gonna Do)' (Morris Broadnax, Clarence Paul, Stevie Wonder) duet with Deniece Williams – 3:39; 03 'You're a Special Part of My Life' (Lani Groves, Clarence McDonald, J.D. Williams) duet with Deniece Williams – 2:56; 04 'Ready or Not' (Amber DiLena, Jack Keller) duet with Deniece Williams – 2:50; 05 'Me for You, You for Me' (Fritz Baskett, Clarence McDonald) duet with Deniece Williams – 3:12. B: 01 'Your Precious Love'(Nickolas Ashford, Valerie Simpson) duet with Deniece Williams – 3:22; 02 'Just the Way You Are' (Billy Joel) duet with Deniece Williams – 3:43; 03 'That's What Friends Are For' (Fritz Baskett, Lani Groves, Clarence McDonald, Deniece Williams) duet with Deniece Williams – 3:27; 04 'I Just Can't Get Over You' (Nat Kipner, Winston Sela) duet with Deniece Williams – 4:11; 05 'Touching Me With Love' (Mel Besher, Corey Maass) duet with Deniece Williams – 2:30.

Produced by Jack Gold. Arranged and conducted by Gene Page except Glen Spreen – arranger ('That's What Friends Are For').

Recorded: April 20, 1978, April 26, 1978, April 28, 1978, May 5, 1978, May 12, 1978. Released: July 21, 1978. Gold RIAA certified on July 20, 1978.

1979

JC 35649 **The Best Days of My Life**

A: 01 'Would You Like to Spend the Night with Me' (L. Russell Brown, Irwin Levine) Greg Phillinganes: synthesizer solo – 3:02; 02 'As Time Goes By' (Herman Hupfeld) sax solo: Plas Johnson – 4:35; 03 'The Best Days of My Life' (Cheryl Christiansen, Arnold Goland, Jack Gold) – 3:30; 04 'Gone, Gone, Gone' (L. Russell Brown, Lisa Hayward) – 3:32; 05 'The Bottom Line' (Dennis Lambert, Brian Potter) Bill Green: sax solo – 3:56. B: 01 'The Last Time I Felt Like This' (Alan Bergman, Marilyn Bergman, Marvin Hamlisch) duet with Jane Olivor – 2:57 02 'Begin the Beguine' (Cole Porter) – 4:16 03 'How Can I Make It on My Own' (Terry Bradford, Nat Kipner) – 4:00 04 'There You Are' (Nancy Goland) Greg Phillinganes: synthesizer solo – 4:12 05 'We're in Love' (Patti Austin) – 3:45.

Produced by Jack Gold. Arranged and conducted by Gene Page.

Recorded: August 23, 1978, September 5, 1978, September 14, 1978, September 15, 1978, November 10, 1978. Released: January 29, 1979.

JC 36216 **Mathis Magic**

A: 01 'No One But the One You Love' (Cheryl Christiansen, Arnold Goland, Jack Gold) vocal harmony: Stephanie Lawrence – 3:14; 02 'Night and Day' from *Gay Divorce* (Cole Porter) Michael Boddicker: synthesizer, Eddie Bongo: congas – 5:03; 03 'Love' (Gerard Kenny, Drey Shepperd) – 3:48; 04 'My Body Keeps Changing My Mind' (Leslie Pearl) – 3:42; 05 'New York State of Mind' (Billy Joel) Oscar Brashear: flugelhorn, Paul Smith: piano – 5:18. B: 01 'She Believes in Me' (Steve Gibb) – 4:22; 02 'That Old Black Magic' (Harold Arlen, Johnny Mercer) Terry Harrington: tenor saxophone, Eddie Bongo: congas – 5:43; 03 'You Saved My Life' (Chris Arnold, Geoff Morrow) duet with Stephanie Lawrence – 2:50; 04 'To The Ends Of The Earth' (Joe Sherman, Noel Sherman) Michael Boddicker: synthesizer, Eddie Bongo: congas – 2:53; 05 'Heart, Soul, Body and Mind' (Ben Peters) – 4:10.

Produced by Jack Gold. Arranged and conducted by Gene Page.

Recorded: June 5, 1979, July 9, 1979, July 23, 1979, September 5, 1979. Released: September 17, 1979.

1980

JC 36505 **Different Kinda Different**

A: 01 'Different Kinda Different' (Marilyn McLeod, Pam Sawyer) duet with Paulette – 3:25; 02 'With You I'm Born Again' from *Fast Break* (Carol Connors, David Shire) – 4:03; 03 'I'll Do It All for You' (Roger Cook, Steve Davis) duet with Paulette, Gary Herbig: sax solo – 3:29; 04 'Never Givin' Up on You' (Steve Dorff, Jack Gold, Gary Harju, Larry Herbstritt) – 3:15; 05 'Deep Purple' (Peter DeRose, Mitchell Parish) Ernie Watts: sax solo – 3:31. B: 01 'I Will Survive' (Dino Fekaris, Freddie Perren) – 3:59; 02 'Paradise' (Teddy Randazzo) – 3:07; 03 'The Lights of Rio' (Arnold Goland, Jack Gold) Chris Bennett: carnival girl – 3:50; 04 'Love Without Words' (Sammy Cahn, John Lewis Parker) – 3:32; 05 'Temptation' from *Going Hollywood* (Nacio Herb Brown, Arthur Freed) – 3:14.

Produced by Jack Gold. Arranged and conducted by Gene Page.

Recorded: July 18, 1979, February 28, 1980, March 5, 1980, April 7, 1980. Released: June 16, 1980.

1981

CANCELLED FC 37383 **I Love My Lady**

A: 01 'Fall in Love (I Want to)' – 6:00; 02 'It's Alright to Love Me' – 4:20 03 'Something to Sing About' – 4:13; 04 'I Love My Lady' – 5:26. B: 01 'Take Me' – 6:50; 02 'Judy' – 3:11; 03 'Stay with Me' – 3:38; 04 'Love and Be Loved' – 4:54.

Produced by Bernard Edwards and Nile Rodgers. Arranged and conducted by Nile Rodgers. All songs written by Bernard Edwards and Nile Rodgers.

Recorded: December 23, 1980, December 31, 1980, January 6, 1981, January 7, 1981, January 21, 1981, January 27, 1981, February 17, 1981, February 18, 1981.

Scheduled to be released: September, 1981, cancelled. Released for the first time on December 8, 2017 in the box set *The Voice of Romance: The Columbia Original Album Collection.*

1982
FC 37748 **Friends in Love**

01 'Got You Where I Want You' (Jim Andron, Candy Parton) duet with Dionne Warwick – 3:43; 02 'I Remember You and Me' (Jim Andron, Candy Parton) – 3:46; 03 'When the Lovin' Goes Out of the Lovin'' (Richard Parker, Bobby Whiteside) – 4:19 04 'Somethin's Goin' On' (Norman Sallitt) – 3:21; 05 'What Do You Do with the Love' (Richard Kerr, Candy Parton) – 3:28 06 'Friends in Love' (Bill Champlin, David Foster, Jay Graydon) duet with Dionne Warwick – 4:03; 07 'What's Forever For' (Rafe Van Hoy) – 3:22; 08 'Warm' (David Buskin) – 4:39; 09 'Memory' from *Cats* (T. S. Eliot, Trevor Nunn, Andrew Lloyd Webber) – 3:00; 10 'Lately' (Stevie Wonder) – 4:05.

Produced by Jack Gold except Jay Graydon – producer ('Got You Where I Want You,' 'Friends in Love'). Barry Fasman – producer and Charles Koppelman – executive producer ('When the Lovin' Goes Out of the Lovin''). Arranged and conducted by Gene Page except Jay Graydon – arranger, conductor ('Got You Where I Want You,' 'Friends in Love'). Artie Butler – arranger, conductor ('I Remember You and Me'). Barry Fasman – rhythm and strings arranger ('When the Lovin' Goes Out of the Lovin''). Arnold Goland – arranger, conductor ('Somethin' Goin' On').

Recorded: July 10, 1981, September 2, 1981, October 21, 1981, November 3, 1981, January 1982. Released: April 5, 1982.

1983
10042 **Unforgettable: A Musical Tribute to Nat King Cole**

01 'Unforgettable' (instrumental)/'Sweet Lorraine' (Irving Gordon/Cliff Burwell, Mitchell Parish) – 3:12; 02 'Nature Boy' (Eden Ahbez) – 3:27; 03 'Orange Colored Sky' (Milton DeLugg, Willie Stein) – 2:11; 04 'Too Young' (Sylvia Dee, Sidney Lippman) – 3:19; 05 Medley – 5:50 a. 'Route 66' (Bobby Troup) b. '(I Love You) For Sentimental Reasons' (Ivory 'Deek' Watson, William Best) c. 'Red Sails in the Sunset' (Hugh Williams, Jimmy Kennedy) d. 'Walkin' My Baby Back Home' (Fred E. Ahlert, Roy Turk) e. 'It's Only a Paper Moon' (Harold Arlen, E. Y. Harburg, Billy Rose); 06 'Stardust' (Hoagy Carmichael, Mitchell Parish) – 3:24; 07 'Unforgettable' (instrumental) (Irving Gordon) – 0:12; 08 Medley (solo performance by Natalie Cole) – 6:20 a. 'Straighten Up and Fly Right' (Nat King Cole, Irving Mills) b. 'Mona Lisa' (Ray Evans, Jay Livingston) c. 'L-O-V-E' (Milt Gabler, Bert Kaempfert) d. 'Dance, Ballerina, Dance' a.k.a. 'Ballerina' (Bob Russell, Carl Sigman) e. 'Ramblin' Rose' (Joe Sherman, Noel Sherman) f. 'The Christmas Song' (Bob Wells, Mel Torme);

09 'To the Ends of the Earth' (Joe Sherman, Noel Sherman) – 3:27; 10 'That Sunday, That Summer' (Joe Sherman, George David Weiss) – 3:22; 11 Medley (performed with Natalie Cole) – 5:42 a. 'Let There Be Love' (Ian Grant, Lionel Rand) b. 'When I Fall in Love' (Edward Heyman, Victor Young); 12 'Unforgettable' (Irving Gordon) – 4:05.

Produced by BBC. Arranged by Ronnie Hazlehurst except Allyn Ferguson – arranger ('Orange Colored Sky,' 'Unforgettable'). Neil Richardson – arranger ('Nature Boy, Medley a. 'Let There Be Love' b. 'When I Fall in Love'). D'Arneill Pershing – arranger ('To the Ends of the Earth,' Too Young'). Brian Rogers – arranger ('Stardust.' Original arrangement by Gordon Jenkins). Joe Guercio – arranger (a. 'Straighten Up and Fly Right' b. 'Mona Lisa' c. 'L-O-V-E' d. 'Dance, Ballerina, Dance' a.k.a. 'Ballerina' e. 'Ramblin' Rose' f. 'The Christmas Song'). Jim Ganduglia – musical director.
Recorded: May 20, 1983. Released: 1983 in the UK.

1984
FC 38718 A Special Part of Me

01 'Simple' (Marvin Morrow, Keith Stegall) – 3:43; 02 'Love Won't Let Me Wait' (Vinnie Barrett, Bobby Eli) duet with Deniece Williams – 4:16; 03 'The Best Is Yet to Come' (Alan Roy Scott, Brian Short) – 4:14; 04 'Lead Me to Your Love' (Michel Colombier, Kathy Wakefield) – 4:21; 05 'You're a Special Part of Me' (Angela Bofill, Loree Gold) duet with Angela Bofill – 4:13; 06 'Love Never Felt So Good' (Paul Anka, Michael Jackson, Kathy Wakefield) – 4:20; 07 'Priceless' (Leon Ware) – 4:05; 08 'One Love' (Eric Kaz, Wendy Waldman) – 3:58; 09 'Right Here and Now' (Barry Mann, Cynthia Weil) – 3:27.

Produced by Denny Diante. Arrangements by Michel Colombier except Jerry Hey – horn arrangements ('Simple,' 'Love Never Felt So Good,' 'Right Here and Now').
Recorded: March 9, 1983, April 13, 1983, August 16, 1983, August 22, 1983. Released: January 22, 1984.

FC 38699 Johnny Mathis Live

01 'I Believe in Love' (Alan Bergman, Marilyn Bergman, Kenny Loggins) – 3:31; 02 'Misty' (Johnny Burke, Erroll Garner) – 3:07; 03 'Begin the Beguine' (Cole Porter) – 3:47; 04 'Fly Away' (Peter Allen, David Foster, Carole Bayer Sager) – 3:46; 05 'A Certain Smile' (Sammy Fain, Paul Francis Webster) – 3:44; 06 'Memory' (T. S. Eliot, Trevor Nunn, Andrew Lloyd Webber) – 3:00; 07 'The Twelfth of Never' (Jerry Livingston, Paul Francis Webster) – 3:06; 08 'Try to Win a Friend' (Larry Gatlin) – 3:30; 09 '99 Miles from L.A.' (Hal David, Albert Hammond) – 3:35; 10 'Chances Are' (Robert Allen, Al Stillman) – 3:10; 11 'Orange Colored Sky' (Milton DeLugg, Willie Stein) – 3:09; 12 'When a Child Is Born' (Ciro Dammicco, Fred Jay) – 3:41.

Produced by Denny Diante. Jim Barnett – arranger ('I Believe in Love'). Jim Barnett and Gene Page – arrangers ('When a Child Is Born'). Glenn Osser – arranger ('Misty'). Gene Page and Victor Vanacore – arrangers ('Begin the Beguine'). Larry Steelman – arranger ('Fly Away,' 'A Certain Smile'). Gene Page and Larry Steelman – arrangers ('Memory'). Gil Reigers – arranger ('Try to Win a Friend'). Michel Colombier and Gil Reigers – arrangers ('The Twelfth of Never,' '99 Miles from L.A.'). Ray Conniff – arranger ('Chances Are'). Allyn Ferguson – arranger ('Orange Colored Sky').
Recorded: May 12-14, 1983, August 22, 1983, July 1984. Released: October 15, 1984.

1985
FC 39601 **Right from the Heart**
01 'Touch by Touch' (Brent Mason, Keith Stegall) – 4:21; 02 'Love Shock' (Michel Colombier, Denny Diante, Kathy Wakefield) – 4:19; 03 'Just One Touch' (Robbie Buchanan, Diane Warren) – 4:02; 04 'Hooked on Goodbye' (Colombier, Diante, Wakefield) – 4:02; 05 'I Need You (The Journey)' (Colombier, Wakefield) – 5:09; 06 'Step by Step' (Brian Fairweather, Wakefield) – 4:34; 07 'Right from the Heart' from *Ryan's Hope* (Earl Rose, Wakefield) – 4:25; 08 'Falling in Love' (Douglas Getschal, John Robinson) – 4:28; 09 'Here We Go Again' (Dave DeLuca, Marvin Morrow) – 4:04; 10 'Hold On' (Colombier, Diante, Wakefield) – 4:31.
Produced by Denny Diante. Arranged by Michel Colombier except Robbie Buchanan – arranger ('Just One Touch'). Brian Fairweather – arranger ('Step by Step'). Douglas Getschal – arranger ('Falling in Love'). John Robinson – arranger ('Falling in Love'). Sidney Weiss – concertmaster.
Recorded: June 29, 1984, July 19, 1984, July 27, 1984 – 'Falling in Love', August 14, 1984, October 24, 1984, December 6, 1984, January 3, 1985, February 8, 1985. Released: March 18, 1985.

1986
FC 40447 **Christmas Eve with Johnny Mathis**
01 'It's Beginning to Look a Lot Like Christmas' (Meredith Willson) – 2:14; 02 'Toyland' from *Babes in Toyland* (Glen MacDonough, Victor Herbert) – 3:41; 03 'It's the Most Wonderful Time of the Year' (Edward Pola, George Wyle) – 2:45; 04 'Jingle Bells' (James Pierpont) – 2:54; 05 Medley – 5:09 a. 'Christmas Is for Everyone' (Richard Loring, Dorothy Wayne) b. 'Where Can I Find Christmas?' *from The Bear Who Slept Through Christmas* (Doug Goodwin) 06 Medley from *Santa Claus: The Movie* – 4:03 a. 'Every Christmas Eve' (Leslie Bricusse, Henry Mancini) b. 'Giving (Santa's Theme)' (Bricusse, Mancini); 07 'The Christmas Waltz' (Sammy Cahn, Jule Styne) – 2:36; 08 'We Need a Little Christmas' from *Mame* (Jerry Herman) – 1:54; 09 Medley – 3:44 a. 'Caroling,

Caroling' (Alfred Burt, Wilha Hutson) b. 'Happy Holiday' from *Holiday Inn* (Irving Berlin);
10 'It's Christmas Time Again' (Sonny Burke, John Elliot, James K. Harwood) – 4:28.
Produced by Denny Diante. Arranged and conducted by Ray Ellis except Jeremy
Lubbock – arranger, conductor ('It's Beginning to Look a Lot Like Christmas,' 'It's the
Most Wonderful Time of the Year,' 'It's Christmas Time Again,' Medley a. 'Caroling,
Caroling' b. 'Happy Holiday'). Henry Mancini – arranger, conductor (Medley
a. 'Every Christmas Eve' b. 'Giving (Santa's Theme)'). Recorded: July 1986.
Released: September 23, 1986.

FC 40372 **The Hollywood Musicals**
01 'You Stepped Out of a Dream' from *Ziegfeld Girl* (1941) (Nacio Herb Brown, Gus
Kahn) – 3:30; 02 'Taking a Chance on Love' from *Cabin in the Sky* (1943) (Vernon
Duke, Ted Fetter, John LaTouche) Henry Mancini: piano solo – 3:00; 03 'When You
Wish Upon a Star' from *Pinocchio* (1940) (Leigh Harline, Ned Washington) – 3:40;
04 'True Love' from *High Society* (1956) (Cole Porter) – 3:06; 05 'Whistling Away the
Dark' from *Darling Lili* (1970) (Henry Mancini, Johnny Mercer) – 3:19; 06 'Time After
Time' from *It Happened in Brooklyn* (1947) (Sammy Cahn, Jule Styne) – 3:27; 07
'It Might as Well Be Spring' from *State Fair* (1945) (Oscar Hammerstein II, Richard
Rodgers) Henry Mancini: piano solo – 4:34; 08 'I Had the Craziest Dream' from
Springtime in the Rockies (1942) (Mack Gordon, Harry Warren) – 3:05; 09 'Long Ago
(and Far Away)' from *Cover Girl* (1944) (Ira Gershwin, Jerome Kern) – 4:00; 10 'Crazy
World' from *Victor Victoria* (1982) (Leslie Bricusse, Henry Mancini) – 3:00; 11 Johnny
Burke/Jimmy Van Heusen Medley – 7:05 a. 'Moonlight Becomes You' from *Road to
Morocco* (1942) b. 'It Could Happen to You' from *And the Angels Sing* (1944) c. 'But
Beautiful' from *Road to Rio* (1947).
Produced by Denny Diante. Arranged and conducted by Henry Mancini.
Recorded: April 6, 1986. Released: October 17, 1986.

1988
CK 44156 **Once in a While**
01 'I'm on the Outside Looking In' (Teddy Randazzo, Bobby Weinstein) – 3:24;
02 'It Wouldn't Have Made Any Difference' (Todd Rundgren) – 4:01; 03 'Two Strong
Hearts' (Andy Hill, Bruce Woolley) duet with Dionne Warwick – 4:00; 04 'Once in
a While' (Michael Edwards, Bud Green) – 3:28; 05 'Fallen' (Lauren Wood) – 3:33;
06 'Daydreamin'' (Noel Closson, Preston Glass, Larry Graham) – 4:30; 07 'From a
Whisper to a Scream' (Steven Birch, Glass) – 4:25; 08 'Ain't No Woman (Like the
One I've Got)' (Dennis Lambert, Brian Potter) – 4:08; 09 'Just Like You' (Jeff Pescetto)
– 3:50; 10 'Love Brought Us Here Tonight' (Stephen Geyer, Allan Rich, Smokey
Robinson) – 4:04.

Executive Producer: Jay Landers. Produced by Preston Glass, Robert Kraft and Peter Bunetta & Rick Chudacoff. Arranged by Preston Glass.
Recorded: December 1987-March 1988. Released: May 23, 1988.

1989
CK 44336 In the Still of the Night

01 'In the Still of the Night' (Fred Parris) featuring Take 6 – 2:38; 02 'It's All in the Game' (Charles Dawes, Carl Sigman) featuring Take 6 – 2:33; 03 'Since I Fell for You (Buddy Johnson) – 3:09; 04 'You Belong to Me' (Pee Wee King, Chilton Price, Redd Stewart) – 3:40; 05 'True Love Ways' (Buddy Holly, Norman Petty) – 2:58; 06 'Since I Don't Have You' (James Beaumont, Walter Lester, Joseph Rock, John Taylor, Joseph Verscharen, Janet Vogel) – 2:39; 07 'Then You Can Tell Me Goodbye' (John D. Loudermilk) – 4:37; 08 'The End of the World' (Sylvia Dee, Arthur Kent) – 3:07; 09 'All Alone Am I' (Arthur Altman, Manos Hadjidakis) – 3:24; 10 'For Your Love' (Ed Townsend) – 3:37.
Executive Producer: Jay Landers. Produced by Peter Bunetta & Rick Chudacoff. Arranged by Cedric Dent and Mervyn Warren.
Recorded: May–November 1988. Released: August 8, 1989.

CANCELLED The Island

01 'The Island' (Alan and Marilyn Bergman, Ivan Lins, Vítor Martins) – 4:00; 02 'Who's in Love Here' (Lins, Martins, Brenda Russell) – 4:24; 03 'Like a Lover' (A. Bergman, M. Bergman, Dori Caymmi, Nelson Motta) – 4:01; 04 'So Many Stars' (A. Bergman, M. Bergman, Sergio Mendes) – 4:02; 05 'Photograph' (Caymmi, Paulo César Pinheiro, Tracy Mann) – 4:35; 06 'Who's Counting Heartaches' (Ina Wolf, Peter Wolf) duet with Dionne Warwick – 4:20; 07 'Your Smile' (Caymmi, Pinheiro, I. Wolf) – 4:26; 08 'Wanting More' (Fernando Leporace, Mann) – 3:23; 09 'We Can Try Love Again' (Caymmi, Mann) – 4:32; 10 'Flower of Bahia' (Caymmi, Mann, Pinheiro) – 4:11.
Executive Producer: Jay Landers. Produced by Sergio Mendes. Arranged by Dori Caymmi except Robbie Buchanan – arranger ('Who's in Love Here,' 'Who's Counting Heartaches,' 'Your Smile,' 'Wanting More').
Recorded: April 19, 1989, August 17, 1989, August 18, 1989, August 21, 1989, August 30, 1989, September 11, 1989. Released for the first time on December 8, 2017 in the box set *The Voice of Romance: The Columbia Original Album Collection*.

1990
CK 46069 In a Sentimental Mood: Mathis Sings Ellington

01 'Overture – A Musical Tribute to Duke Ellington' (Byron Olson) Fred Hersch; piano solo – 2:16; 02 'Lush Life' (Billy Strayhorn) – 4:15; 03 Medley a. 'Don't You

Know I Care (Don't You Care I Know)' (Mack David, D. Ellington) b. 'I Didn't Know About You' (D. Ellington, Bob Russell) – 4:47; 04 'Things Ain't What They Used to Be' (instrumental) (Mercer Ellington, Ted Persons) – 1:17; 05 'In a Sentimental Mood' (D. Ellington, Manny Kurtz, Irving Mills) Fred Hersch: piano solo – 4:05; 06 'What Am I Here For' (D. Ellington, Frankie Lane) Bill Berry: trumpet solo – 4:22; 07 'I Got It Bad (and That Ain't Good)' (instrumental) (D. Ellington, Paul Francis Webster) – 1:43; 08 'Something to Live For' (D. Ellington, Billy Strayhorn) Ronny Ross: baritone saxophone solo – 3:37; 09 'Solitude' (Eddie DeLange, D. Ellington, Irving Mills) – 3:40; 10 'Perdido' (instrumental) (Ervin Drake, Hans Lengsfelder, Juan Tizol) – 1:05; 11 'Prelude to a Kiss' (D. Ellington, Irving Gordon, Irving Mills) – 2:52; 12'In a Mellow Tone' (D. Ellington, Milt Gabler) – 3:19; 13 'Don't Get Around Much Anymore' (D. Ellington, Bob Russell) – 3:16; 14 'Satin Doll' (instrumental) (D. Ellington) – 1:07; 15 'Come Sunday' (D. Ellington) – 3:24; 16 'Do Nothing till You Hear from Me' (D. Ellington, Bob Russell) Bill Berry: trumpet solo – 4:39; 17 'Caravan' (instrumental) (D. Ellington, Irving Mills, Juan Tizol) – 0:54; 18 'Day Dream' (D. Ellington, John LaTouche, Billy Strayhorn) – 3:26.

Executive Producer: Jay Landers. Produced by Mike Berniker. Arranged by Brad Dechter except Byron Olson – arranger ('Overture – A Musical Tribute to Duke Ellington,' 'Lush Life,' 'In a Sentimental Mood,' 'I Got It Bad (and That Ain't Good),' 'Something to Live For,' 'Solitude,' 'Caravan,' 'Day Dream'). Harry Rabinowitz – conductor.

Recorded: February–June 1990. Released: October 9, 1990.

1991
CK 47982 **Better Together: The Duet Album**

01 'Better Together' performed with Regina Belle (Randy Bowland) duet with Regina Belle – 4:37; 02 'You Brought Me Love' (Andy Goldmark) duet with Patti Austin – 4:07; 03 'Too Much, Too Little, Too Late' (Nat Kipner, John Vallins) duet with Deniece Williams – 2:59; 04 'It's All in the Game' (Charles Dawes, Carl Sigman) performed with Take 6 – 2:33; 05 'Love Won't Let Me Wait' (Vinnie Barrett, Bobby Eli) duet with Deniece Williams – 4:16; 06 'You're a Special Part of Me' (Angela Bofill, Loree Gold) duet with Angela Bofill – 4:13; 07 'The Last Time I Felt Like This' (Alan and Marilyn Bergman, Marvin Hamlisch) duet with Jane Olivor – 2:57; 08 'Friends in Love' (Bill Champlin, David Foster, Jay Graydon) duet with Dionne Warwick – 4:03; 09 'In the Still of the Night' (Fred Parris) performed with Take 6 – 2:38; 10 'You're All I Need to Get By' (Nickolas Ashford, Valerie Simpson) duet with Deniece Williams – 2:40; 11 Who's Counting Heartaches' (Ina Wolf, Peter Wolf) duet with Dionne Warwick – 4:20.

Executive Producer: Jay Landers. Produced by Nick Martinelli, Thom Bell, Jack

Gold, Peter Bunetta & Rick Chudacoff, Denny Diante, Jay Graydon and Sergio Mendes. Nick Martinelli and Randy Bowland – arrangers ('Better Together'). Thom Bell – arranger ('You Brought Me Love').
Recorded: 1977–1991. Released: October 10, 1991.

1993
CK 53204 **How Do You Keep the Music Playing? The Songs of Michel Legrand and Alan & Marilyn Bergman**
01 'How Do You Keep the Music Playing?' from *Best Friends* (Introduction) – 1:26; 02 'The Summer Knows' from *Summer of '42* – 4:19; 03 'Something New in My Life' from *Micki & Maude* – 4:10; 04 'What Are You Doing the Rest of Your Life?' from *The Happy Ending* – 5:58; 05 'The Way She Makes Me Feel' from *Yentl* – 4:01; 06 'I Was Born in Love with You' from *Wuthering Heights* (1970) – 4:45; 07 'On My Way to You' – 5:01; 08 'After the Rain' – 4:08; 09 'The Windmills of Your Mind' from *The Thomas Crown Affair* – 4:30; 10 'Summer Me, Winter Me' – 3:38; 11'How Do You Keep the Music Playing?' from *Best Friends* – 4:42.
Executive Producer: Jay Landers. Produced by Michel Legrand and Alan & Marilyn Bergman. Arranged and conducted by Michel Legrand.
Recorded: October 1992-February 1993. Released: May 4, 1993.

1996
CK 67509 **All About Love**
01 'Let Your Heart Remember' (Stephen Bishop, Jeff Jones) – 4:36; 02 'I Will Walk Away' (Gerry Goffin, Carole King) – 3:59; 03 'Every Beat of My Heart' (Earl Rose, Brian McKnight) – 3:58; 04 'Why Goodbye' (Diane Warren) – 4:50; 05 'Like No One in the World' (Burt Bacharach, John Bettis) – 4:31; 06 'One More Night' (Stephen Bishop) – 3:26; 07 'Let Me Be the One' (Burt Bacharach, Denise Rich, Taja Sevelle) – 5:00; 08 'Welcome Home' (Ray Chafin, Dobie Gray, Bud Reneau) – 3:20; 09 'Sometimes Love's Not Enough' (Kenny Denton, Danny Saxon) – 4:37; 10 'Could It Be Love This Time' (Mark Radice) – 3:18.
Produced by Phil Ramone. Arranged by Mark Portmann.
Recorded: 1996. Released: May 7, 1996.

1998
CK 68893 **Because You Loved Me: The Songs of Diane Warren**
01 'Un-Break My Heart' – 5:01; 02 'Love Will Lead You Back' – 5:09; 03'Don't Take Away My Heaven' – 4:38; 04 'If You Asked Me To' – 4:13; 05 'By the Time This Night Is Over' (Michael Bolton, Andy Goldmark, Warren) – 4:39; 06 'Because You Loved Me' – 4:37; 07 'All I Want Is Forever' – 4:28; 08 'Set the Night to Music' – 5:10;

09 'Live for Loving You' (Emilio Estefan Jr., Gloria Estefan, Warren) – 5:39; 10 'Missing You Now' (Walter Afanasieff, Michael Bolton, Warren) – 4:24. Produced by Humberto Gatica. Arranged by Lester Mendez except Danny Luchansky – arrangement ('Missing You Now,' 'Set the Night to Music'). David Foster – arrangement ('Because You Loved Me'). Tony Smith – arrangement ('By the Time This Night Is Over,' 'Love Will Lead You Back'). Rick Hunt – arrangement ('Un-Break My Heart'). All songs by Diane Warren except where otherwise indicated. Recorded: 1998. Released: October 20, 1998.

2000
CK 63897 **Mathis on Broadway**

01 'On Broadway' from *Smokey Joe's Cafe* (Barry Mann, Cynthia Weil, Jerry Leiber, Mike Stoller) – 3:24; 02 'Life Is Just a Bowl of Cherries' from *Fosse* (featuring Forever Plaid) (Lew Brown, Ray Henderson) – 2:46; 03 'Loving You' from *Passion* (Stephen Sondheim) – 4:38; 04 'They Live in You' from *The Lion King* (Lebo M., Mark Mancina, Jay Rifkin) – 4:13; 05 'Bring Him Home' from *Les Misérables* (Alain Boublil, Herbert Kretzmer, Claude-Michel Schönberg) – 3:23; 06 Medley (featuring Betty Buckley) a. 'Children Will Listen' from *Into the Woods* (Stephen Sondheim) b. 'Our Children' from *Ragtime* (Lynn Ahrens, Stephen Flaherty) – 5:45 07 'All I Ask of You' from *The Phantom of the Opera* (Charles Hart, Andrew Lloyd Webber, Richard Stilgoe) – 4:15; 08 'Once Upon a Dream' from *Jekyll & Hyde* (Leslie Bricusse, Steve Cuden, Frank Wildhorn) – 5:10; 09 'Seasons of Love' from *Rent* (featuring Nell Carter) (Jonathan Larson) – 4:08.

Executive Producer: Jay Landers. Produced by Richard Jay-Alexander with William Ross, Randy Waldman, Jorge Calandrelli and Jonathan Tunick. Arranged and conducted by William Ross except Megan Cavallari – arranger ('Once Upon a Dream'). Jorge Calandrelli – arranger, conductor ('Life Is Just a Bowl of Cherries'). Jonathan Tunick – arranger, conductor ('Loving You'). Randy Waldman – arranger Lebo M. – choir arranger and conductor ('They Live in You'). Randy Waldman – arranger Megan Cavallari – choir arranger and conductor ('Seasons of Love'). Recorded: 2000. Released: April 25, 2000.

2002
CK 86814 **The Christmas Album**

01 'Joy To The World' (Lowell Mason, Isaac Watts) – 2:01; 02 'Heavenly Peace' (Dean Pitchford, Tom Snow) – 3:30; 03 'Away in a Manger' (William J. Kirkpatrick) – 2:30; 04 'A Christmas Love Song' (Alan and Marilyn Bergman, Johnny Mandel) – 3:35; 05 'Frosty the Snowman' (Steve Nelson, Jack Rollins) – 2:31; 06 'Have a Holly Jolly Christmas' (Johnny Marks) – 2:00; 07 'O Little Town of Bethlehem' (Phillip Brooks,

Lewis H. Redner) – 2:44; 08 'I've Got My Love to Keep Me Warm' (Irving Berlin) – 3:34 09 Medley a. 'Snowfall' (Claude Thornhill) b. 'Christmas Time Is Here' (Vince Guaraldi, Lee Mendelson) – 5:00; 10 'Merry Christmas' (Fred Spielman, Janice Torre) – 3:12.

Executive Producer: Jay Landers. Produced by Robbie Buchanan. Arranged by Bob Krogstad except Robbie Buchanan – arranger ('Heavenly Peace,' 'Away in a Manger'). Alan Broadbent – arranger ('A Christmas Love Song'). Ray Ellis – arranger ('Have a Holly Jolly Christmas'). Jonathan Tunick – arranger ('O Little Town of Bethlehem,' 'Merry Christmas').

Recorded: 2002. Released: October 15, 2002.

2005
CK 86029 **Isn't It Romantic: The Standards Album**

01 'Isn't It Romantic?' (Lorenz Hart, Richard Rodgers) – 3:45; 02 'Love Is Here to Stay' (George Gershwin, Ira Gershwin) – 4:41; 03 'Day by Day' (Sammy Cahn, Axel Stordahl, Paul Weston) – 2:41; 04 'Dindi' (Ray Gilbert, Antonio Carlos Jobim, Aloysio de Oliveira) – 4:10; 05 'There's a Kind of Hush' (Les Reed, Geoff Stephens) – 4:13; 06 'This Can't Be Love' (Lorenz Hart, Richard Rodgers) – 2:53; 07 'Cottage for Sale' (Larry Conley, Willard Robison) – 5:15; 08 'Almost Like Being in Love' (Alan Jay Lerner, Frederick Loewe) – 3:39; 09 'The Rainbow Connection' (Kenny Ascher, Paul Williams) – 3:41; 10 'Over the Rainbow' (Harold Arlen, E.Y. Harburg) duet with Ray Charles – 4:52.

Executive Producer: Jay Landers. Produced by Jorge Calandrelli except John Burk, Terry Howard, Herbert Walt – producers ('Over the Rainbow'). Arranged and conducted by Jorge Calandrelli.

Recorded: 2004. Released: February 1, 2005.

2008
88697 10038-2 **A Night to Remember**

01 'Just the Two of Us' (Ralph MacDonald, William Salter, Bill Withers) Kenny G: saxophone – 4:07; 02 'You Make Me Feel Brand New' (Thom Bell, Linda Creed) duet with Yolanda Adams – 5:12; 03 'Walk on By' (Burt Bacharach, Hal David) – 3:03; 04 'Hey Girl' (Gerry Goffin, Carole King) – 4:33; 05 'The Closer I Get to You' (Reggie Lucas, James Mtume) – 4:43; 06 'Where Is the Love' (Ralph MacDonald, William Salter) – 3:22; 07 'All This Love' (El DeBarge) – 5:20; 08 'Always' (David Lewis, Jonathan Lewis, Wayne Lewis) duet with Mone't – 4:10; 09 'We're in This Love Together' (Roger Murrah, Keith Stegall) Dave Koz: saxophone – 3:39; 10 'How 'Bout Us' (Dana Walden) – 4:29; 11 'Always and Forever' (Rod Temperton) – 4:25; 12 'A Night to Remember' (Walter Afanasieff, Jay Landers) duet with Gladys Knight – 4:13.

Executive Producer: Jay Landers. Produced by Walter Afanasieff. Arranged by Walter Afanasieff.
Recorded: 2008. Released: April 29, 2008.

2010
88967 56314-2 Let It Be Me: Mathis in Nashville
01 'What a Wonderful World' (Bob Thiele, George David Weiss) duet with Lane Brody – 4:04; 02 'Let It Be Me' (Gilbert Bécaud, Mann Curtis) duet with Alison Krauss – 3:29; 03 'Make the World Go Away' (Hank Cochran) – 3:17; 04 'Crazy' (Willie Nelson) – 3:27; 05 'Southern Nights' (Allen Toussaint) – 3:33; 06 'You Don't Know Me' (Cindy Walker, Eddy Arnold) – 3:30; 07 'Lovin' Arms' (Tom Jans) Vince Gill: harmony vocal – 3:06; 08 'Shenandoah' (traditional) – 4:35; 09 'We Must Be Lovin' Right' (Clay Blaker, Roger Brown) – 3:32; 10 'I Can't Stop Loving You' (Don Gibson) – 3:12; 11 'Love Me Tender' (adaptation of Civil War song 'Aura Lee' by Ken Darby, who published it under the pseudonym 'Vera Matson', the name of his wife) – 3:37; 12 'Please Help Me, I'm Falling' (Hal Blair, Don Robertson) – 2:55; 13 'What a Wonderful World' (Christmas Version) (Bob Thiele, George David Weiss) duet with Lane Brody – 4:31
Executive Producer: Jay Landers. Produced by Fred Mollin. Arranged and conducted by Matthew McCauley.
Recorded: 2010. Released: September 21, 2010.

2013
88883 77205-2 Sending You a Little Christmas
01 'The Christmas Song (Chestnuts Roasting on an Open Fire) (Mel Tormé, Robert Wells) duet with Billy Joel – 3:56; 02 'Have Yourself a Merry Little Christmas' (Ralph Blane, Hugh Martin) duet with Natalie Cole – 3:41; 03 'This Christmas' (Donny Hathaway, Nadine McKinnor) – 4:05; 04 'Sending You a Little Christmas' (James Brickman, William Mann, Victoria Shaw) Jim Brickman: piano – 3:53; 05 'Mary's Boy Child' (Jester Hairston) – duet with Gloria Estefan 3:09; 06 'This Is a Time for Love' (Dobie Gray, Bud Reneau) – 4:03; 07 'Do You Hear What I Hear?' (Gloria Shayne Baker, Noël Regney) duet with Susan Boyle – 3:52; 08 'Home for the Holidays (Robert Allen, Al Stillman) performed with The Jordanaires– 3:07; 09 'Merry Christmas Darling' (Richard Carpenter, Frank Pooler) – 3:13; 10 'Decorate the Night' (Ray Chafin, Dobie Gray, Bud Reneau) – 3:33; 11 Medley a. 'I'll Be Home for Christmas' (Kim Gannon, Walter Kent, Buck Ram) b. 'White Christmas' (Irving Berlin) performed with Vince Gill and Amy Grant – 3:36; 12 'Count Your Blessings (Instead of Sheep)' (Irving Berlin) – 3:25.
Produced by Fred Mollin. Arranged by Gordon Goodwin. Conducted by Gordon Goodwin, Scott Lavender and Matthew McCauley.
Recorded: 2013. Released: October 29, 2013.

2017
88985 44249-2 **Johnny Mathis Sings the Great New American Songbook**

01 'Hallelujah' (Leonard Cohen) – 5:30; 02 'Once Before I Go' (Peter Allen, Dean Pitchford) – 3:49; 03 'Blue Ain't Your Color' (Steven Lee Olsen, Hillary Lindsey, Clint Lagerberg) – 3:44; 04 'You Raise Me Up' (Brendan Graham, Rolf Løvland) – 4:01; 05 'Say Something' (Ian Axel, Chad King, Mike Campbell) – 3:15; 06 'Just the Way You Are' (Philip Lawrence, Ari Levine, Bruno Mars, Khari Cain, Saint Cassius) – 3:27; 07 'I Believe I Can Fly' (R. Kelly) – 4:47; 08 'Remember When' (Alan Jackson) – 3:55; 09 'Happy' (Pharrell Williams) – 3:25; 10 'Hello' (Adele Adkins, Greg Kurstin) – 5:17; 11 'Run to You' (Allan Rich, Jud Friedman) – 4:29.

Executive Producer: Clive Davis. Produced by Kenneth 'Babyface' Edmonds. William Ross – all string arrangements except Demonte Posey – string arrangements ('Hello,' 'Remember When'). Chloé Flower – piano arrangement ('You Raise Me Up'). Recorded: 2017. Released: September 29, 2017.

Appendix Two: A Listener's Guide to Johnny Mathis

I. Box Sets

It's possible to acquire virtually all of Johnny Mathis's records by investing in a series of box sets. The consistently high quality and variety of the music make it a worthwhile investment, although box sets never come cheap.

The ultimate Mathis box set is *The Voice of Romance: The Columbia Original Album Collection* (Columbia Records, 2017). It includes 68 discs that cover Mathis's work for Columbia, excluding the singles. 62 albums have been remastered and the lost albums *I Love My Lady* and *The Island* are also included, along with a double disc of rarities. There's also a hand-signed certificate and a 200-page book with photos and an essay by James Ritz. The only problem is the lack of original liner notes to some of the albums and the discography is also flawed.

The non-album Columbia singles have been gathered on the decidedly more modest 4-CD box *Johnny Mathis: The Singles* (Columbia Records, 2015). It's a good choice for the beginner who wants to experience the evolution of Mathis's music without taking the deep plunge into the Columbia album collection. The booklet includes notes by Mathis.

Mathis also penned the notes for *The Complete Global Albums Collection* (Sony Music Entertainment Legacy Recordings, 2014). It's a 13-CD collection that includes all his Global albums plus singles and rarities. Although the singles don't reach the commercial and artistic heights of the Columbia counterpart, the albums underline that Mathis always delivered musically at Global and the aborted *Broadway* album project, which is also included, deserves the same status as his lost albums on Columbia: *The Island* and *I Love My Lady*.

There's also a box set available that gathers Mathis's Christmas albums on three discs: *The Complete Christmas Collection 1958-2010* (Real Gone Music, 2015). Having the albums together is a convenient way of tracing the evolution of Mathis's take on Christmas music and the notes by Joe Marchese are another bonus, but listeners who already own the complete Columbia and Global collections should be aware that Mathis's Christmas music is already included in those boxes.

For those who want a concise overview of Mathis's career, it's worth tracking down *The Music of Johnny Mathis: A Personal Collection* (Columbia Records, 1993). It's a nicely packaged set that includes a 96-page book with an excellent essay by Todd Everett and track-by-track notes by Gene Lees and Mathis himself. The only major drawback is that it ends in the 90s and thus excludes Mathis's work in the 21st century. It wouldn't be that big a problem with many other artists. It's not an uncommon experience that the quality of a box declines as the selection gets to the phase of maturity and old age. This is not so with Mathis, whose late recordings supervised by Jay Landers constitute some of his most important work.

Listeners who want the complete picture of Mathis's artistry might try the 4-CD box set *60th + 1 Anniversary: Classic Singles & Favorite Songs* (2017), released by TJL Productions, since it covers all stages of Mathis's career, including the Landers era. It also has a beautiful, career-spanning essay by Joe Marchese. Unfortunately, it's a limited release and hard to track down.

II. Selected Albums

A fine alternative to the box sets is the series of reissues of Mathis's music released on BGO Records and Real Gone Music. They come with insightful notes by Charles Waring (BGO) and Joe Marchese (Real Gone Music). The advantage of the BGO releases is that they bundle four albums together on 2CD-sets, while Real Gone Music mostly combine two albums with bonus tracks or add bonus tracks to a single release. However, in terms of packaging, Real Gone Music has gone the extra mile in order to present the definitive editions of the albums. The music has been remastered from the original tapes and the bonus tracks are carefully curated, while the notes include first-hand interviews with Mathis and important collaborators, including producers Thom Bell and Jerry Fuller. The booklets also include rare photography and scans of original album art and labels and the most thorough and correct discographies available. Finally, the label even commissioned new artwork for the lost albums *The Island* and *I Love My Lady*.

Especially recommended from Real Gone Music are the albums that make up the Jerry Fuller tetralogy: *The First Time Ever (I Saw Your Face)*, *Songs Sung Blue, Me and Mrs. Jones* and *Killing Me Softly With Her Song*). Other noteworthy albums are *Sings the Music of Bacharach and Kaempfert, I Love My Lady* and *Life Is A Song Worth Singing: The Complete Thom Bell Sessions* (sadly out of print). Two BGO Releases worth highlighting are the packages with *You Light Up My Life / That's What Friends Are For (With Deniece Williams) / The Best Days Of My Life / Mathis Magic* and *The Heart Of A Woman + Bonus Tracks / When Will I See You Again / I Only Have Eyes For You / Mathis Is*.

Many important Mathis albums still haven't been reissued by BGO Records or Real Gone Music, though they might be available in the future.

So far, many of his essential classic albums from his early Columbia years and the Jay Landers productions are missing, but these records are still relatively easy to track down.

Mathis has made so many excellent albums that it's hard to choose among them, but here is a list with ten albums I would bring to the proverbial desert island: *Merry Christmas* (1958), *Open Fire, Two Guitars* (1959), *Heavenly* (1959), *Broadway* (1964), *I'm Coming Home* (1973), *That's What Friends Are For* (1978), *I Love My Lady* (1982), *How Do You Keep the Music Playing? The Songs of Michel Legrand and Alan & Marilyn Bergman* (1993), *All About Love* (1996) and *Isn't It Romantic: The Standards Album (2005)*.

III. Imaginary Songbooks

Of course, Mathis's music is easily available on streaming services, but you lose the feeling of having a physical record and not least the liner notes. If there's one advantage of streaming services, besides having all the music at your fingertips, it's the opportunity of being able to compile imaginary albums that Mathis never released. Gathering his interpretations of Cole Porter, Rodgers & Hammerstein and Rodgers & Hart underlines the major work Mathis has done to keep The Great American Songbook alive. Mathis has also helped to promote lesser-known composers of standards. His recordings of the music of Bart Howard are a beautiful homage to an unsung master and Howard's songs deserve to be heard in sequence. Mathis has also recorded composers whose songs have become modern standards. With ten songs, the Bacharach part of *Johnny Mathis Sings the Music of Bacharach & Kaempfert* isn't enough. Add nine more songs to get a better picture of the scope of their collaboration.

Another kindred spirit is Stephen Sondheim. Mathis somehow manages to find the right balance between melodrama and musical elegance in Sondheim's music. His interpretations are both touching and sophisticated. Speaking of elegance and sophistication, few singers are better at bringing out the cool, playful musicality of Cole Porter. The critic Will Friedwald, who doesn't get Mathis, has said that he can't fathom why anybody would hear Mathis sing Cole Porter. Hearing a sequence of his interpretations of Porter is the best argument against Friedwald's preposterous claim.

In fact, hearing Mathis tackle any songbook is a pleasure. Here are six songbooks that haven't made it to disc. The playlists are available on Spotify, but it would be easy to compile a similar playlist on another streaming service by using the information overleaf.

Johnny Mathis Sings **Cole Porter**
1. Easy To Love from *Johnny Mathis* (1956)
2. Looking At You from *Wonderful, Wonderful* (1957)
3. All Through The Night from *Wonderful, Wonderful* (1957)
4. It's De-Lovely from *Swing Softly* (1958)
5. You'd Be So Nice To Come Home To from *Swing Softly* (1958)
6. In The Still Of The Night from *Open Fire, Two Guitars* (1959)
7. I Concentrate On You from *Open Fire, Two Guitars* (1959)
8. You Do Something To Me from *Rhythms of Broadway* (1960)
9. Let's Misbehave from *Rhythms of Broadway* (1960)
10. Let's Do It from *Rhythms of Broadway* (1960)
11. I Am In Love from *Rhythms of Broadway* (1960)
12. Ace In The Hole from *Live It Up!* (1961)
13. I Love You from *Johnny* (1963)
14. Get Out Of Town from *Broadway* (recorded in 1964 and released in 2012)
15. Ridin' High from *Broadway* (recorded in 1964 and released in 2012)
16. Night and Day from *Mathis Magic* (1979)
17. Begin The Beguine from *The Best Days Of My Life* (1979)
18. Begin The Beguine from *Mathis Live* (1984)
19. True Love from *The Hollywood Musicals* (1986)

Johnny Mathis Sings **Bart Howard**
1. In Other Words (Fly Me To The Moon) from *Johnny Mathis* (1956)
2. Let Me Love You from *Wonderful, Wonderful* (1957)
3. Year After Year from *Wonderful, Wonderful* (1957)
4. To Be In Love from *Swing Softly* (1958)
5. I'll Be Easy To Find from *Heavenly* (1959)
6. Nobody Knows (How Much I Love You) from *Faithfully* (1959)
7. Where Do You Think You're Going from *Faithfully* (1959)
8. Miracles from *Johnny* (1963)
9. The Joy of Loving You from I'll Search My Heart (1964)
10. Forget Me Not from *Tender Is The Night* (1964)
11. Tomorrow Song from *Tender Is The Night* (1964)
12. Sky Full Of Rainbows from *The Wonderful World of Make Believe* (1964)
13. What Do You Feel In Your Heart from *This Is Love* (1964)
14. Fantastic from *This Is Love* (1964)
15. A Thousand Blue Bubbles from *Love Is Everything* (1965)

Johnny Mathis Sings **Rodgers and Hammerstein**
1. It Might As Well Be Spring from *Johnny Mathis* (1956)
2. You Are Beautiful (1958) from *The Singles* (2015)
2. Hello, Young Lovers from *Heavenly* (1959)
3 I Have Dreamed from *Ballads of Broadway* (1960)
4. A Cockeyed Optimist from *Rhythms of Broadway* (1960)
5. Love Look Away from *I'll Buy You A Star* (1961)
6. Getting To Know You from *Romantically* (1963)
7. The Sound Of Music from *Romantically* (1963)
8. Shall We Dance from *The Complete Global Albums Collection: Singles and Unreleased Vol. Two* (2014). Previously unreleased single.
9. My Favorite Things from *Give Me Your Love For Christmas* (1969)
10. We Kiss In A Shadow. Previously unreleased bonus track from *Friends In Love* (1982)
11. It Might As Well Be Spring from *The Hollywood Musicals* (1986)

Johnny Mathis Sings **Rodgers and Hart**
1. My Funny Valentine from *Open Fire, Two Guitars* (1959)
2. My Romance from *Ballads of Broadway* (1960)
3. Dancing On The Ceiling from *Ballads of Broadway* (1960)
4. I Married An Angel from *Ballads of Broadway* (1960)
5. Spring Is Here from *Ballads of Broadway* (1960)
6. I Wish I Were In love Again from *Rhythms of Broadway* (1960)
7. Johnny One-Note from *Live it Up!* (1961)
8. The Most Beautiful Girl In The World from *Johnny* (1963
9. Manhattan from *Broadway* (recorded in 1964 and released in 2012)
10. A Ship Without A Sail from *Tender Is The Night* (1964)
11. Lover from *The Complete Global Albums Collection: Singles and Unreleased Vol. Two* (2014). Previously unreleased single.
12. Where Or When from *You Light Up My Life* (1978)
13. Isn't It Romantic from *Isn't It Romantic: The Standards Album* (2005)
14. This Can't Be Love from *Isn't It Romantic: The Standards Album* (2005)

Johnny Mathis Sings **Stephen Sondheim**
1. Tonight from *Faithfully* (1959)
2. Maria from *Faithfully* (1959)
3. Small World (1959) from *The Singles* (2015)
4. Everything's Coming Up Roses from *Rhythms of Broadway* (1960)
5. Somewhere from *Tender Is The Night* (1964)

6. Some People from *The Complete Global Albums Collection: Singles and Unreleased Vol. Two* (2014). Previously unreleased single.

7. Something's Coming from *The Shadow Of Your Smile* (1966)

8. Send In The Clowns from *I Only Have Eyes For You* (1976)

9. Goodbye For Now. Previously unreleased bonus track from *Friends In Love* (1982)

10. I Have A Love / One Hand, One Heart from *Barbra: Back To Broadway* (1993)

11. Loving You from *Mathis on Broadway* (2000)

12. Children Will Listen / Our Children from *Mathis on Broadway* (2000)

Johnny Mathis Sings **Bacharach and David**

1. Warm and Tender (1957) from *The Singles* (2015)

2. What The World Needs Now Is Love from *So Nice* (1966)

3. Saturday Sunshine from *Johnny Mathis Sings* (1967)

4. (There's) Always Something There To Remind Me from *Johnny Mathis Sings* (1967)

5. I Say A Little Prayer from *Love Is Blue* (1968)

6. The Look Of Love from Love Is Blue (1968)

7. Don't Go Breakin' My Heart from *Love Is Blue* (1968)

8. Walk On By from *Love Is Blue* (1968)

9. This Guy's In Love With You from *Those Were The Days* (1968)

10. I'll Never Fall In Love Again from *Love Theme From Romeo And Juliet (A Time For Us)* (1969)

11. Christmas Day from *Give Me Your Love For Christmas* (1969)

12. Whoever You Are, I Love You (1969) from *The Singles* (2015)

13. Raindrops Keep Fallin' On My Head from *Raindrops Keep Fallin' On My Head* (1970)

14. Alfie from *Raindrops Keep Fallin' On My Head* (1970)

15. Odds And Ends from *Raindrops Keep Fallin' On My Head* (1970)

16. They Long To Be Close To You from *Close To You* (1970)

17. Ten Times Forever More from *Love Story* (1971)

18. Make It Easy On Yourself from *Song Sung Blue* (1972)

19. Walk On By from *A Night To Remember* (2008)

Endnotes

1   Karen Heller: 'Johnny Mathis, the voice of the '50s, was always ahead of his time. Now he's ready to talk about it.' In *The Washington Post*, August 2, 2018. *www.washingtonpost.com*

2   Vincent L. Stephens: 'Johnny Mathis (Easy) Listening party! An appreciation in three parts' in Riffs, Beats and Codas, April 11, 2018: *www.riffsbeatsandcodas.com*

3   Ibid.

4   Interview with Johnny Mathis, March 2021.

5   Ibid.

6   Ibid.

7   Jasper, Tony: *Johnny: The Authorised Biography of Johnny Mathis*, W.H. Allen, 1983, p. 18.

8   Interview with Johnny Mathis, March 2021.

9   Steven Gaydos: Johnny Mathis Remembers His Jazz Roots, *Variety*, Jan 4, 2019: *variety.com*

10   Will Friedwald: 'Johnny Mathis' p. 689 in *A Biographical Guide to the Great Jazz and Pop Singers*, Pantheon Books, 2010

11   Johnny Mathis: Wonderful! Wonderful! CBS News, May 14, 2017: *www.cbsnews.com*

12   Interview with Johnny Mathis, March 2021.

13   Ibid.

14   Ibid.

15   Ibid.

16   Ibid.

17   Jasper, Tony: *Johnny: The Authorised Biography of Johnny Mathis*, W.H. Allen, 1983, p. 31.

18   Ibid. p. 62

19   George Avakian: Liner notes to *Johnny Mathis*, Columbia Records, 1956

20   Interview with Johnny Mathis, March 2021

21   Steven Gaydos: Johnny Mathis Remembers His Jazz Roots, *Variety*, Jan 4, 2019: *variety.com*

22   Interview with Johnny Mathis, March 2021.

23   Ibid.

24   Mitch Miller Interview, by Karen Herman on July 24, 2004 for *The Interviews: An Oral History of Television*. Visit *TelevisionAcademy. com/Interviews* for more information

25 Ann Schau: 'Percy Faith' in *The Canadian Encyclopedia*, January 29, 2008: *www.thecanadianencyclopedia.ca*

26 Liner notes to *Wonderful, Wonderful*, Columbia Records, 1957

27 Michael P. Coleman: The Hub's Exclusive Conversation with Johnny Mathis, Sac Cultural Hub, 07.01.2015: *www.sacculturalhub.com*

28 Michael P. Coleman: The Hub's Exclusive Conversation with Johnny Mathis, Sac Cultural Hub, 07.01.2015: *www.sacculturalhub.com*

29 Ibid.

30 Ibid

31 Tony Mottola obituary, *The Independent*, Tuesday 17, August 2004: *www.independent.co.uk*

32 Sam Roberts: Al Caiola, Guitarist With Top 40 Instrumental Hits, Dies at 96, The New York Times, November 24, 2016: *www.nytimes.com*

33 Liner notes to Open Fire, Two Guitars, Columbia Records, 1959

34 Mikael Wood: Johnny Mathis, 'Open Fire, Two Guitars', 35 life-affirming albums to help get you through self-quarantine, according to music experts, *Los Angeles Times*, March 25, 2020: *www.latimes.com*

35 Erwin Price: 'Abe (Glenn) Osser: A Tremendous Enthusiasm For Life' in *Allegro*, Volume 114, No. 6
June, 2014:

36 Joseph H. Manning: 'Making 'Misty': The Legendary Johnny Mathis Recording' in *Mornings on Maple Street*, 2010: *morningsonmaplestreet.com*

37 James Ritz. P. 17-18. Liner notes to *Johnny Mathis: The Voice of Romance: The Columbia Original Album Collection*, Columbia Records, 2017.

38 Jonathan Osser: 'Remembering Abe Osser' in *Allegro*, Volume 114, No. 6, June, 2014:

39 Joseph H. Manning: 'Making 'Misty': The Legendary Johnny Mathis Recording' in *Mornings on Maple Street*, 2010: *morningsonmaplestreet.com*

40 Ibid.

41 Ibid.

42 Ibid.

43 Steve Voce: 'Ralph Burns' in *The Independent*, Friday 23 November, 2001: *www.independent.co.uk*

44 Will Friedwald: 'Johnny Mathis' p. 689 in *A Biographical Guide to the Great Jazz and Pop Singers*, Pantheon Books, 2010

45   Rosemary Riddle: 'Nelson Riddle': *www.nelsonriddlemusic.com*

46   Ibid.

47   Joe Viglione: *AllMusic* review of *I'll Buy You Star*: *www.AllMusic.com*

48   Buddy Seigal: Q&A; / With Johnny Mathis : Respect For a Voice-Activated Career in *Los Angeles Times*, Oct. 12, 1995: *www.latimes.com*

49   Marc Myers: Johnny Mathis: Don Costa Sessions in *JazzWax.com*. Reprinted by *All About Jazz*, June 13, 2009: *news.allaboutjazz.com*

50   Ibid.

51   Joe Marchese: Liner notes to *Johnny Mathis: 60th + 1 Anniversary Classic Singles & Favorite Songs*, TJL Productions, 2017

52   Johnny Mathis: Liner notes to *The Complete Global Albums Collection*, Sony Music Entertainment Legacy Recordings, 2014.

53   Ibid.

54   Ibid.

55   Carmel Dagan: 'Jack Feierman, Conductor and Musical Director, Dies at 91' in *Variety*, February 25, 2016: *variety.com*

56   Johnny Mathis: Liner notes to *The Complete Global Albums Collection*, Sony Music Entertainment Legacy Recordings, 2014.

57   Wayne Whitwam: Black Orpheus: The Film and Bossa Nova in RootsWorld: *www.rootsworld.com*

58   Johnny Mathis: Liner notes to *The Complete Global Albums Collection*, Sony Music Entertainment Legacy Recordings, 2014

59   Greg Adams: *AllMusic* review of The Wonderful World of Make Believe: *www.allmusic.com*

60   Johnny Mathis: Liner notes to *This Is Love*, Mercury, 1964

61   Al Campbell: *AllMusic* review of *Love is Everything/Broadway*: *www.allmusic.com*

62   Johnny Mathis: Liner notes to *The Complete Global Albums Collection*, Sony Music Entertainment Legacy Recordings, 2014

63   James Ritz: Liner notes to *Love Is Everything/Broadway*, Sony Music, 2012.

64   Joe Viglione: *AllMusic* review of *Johnny Mathis Sings*: *www.allmusic.com*

65   Ibid.

66   Ibid.

67   Didier C. Deutsch: Liner notes to *Johnny Mathis: The Singles*, Columbia/Legacy, 2015

68   Johnny Mathis: Liner notes to *Johnny Mathis: The Singles*, Columbia/Legacy, 2015

69   Vera Conniff: *Ray Conniff's Short Biography By Vera Conniff* (1997): *www.rayconniff.com*

70   Ibid.

71   Johnny Mathis: Liner notes to *Johnny Mathis: The Singles*, Columbia/Legacy, 2015

72   Jason Ankeny: *AllMusic* biography of Ray Ellis: *www.allmusic.com*

73   Michael P. Coleman: The Hub's Exclusive Conversation with Johnny Mathis, Sac Cultural Hub, 07.01.2015: *www.sacculturalhub.com*

74   Johnny Mathis: Liner notes to *Merry Christmas*, Columbia Records, 1958

75   Johnny Mathis: Liner notes to *The Complete Global Albums Collection*, Sony Music Entertainment Legacy Recordings, 2014

76   Interview with Robbie Buchanan, December 2020

77   Johnny Mathis in James Ritz: Liner notes to *Johnny Mathis: The Voice of Romance: The Columbia Original Album Collection*, Columbia Records, 2017

78   Charles Waring: Liner notes to *Up, Up And Away/Love Is Blue/Those Were The Days/Sings The Music Of Bert Kaempfert*, BGO Records, 2021

79   Clive Davis with James Willwerth: *Clive: Inside the Record Business*, p. 240-249, Ballentine Books, 1975

80   Interview with Johnny Mathis, March 2021

81   Clive Davis with James Willwerth: *Clive: Inside the Record Business*, p. 244, Ballentine Books, 1975

82   Roger Catlin: Johnny Mathis: The TVD Interview in *The Vinyl District*, March 29, 2018: *www.thevinyldistrict.com*

83   Joe Marchese: Liner notes to *Johnny Mathis Sings the Music of Bacharach and Kaempfert*, Real Gone Music, 2018

84   Ibid.

85   Ibid.

86   Ibid.

87   Ibid.

88   Joe Marchese: Liner notes to *Johnny Mathis Sings the Music of Bacharach and Kaempfert*, Real Gone Music, 2018

89   Interview with Johnny Mathis, March 2021

90   Tony Jasper: *Johnny: The Authorised Biography of Johnny Mathis*, W.H. Allen, 1983, p. 91

91   Joe Marchese: Liner notes to *Johnny Mathis Sings the Music of Bacharach and Kaempfert*, Real Gone Music, 2018

92   Ibid.

93   Ibid.

94   Joe Marchese: Liner notes to *You've Got A Friend*, Real Gone Music, 2018

95   Vincent L. Stephens: 'Johnny Mathis (Easy) Listening party! An appreciation in three parts (Part 2)' in *Riffs, Beats, & Codas*, April 11, 2018: *www.riffsbeatsandcodas.com*

96   Jerry Fuller biography: *jerryfuller.net*

97   Joe Marchese: Liner notes to *The First Time Ever (I Saw Your Face) / Song Sung Blue*, Real Gone Music, 2018

98   Tony Jasper: *Johnny: The Authorised Biography of Johnny Mathis*, W.H. Allen, 1983, p. 144

99   Joe Marchese: Liner notes to *The First Time Ever (I Saw Your Face) / Song Sung Blue*, Real Gone Music, 2018

100 Tony Jasper: *Johnny: The Authorised Biography of Johnny Mathis*, W.H. Allen, 1983, p. 145

101 Joe Marchese: Liner notes to *The First Time Ever (I Saw Your Face) / Song Sung Blue*, Real Gone Music, 2018

102 Christian John Wikane: 'Coming Back to 'Coming Home': An Interview with Johnny Mathis and Thom Bell' in *PopMatters*, 2 March 2015: *popmatters.com*

103 Ibid.

104 Joe Marchese: Liner notes to *Life Is a Song Worth Singing: The Complete Thom Bell Sessions*, Real Gone Music, 2015

105 Ibid.

106 Interview with Johnny Mathis, March 2021

107 Charles Waring: Liner notes to *The Heart Of A Woman plus bonus tracks / When Will I See You Again / I Only Have Eyes For You / Mathis Is*, BGO Records, 2021.

108 Interview with Johnny Mathis, March 2021

109 Jeff Burger: 'An Interview with Motown Great Johnny Bristol,' May 7, 1975: By Jeff Burger: *byjeffburger.com*

110 Trudy Gallant: *Motown Revue Reunion*, 1989 (6:05-6:19): *abj.matrix.msu.edu*

111 Jeff Burger: 'An Interview with Motown Great Johnny Bristol,' May 7, 1975: By Jeff Burger: *byjeffburger.com*

112 Joe Marchese: Liner notes *The Heart of a Woman / Feelings*, Real Gone Music, 2019

113 Ibid.

114 Charles Waring: Liner notes to *The Heart Of A Woman plus bonus tracks / When Will I See You Again / I Only Have Eyes For You / Mathis Is*, BGO Records, 2021.

115 Johnny Mathis: Liner notes to *Johnny Mathis: The Singles*, Columbia/Legacy, 2015

116 David Ritz: Liner notes to *Barry White: Just for You*, Mercury, 2008

117 Charles Waring: Liner notes to *You Light Up My Life/That's What Friends Are For/The Best Days of My Life/Mathis Magic*, BGO Records, 2021

118 Christian John Wikane: 'Better Late Than Never: An Interview with Johnny Mathis' in *PopMatters*, 23 April 2019: *Popmatters.com*

119 Ibid.

120 Joe Marchese: Liner notes to *I love My Lady*, Real Gone Music, 2019

121 Ibid.

122 Tony Jasper: *Johnny: The Authorised Biography of Johnny Mathis*, W.H. Allen, 1983, p. 99

123 Joe Marchese: Liner notes to *I love My Lady*, Real Gone Music, 2019

124 Interview with Johnny Mathis, March 2021

125 Ibid.

126 James Ritz. P. 27. Liner notes to *Johnny Mathis: The Voice of Romance: The Columbia Original Album Collection*, Columbia Records, 2017

127 Tom Breihan: 'The Number Ones: Johnny Mathis & Deniece Williams' 'Too Much, Too Little, Too Late'' in *Stereogum*, December 13, 2019: *www.stereogum.com*

128 Tony Jasper: *Johnny: The Authorised Biography of Johnny Mathis*, W.H. Allen, 1983, p. 87

129 Interview with Johnny Mathis, March 10th, 2021

130 Ibid.

131 Ibid.

132 Ibid.

133 Vincent L. Stephens: 'Johnny Mathis (Easy) Listening party! An appreciation in three parts (Part 3)' in *Riff, Beats, & Codas*, April 11, 2018: *www.riffsbeatsandcodas.com*

134 Charles Waring: Liner notes to *Different Kinda Different/Friends In Love/A Special Part Of Me/Live*, BGO Records, not released yet.

135 Interview with Kathleen Wakefield, April 2021

136 Ibid.

137 Johnny Mathis: Liner notes to *The Complete Global Albums Collection*, Sony Music Entertainment Legacy Recordings, 2014

138 Interview with Henry Mancini, January 1, 1974: *www. nationaljazzarchive.org.uk*

139 Tony Jasper: *Johnny: The Authorised Biography of Johnny Mathis*, W.H. Allen, 1983, p. 166

140 Interview with Gil Reigers, March 2022

141 Ibid.

142 Ibid.

143 Ibid.

144 Interview with Mark Portmann, May 2021

145 Ibid.

146 Ibid.

147 Ibid.

148 Ibid.

149 Ibid.

150 Ibid.

151 Ibid.

152 Songwriters Hall of Fame: Diane Warren: *www.songhall.org*

153 Jack Hurst: 'The Ballad of Diane Warren' in *Chicago Tribune*, August 22, 1999: *www.chicagotribune.com*

154 Interview with Jay Landers, May 2021

155 Ibid.

156 Johnny Mathis. Track-by-track comments to *The Music of Johnny Mathis: A Personal Collection*, Sony Music, 1993

157 Ibid.

158 Interview with Jay Landers, May 2021

159 Joe Marchese: Liner notes to *The Island*, 2019

160 Johnny Mathis. Track-by-track comments to *The Music of Johnny Mathis: A Personal Collection*, Sony Music, 1993

161 Ibid.

162 Interview with Jay Landers, May 2021

163 Stéphane Lerouge interview with Michel Legrand translated by Martin Davies in *Le Cinéma de Michel Legrand*, EmArcy, 2007

164 Johnny Green: 'Forever Johnny' in *The New Yorker*, July 3, 2000, p. 57

165 Alan and Marilyn Bergman: *Testimony in the notes to Le Cinéma de Michel Legrand*, EmArcy, 2007

166 Norman Jewison: *Testimony in the notes to Le Cinéma de Michel Legrand*, EmArcy, 2007

167 Interview with Jay Landers, May 2021

168 Interview with Jorge Calandrelli, June 2021

169 Ibid.

170 Ibid.

171 Ibid.

172 Ibid.

173 Ibid.

174 Ibid.

175 Ibid.

176 Ibid.

177 Interview with Johnny Mathis, March 2021

178 Charles Waring: Liner notes for *Different Kinda Different/Friends in Love/A Special Part of Me/Live*, BGO Records, 2021

179 Interview with Fred Mollin, June 2021

180 Interview with Jay Landers, May 2021

181 Interview with Fred Mollin, June 2021

182 Vincent L. Stephens: 'Johnny Mathis (Easy) Listening party! An appreciation in three parts (Part 3)' in *Riff, Beats, & Codas*, April 11, 2018: *www.riffsbeatsandcodas.com*

183 Stephen Thomas Erlewine: *AllMusic* review of *Let It Be Me: Mathis in Nashville*: *www.allmusic.com*

184 Interview with Fred Mollin, June 2021

185 Ibid.

186 Interview with Gil Reigers, March 2022

187 Interview with Fred Mollin, June 2021

188 Interview with Jay Landers, May 2021

189 Vincent L. Stephens: 'Johnny Mathis (Easy) Listening party! An appreciation in three parts (Part 3)' in *Riff, Beats, & Codas*, April 11, 2018: *www.riffsbeatsandcodas.com*

On Track series
Alan Parsons Project – Steve Swift 978-1-78952-154-2
Tori Amos – Lisa Torem 978-1-78952-142-9
Asia – Peter Braidis 978-1-78952-099-6
Badfinger – Robert Day-Webb 978-1-878952-176-4
Barclay James Harvest – Keith and Monica Domone 978-1-78952-067-5
The Beatles – Andrew Wild 978-1-78952-009-5
The Beatles Solo 1969-1980 – Andrew Wild 978-1-78952-030-9
Blue Oyster Cult – Jacob Holm-Lupo 978-1-78952-007-1
Blur – Matt Bishop – 978-178952-164-1
Marc Bolan and T.Rex – Peter Gallagher 978-1-78952-124-5
Kate Bush – Bill Thomas 978-1-78952-097-2
Camel – Hamish Kuzminski 978-1-78952-040-8
Caravan – Andy Boot 978-1-78952-127-6
Cardiacs – Eric Benac 978-1-78952-131-3
Eric Clapton Solo – Andrew Wild 978-1-78952-141-2
The Clash – Nick Assirati 978-1-78952-077-4
Crosby, Stills and Nash – Andrew Wild 978-1-78952-039-2
The Damned – Morgan Brown 978-1-78952-136-8
Deep Purple and Rainbow 1968-79 – Steve Pilkington 978-1-78952-002-6
Dire Straits – Andrew Wild 978-1-78952-044-6
The Doors – Tony Thompson 978-1-78952-137-5
Dream Theater – Jordan Blum 978-1-78952-050-7
Electric Light Orchestra – Barry Delve 978-1-78952-152-8
Elvis Costello and The Attractions – Georg Purvis 978-1-78952-129-0
Emerson Lake and Palmer – Mike Goode 978-1-78952-000-2
Fairport Convention – Kevan Furbank 978-1-78952-051-4
Peter Gabriel – Graeme Scarfe 978-1-78952-138-2
Genesis – Stuart MacFarlane 978-1-78952-005-7
Gentle Giant – Gary Steel 978-1-78952-058-3
Gong – Kevan Furbank 978-1-78952-082-8
Hall and Oates – Ian Abrahams 978-1-78952-167-2
Hawkwind – Duncan Harris 978-1-78952-052-1
Peter Hammill – Richard Rees Jones 978-1-78952-163-4
Roy Harper – Opher Goodwin 978-1-78952-130-6
Jimi Hendrix – Emma Stott 978-1-78952-175-7
The Hollies – Andrew Darlington 978-1-78952-159-7
Iron Maiden – Steve Pilkington 978-1-78952-061-3
Jefferson Airplane – Richard Butterworth 978-1-78952-143-6
Jethro Tull – Jordan Blum 978-1-78952-016-3
Elton John in the 1970s – Peter Kearns 978-1-78952-034-7
The Incredible String Band – Tim Moon 978-1-78952-107-8

Iron Maiden – Steve Pilkington 978-1-78952-061-3
Judas Priest – John Tucker 978-1-78952-018-7
Kansas – Kevin Cummings 978-1-78952-057-6
The Kinks – Martin Hutchinson 978-1-78952-172-6
Korn   Matt Karpe 978-1-78952-153-5
Led Zeppelin – Steve Pilkington 978-1-78952-151-1
Level 42 – Matt Philips 978-1-78952-102-3
Little Feat – 978-1-78952-168-9
Aimee Mann – Jez Rowden 978-1-78952-036-1
Joni Mitchell – Peter Kearns 978-1-78952-081-1
The Moody Blues – Geoffrey Feakes 978-1-78952-042-2
Motorhead – Duncan Harris 978-1-78952-173-3
Mike Oldfield – Ryan Yard 978-1-78952-060-6
Opeth – Jordan Blum 978-1-78-952-166-5
Tom Petty – Richard James 978-1-78952-128-3
Porcupine Tree – Nick Holmes 978-1-78952-144-3
Queen – Andrew Wild 978-1-78952-003-3
Radiohead – William Allen 978-1-78952-149-8
Renaissance – David Detmer 978-1-78952-062-0
The Rolling Stones 1963-80 – Steve Pilkington 978-1-78952-017-0
The Smiths and Morrissey – Tommy Gunnarsson 978-1-78952-140-5
Status Quo the Frantic Four Years – Richard James 978-1-78952-160-3
Steely Dan – Jez Rowden 978-1-78952-043-9
Steve Hackett – Geoffrey Feakes 978-1-78952-098-9
Thin Lizzy – Graeme Stroud 978-1-78952-064-4
Toto – Jacob Holm-Lupo 978-1-78952-019-4
U2 – Eoghan Lyng 978-1-78952-078-1
UFO – Richard James 978-1-78952-073-6
The Who – Geoffrey Feakes 978-1-78952-076-7
Roy Wood and the Move – James R Turner 978-1-78952-008-8
Van Der Graaf Generator – Dan Coffey 978-1-78952-031-6
Yes – Stephen Lambe 978-1-78952-001-9
Frank Zappa 1966 to 1979 – Eric Benac 978-1-78952-033-0
Warren Zevon – Peter Gallagher 978-1-78952-170-2
10CC – Peter Kearns 978-1-78952-054-5

Decades Series
The Bee Gees in the 1960s – Andrew Mon Hughes et al 978-1-78952-148-1
The Bee Gees in the 1970s – Andrew Mon Hughes et al 978-1-78952-179-5
Black Sabbath in the 1970s – Chris Sutton 978-1-78952-171-9
Britpop – Peter Richard Adams and Matt Pooler 978-1-78952-169-6
Alice Cooper in the 1970s – Chris Sutton 978-1-78952-104-7
Curved Air in the 1970s – Laura Shenton 978-1-78952-069-9

Bob Dylan in the 1980s – Don Klees 978-1-78952-157-3
Fleetwood Mac in the 1970s – Andrew Wild 978-1-78952-105-4
Focus in the 1970s – Stephen Lambe 978-1-78952-079-8
Free and Bad Company in the 1970s – John Van der Kiste 978-1-78952-178-8
Genesis in the 1970s – Bill Thomas 978178952-146-7
George Harrison in the 1970s – Eoghan Lyng 978-1-78952-174-0
Marillion in the 1980s – Nathaniel Webb 978-1-78952-065-1
Mott the Hoople and Ian Hunter in the 1970s – John Van der Kiste 978-1-78-952-162-7
Pink Floyd In The 1970s – Georg Purvis 978-1-78952-072-9
Tangerine Dream in the 1970s – Stephen Palmer 978-1-78952-161-0
The Sweet in the 1970s – Darren Johnson from Gary Cosby collection 978-1-78952-139-9
Uriah Heep in the 1970s – Steve Pilkington 978-1-78952-103-0
Yes in the 1980s – Stephen Lambe with David Watkinson 978-1-78952-125-2

On Screen series
Carry On... – Stephen Lambe 978-1-78952-004-0
David Cronenberg – Patrick Chapman 978-1-78952-071-2
Doctor Who: The David Tennant Years – Jamie Hailstone 978-1-78952-066-8
James Bond – Andrew Wild – 978-1-78952-010-1
Monty Python – Steve Pilkington 978-1-78952-047-7
Seinfeld Seasons 1 to 5 – Stephen Lambe 978-1-78952-012-5

Other Books
1967: A Year In Psychedelic Rock – Kevan Furbank 978-1-78952-155-9
1970: A Year In Rock – John Van der Kiste 978-1-78952-147-4
1973: The Golden Year of Progressive Rock 978-1-78952-165-8
Babysitting A Band On The Rocks – G.D. Praetorius 978-1-78952-106-1
Eric Clapton Sessions – Andrew Wild 978-1-78952-177-1
Derek Taylor: For Your Radioactive Children – Andrew Darlington 978-1-78952-038-5
The Golden Road: The Recording History of The Grateful Dead – John Kilbride 978-1-78952-156-6
Iggy and The Stooges On Stage 1967-1974 – Per Nilsen 978-1-78952-101-6
Jon Anderson and the Warriors – the road to Yes – David Watkinson 978-1-78952-059-0
Nu Metal: A Definitive Guide – Matt Karpe 978-1-78952-063-7
Tommy Bolin: In and Out of Deep Purple – Laura Shenton 978-1-78952-

Also available from Sonicbond

070-5
Maximum Darkness – Deke Leonard 978-1-78952-048-4
Maybe I Should've Stayed In Bed – Deke Leonard 978-1-78952-053-8
The Twang Dynasty – Deke Leonard 978-1-78952-049-1

and many more to come!

Would you like to write for Sonicbond Publishing?

At Sonicbond Publishing we are always on the look-out for authors, particularly for our two main series:

On Track. Mixing fact with in depth analysis, the On Track series examines the work of a particular musical artist or group. All genres are considered from easy listening and jazz to 60s soul to 90s pop, via rock and metal.

On Screen. This series looks at the world of film and television. Subjects considered include directors, actors and writers, as well as entire television and film series. As with the On Track series, we balance fact with analysis.

While professional writing experience would, of course, be an advantage the most important qualification is to have real enthusiasm and knowledge of your subject. First-time authors are welcomed, but the ability to write well in English is essential. Sonicbond Publishing has distribution throughout Europe and North America, and all books are also published in E-book form. Authors will be paid a royalty based on sales of their book.

Further details are available from www.sonicbondpublishing.co.uk.

To contact us, complete the contact form there or email info@sonicbondpublishing.co.uk